College Success for
Students with Disabilities

College Success for Students with Disabilities

A Guide to Finding and Using Resources, with Real-World Stories

IRENE INGERSOLL

Foreword by Nido R. Qubein

McFarland & Company, Inc., Publishers
Jefferson, North Carolina

LIBRARY OF CONGRESS CATALOGUING-IN-PUBLICATION DATA

Names: Ingersoll, Irene, 1955– author.
Title: College success for students with disabilities : a guide to finding and using resources, with real-world stories / Irene Ingersoll ; foreword by Nido R. Qubein.
Description: Jefferson, North Carolina : McFarland & Company, Inc., Publishers, 2016 | Includes bibliographical references and index.
Identifiers: LCCN 2016003881 | ISBN 9781476662886 (softcover : acid free paper) ∞
Subjects: LCSH: People with disabilities—Education (Higher)—United States. | College students with disabilities—Services for—United States. | College student orientation—United States. | College dropouts—United States—Prevention.
Classification: LCC LC4818.38 .I64 2016 | DDC 378.0087—dc23
LC record available at http://lccn.loc.gov/2016003881

BRITISH LIBRARY CATALOGUING DATA ARE AVAILABLE

ISBN (print) 978-1-4766-6288-6
ISBN (ebook) 978-1-4766-2405-1

Front cover image © 2016 iStock/Steve Cole Images

Printed in the United States of America

McFarland & Company, Inc., Publishers
Box 611, Jefferson, North Carolina 28640
www.mcfarlandpub.com

To the brave students who so willingly shared their personal adversities and triumphs in order to guide future college students with disabilities towards college success, and to the professionals and parents who shared their knowledge and experiences in order to communicate valuable information throughout this text

Acknowledgments

I would like to thank my husband, three sons and extended family for their patience, love and support during the writing of this book.

A special thank you to all the students I worked with over the years at High Point University as the coordinator of disability services. These amazing students inspired me to write this informative book to help all students with disabilities attain their college goals. The exceptional young men and women who stepped up to share their personal struggles and triumphs wanted to help me create a path to success for other students who are experiencing similar situations. Each interview gives the reader insight into their life circumstances, learning challenges, personal choices and inner strength as they overcame obstacles to finally become the successful young adults they are today.

I would like to thank the following professionals who contributed their valuable experiences and information in order to provide guidance for upcoming students: Bruce Pomeroy, Director of Accessibility Services at UNC–Greensboro; Beth Barton, Ph.D., Deputy Director for the Marines' Family Program Division—Educational Transitions Program; Bob Dannehold, owner of Collegeology and a private college counselor in Seattle who volunteers his time to assist veterans returning to college; a college advisor who offered to share valuable information and advice for both students and parents; and Molly Casebere, a counselor who shared valuable information, resources and guidelines for accessing counseling help. Your time and input has been greatly appreciated. Your passion for helping students shines through your work!

I would also like to thank the parents who shared their valuable experiences and insight in helping their children traverse college with academic, physical, or medical adversities. Together we learned what works best and which resources were necessary for a successful outcome.

I would like to thank Carin and Leanne, who believed in my vision for this book and gave me valuable guidance throughout the writing process.

Table of Contents

Foreword
by Nido R. Qubein

Irene Ingersoll is a faithful believer in the potential of students. She focuses on the positive potential of every person and defiantly moves onward with conviction that, given a proper learning process and enough commitment, every student can achieve success. I know, I watched her, with admiration guide one student after another from a position of doubt to a place of achievement. She is a champion for students with disabilities. She deserves our gratitude and admiration.

She knows about how students learn. How they excel. How they can have plenty of success and a feeling of significance, and now she has written a book that will assist many students to discover which resources need to be in place to accept their disability as part of who they are, to discard old labels , and to march forward. Academic demands on a college campus can be frightening and overwhelming to students with special needs. This book tells them they can succeed. It explains to parents the resources needed and gives them hope for a better future. Irene Ingersoll has been in the field, in the trenches. Day after day she personally guided students to successful academic progress, and saw to it that they graduated from college. She has dedicated her life to finding out what works, and what doesn't and why. You will sense that in this work and you will be grateful for her tenacious effort to serve students and their families in such a dedicated manner.

At High Point University I watched with amazement as Mrs. Ingersoll inspired, encouraged and mentored students with learning needs to believe in themselves, to be resilient, to focus on purposeful outcomes and to reach their goals. She is a coach, a model and a teacher. We are grateful for her leadership.

Nido R. Qubein has been since 2005 the president of High Point University, where he orchestrated an internal and external transformation. He is also a motivational speaker and the author of a dozen books on topics ranging from effective communications skills, leadership and sales to personal motivation.

Introduction

As an educator working for the past 35 years with students who have disabilities, I have witnessed a constant determination in these students to achieve their academic goals despite the many challenges they encounter along the way. I have had the exceptional opportunity to work closely with college students who are bright, talented young adults, yet have had to overcome either personal or academic difficulties in their journey to find academic success at the college level. The dream of a college education was always their goal, but in order for this to happen they had to learn which resources and study strategies to put in place. College success is not a given, as all students need to become motivated and independent learners. The three million college students with disabilities face more challenges than the average student, and consequently their graduation rate is much lower than their peers. My background as a college disability coordinator and an academic coach opened my eyes to the amazing strength of character these students build as they overcome academic struggles. Without the right support systems in place, however, students with disabilities may fail out of college or just give up. In order to help close the gap to their graduation success, I have gathered important resources, along with students' personal testimonies of the obstacles they faced in college and which resources they put in place in order to achieve academic success.

My purpose is to let students who struggle with any type of disability know that they *can* be successful on their college journey. Many colleges across the country have created excellent support programs to meet the academic needs of these students as they work to achieve their career goals. Success comes with hard work, motivation, and knowledge of one's specific disability, along with understanding the college resources that are available and how to utilize them. I have always been passionate about helping students achieve their academic goals; this book is a conglomerate of strategies that work to empower students with challenges and will guide them towards college success.

The college environment is demanding and tests the skills of even the well-prepared students. Those entering college with a learning disability, ADHD, medical or psychological diagnosis have an even bigger challenge to overcome. As disability coordinator and college student success coach for High Point University (who also taught a college study skills course), I have helped students successfully maneuver the difficult courses using accommodations along with other college resources. Some of these resources are learning centers, writing labs, math labs, assistive technology, academic coaching, specialized academic support programs, peer mentoring, counseling and group study sessions. Once a student makes the decision to "want to learn," steps can be put into place to help him or her succeed. Students are encouraged to apply for and use their approved accommodations in order to "equal the playing field" in the college academic realm.

The student has the primary responsibility to disclose his or her disability and apply for accommodations by meeting with the disability services program staff at his or her college. Accommodations are put in place to make sure the student has access to all the course information. Utilizing tutors and other resources in order to learn, retain, and retrieve the material becomes a new hurdle to overcome. The information provided in this book will help guide students, parents, high school counselors, and psychologists towards finding the right resources to help empower students to become successful at the college level. I have witnessed the success of many students who would not let their disability hold them back; instead they chose to pursue every resource available to achieve their dream of college success. These students learned to build relationships with staff members and professors who went out of their way to be part of their success team. Learning to ask for help and guidance was key to their success. They understood that going it alone would not work; they had to trust tutors, parents, professors, and college staff to assist them when difficulties arose. Their ultimate reward was a college diploma with endless possibilities for a successful professional career, as they continue to grow and, as Dr. Nido R. Qubein says, "live their lives with purpose."

1

New Hurdles for College Freshmen with Disabilities

Three million college students have disabilities, and this number represents 11 percent of all college students in the United States (NCES, 2015). Many of these students find college more challenging than their peers and they tend to graduate college at a much slower rate. These students need to have support systems in place in order to help them succeed. High school students who have been diagnosed with a disability and receive accommodations should consider requesting accommodations for college. Colleges *want* their students to successfully complete their career goals, and have put many support services and resources in place to assist students as they complete courses within their degree programs.

It is important for students with disabilities to take the time in high school to pursue the right college fit. As students and their parents begin planning for college, they should become familiar with college disability support services and how these services can positively impact them. Students should meet with the disability/accessibility office during their initial college visits to assess whether each college offers the support resources they need for their specific disability. Students should also request accommodations for the college placement exams, such as the SAT, ACT, and PSAT. Students who use accommodations for these tests often improve their overall test scores.

Successful students choose to use their accommodations and other support services available to them. Unfortunately, many students with learning disabilities, ADHD and psychological disabilities often begin their college career without accommodations, and then struggle to turn around a bad academic start. History shows that students with disabilities often struggle and drop out of college. "Nationally, college students with LD have a drop-out rate near 70%, and compared to peers without disabilities, obtain lower GPA's, are more likely to take leaves of absences, and tend to change to easier programs that prepare them for less lucrative careers" (Lightner, Kipps-Vaughan,

Schulte, & Trice, 2011, p. 20). Researching potential college accommodations and academic resources and having them in place from the beginning will increase chances of success.

Transition Plans

Under the IDEA laws, students with a documented disability under an IEP or 504 plan should have a transition plan in place; unfortunately, the quality of transition plans varies considerably. An updated evaluation should be part of this plan to assist colleges with setting up appropriate accommodations. Students should have a recent psychological evaluation or be re-evaluated by a certified psychologist during their junior or senior year of high school to enable college disability services to assess current disabilities and set up appropriate accommodations. The transition plan should consider the student's academic and creative strengths, and the student should select a career path that will enrich them. The plan should also include potential colleges that offer the career programs and support services that meet the student's needs. According to a study by Lightner, et al. (2011), a student's lack of knowledge as to which resources are available and procedures for accessing services on the college level is often what prohibits students from seeking accommodations and support services. Parents, high school counselors and independent counselors need to help these student's research colleges, programs and accommodation procedures to ensure a good college fit and a strong academic start. The results of this combined research should be in the transition plan for career goals.

Steps to Complete Before Attending College

Students with a diagnosed disability (and their parents) should become familiar with the process of requesting and setting up disability accommodations both for college and for the SAT/ACT and PSAT tests, as well as the AP exams. Students who have taken these tests with their approved accommodations, such as extended test time, testing in a separate environment, use of a reader, and enlarged font, have received improved test scores compared to students with similar disabilities who chose not to apply for pre-college testing accommodations.

Specific policies, procedures and documentation are required to receive approved accommodations. The College Board encourages families to work closely with the high school counselors or disability services staff when completing the accommodation request process.

The College Board website has special instructions and forms to be completed by students with disabilities in order to receive testing accommodations for the PSAT, NMSQT and the SAT. "The College Board request process could take up to seven weeks, so start early" (College Board, 2015). The required information should be completed at least two months before the desired testing date in order for the board to process the documentation and approve the requested accommodations, especially since there has been an increase in students requesting accommodations. The high school disability specialist and/or counselor can assist the family in completing these forms and sending in the appropriate documentation.

The College Board website (2015) states:

> If you have a documented disability, you may be eligible for accommodations on SAT Program tests. Visit our Services for Students with Disabilities (SSD) site for information about accommodations, the request process, and required documentation. If you've already been approved by SSD to take the PSAT/ NMSQT or AP Exams with accommodations, you don't need to submit a second request. Start with the following website and follow all directions: https://sat. collegeboard.org/register/for-students-with-disabilities. All students who request accommodations are assigned a seven-digit SSD Eligibility Code. This number is printed on the student's decision and eligibility letters.

Students can also register for a testing date without approved accommodations, and then change to approved accommodations when they receive their approval letter from the board. "*If your accommodations have not been approved yet, you must register as a standard test-taker.* Once your accommodations are approved, check your Admission Ticket online or call 212–713–8333 to confirm that your registration has been updated to reflect the accommodations" (College Board, 2015).

The College Board will also assist students with applying for accommodations for their AP exams. Information can be found on the aforementioned "Serving Students with Disabilities" webpage and also at *https://www.college board.org/ students-with-disabilities/exam-administration/administrating-ap-exams-accommodations.*

The College Board (2105) states: "Note that the College Board exam accommodations for which a student is approved may differ from the accommodations approved by the school." Appropriate documentation from a licensed specialist is needed for approval of requested accommodations.

Students who choose to take the ACT should go to www.act.org/aap/ pdf/ACT-TestAccommodationsChart.pdf and complete all forms. The high school disability specialist or counselor will be able to assist with this process. All guidelines and forms are located on the ACT website. Students can request extended test time and testing at a special testing site (such as their high school). The testing with 50 percent extended time will take five hours and 45 minutes, as opposed to three hours for normal testing. If a student is requesting testing at a special site they need to send in documentation to prove that they are a student who "normally uses more than time-and-a-half on tests (or uses extended time only on writing tests)" *or* "requires testing over multiple days due to the nature of the disability" *or* "normally uses alternate test formats such as Braille, DVDs, or a computer for essays (available only for examinees whose disabilities prevent them from writing independently)" (ACT, 2015).

All approved accommodations for SAT and ACT can be applied to AP (Advanced Placement) course testing.

Students who use their approved SAT/ACT/AP/PSAT accommodations usually improve their test scores from previous testing without accommodations. Some students fear that the colleges will know that they have accommodations and this might interfere with their college acceptance, but this is a falsehood. "College admissions committees will not know that you took the test under modified circumstances, so you shouldn't hesitate to request accommodations if you need them. Depending on your learning disability, accommodations could include extended time to take the test, an assistant to read questions out loud, or a specific seating arrangement (students with ADHD, for example, may be able to take the test in a private room, or a room with fewer students). The basic fee is the same" (Princeton Review, 2015).

If a student is denied accommodations they can appeal the decision, and may need to send in additional support documentation.

Entering College

An increasing number of students with disabilities are joining the multitudes of bright-eyed college freshmen arriving on campus each fall eager to begin their academic journey and work toward their career goals. These students chose a demanding high school curriculum and worked hard to achieve good grades in order to meet the requirements for acceptance into the college of their choice. They have spent countless summer hours anticipating their first year of college. Many have already met new college friends through social media and have purchased those expensive textbooks. These energetic students are now ready for college!

Beginning college is an exciting life change for any student, but can also be overwhelming and emotionally taxing. Students with disabilities often face more academic challenges than their peers and will need to apply for and use college accommodations, whether they suffer from learning disabilities, ADHD, psychological disabilities or medical and physical disabilities.

Requesting and Implementing College Accommodations

Students with disabilities are required to self-disclose and advocate for themselves, starting with requesting appropriate accommodations through the college disability/accessibility services office on campus. This should be done soon after the student turns in their commitment deposit. Documentation for their specific disability should be sent to the disability office along with the completed disability intake forms. Four to six weeks later the student will receive a letter with their approved accommodations, which they need to share with each professor during the first week of classes in order to set up implementation of these accommodations and to begin building a relationship with each professor. This is an important first step in becoming a successful student. Issues may arise during the semester, and students will need to advocate for themselves, such as in Chase's case.

Chase has a medical disability that requires the use of a special motorized wheelchair. He transferred to High Point University (HPU) as a junior and registered with disability services before classes started, and looked forward to his new courses. When he entered one of his classrooms, however, he found that each of the individual desks were mounted to the floor and he was unable to wheel his chair close enough to set up his computer to take notes. Chase met with his professor immediately after class to discuss this problem, and the professor made contact with disability services for assistance in classroom accessibility. That afternoon, Chase met with disability services to discuss his situation. Disability services reached out to campus enhancement and they were able to quickly locate a small table that would easily fit his wheelchair and computer. Chase and the disability director met with a staff member in the classroom to set up the table and make sure it would be comfortable for Chase. The new table would be placed at the front where Chase could easily access it, and if he needed help a couple of students volunteered to assist him. Disability services also met with the rest of his professors and made them aware of his needs. Chase and the disability coordinator walked through his schedule to make sure he could easily maneuver each of his classrooms and had accessible tables put in place wherever they were needed. Professors were encouraged to contact disability services if other classroom accessibility issues arose.

Freshmen students like Chase attend their new classes with open hearts and minds and the excitement of a fresh start. During the first week of classes students meet professors and review the course syllabi. Most students feel that the required assignments are manageable while others may start to feel a quiet panic. The material presented by each professor seems interesting and each new freshman wants to do well. Students are meeting friends and attending social events; unfortunately, keeping academics the main focus can become the first hurdle for many freshmen because many are not sure how to manage all their "free time" and they often procrastinate. That "free time" isn't really free; it is meant for studying, but often students see this as personal fun time. During the fourth or fifth week of college many freshmen experience their first stressful moments because they are behind on their course readings, or they have taken the first test or quiz and results were not as they had hoped. The work is coming at them at a faster pace than in high school, and they are expected to work independently. The "quiet panic" they felt during the first week of classes has now turned into full-blown anxiety.

While this experience is familiar to many college freshmen, students with disabilities often experience more challenges than their peers as they transition to college. They may begin to notice that they are spending twice as much time studying than their friends, yet can't seem to get caught up. Staying organized and learning to manage their time is a major hurdle. Keeping up with the assigned readings, papers and course assignments brings new frustrations. Sleeping patterns and eating habits have also changed, and most students do not get enough sleep or adequate nutrition. Parents are no longer hovering over their shoulder reminding them to take medications and complete assignments on time. Stress and anxiety begin to mount causing some students to call home in a panic and tell their families they want to leave college because they are feeling like a failure.

Josh, for example, was diagnosed with ADHD and a reading disability at a young age. Throughout high school he received accommodations and knew that he would need accommodations in college in order to be successful. He requested them as an incoming freshman, and was approved for classroom and testing accommodations such as peer notes, extended test time, and testing in a separate environment, which he put into place right away. Despite this, Josh began to feel very discouraged after the first six weeks of college. He was struggling in each of his classes, falling behind on reading assignments and unsure of how to even prepare to memorize the massive amounts of information for upcoming mid-term exams. Josh had a good relationship with the disability director and met with her for advice. During their meeting he shared that his high school study strategies were not helping him with the faster pace of college. She gave him a learning styles inventory, and then used the results to tailor new study strategies to his auditory learning style. He had been approved for peer notes, but she discovered he did not go to the website to download the peer notes. The disability specialist walked Josh through the steps on how to access the peer notes, and how to apply for testing in a separate environment. He began accessing peer notes in his history and religion classes, and was given tutors for English and math. Josh and the disability director decided to meet every two weeks for the rest of the semester to evaluate his progress and study strategies in order to keep him on a successful academic path. Josh's grades did improve and he eventually joined a fraternity. He found another excellent resource for academic support through his fraternity brothers. They required study hall hours and upperclassmen tutored students who were struggling in core courses, and gave guidance with organization and time management. Josh was able to complete his degree program and successfully graduate within four years with these support systems in place.

Mid-term is still early enough in the semester that students can turn their academics around if they are willing to stop and assess where they are, then take the appropriate steps to utilize the college resources available to help them succeed. If students with disabilities take the time to self-evaluate to assess their study skills and determine their learning styles, then utilize campus resources and use their approved accommodations they can have a successful semester. Unfortunately, many freshmen just keep plugging along, keeping with their old habits, and getting deeper into academic peril. Often their mid-semester grades are quite low, and they realize that it will take a lot of hard work to turn things around. At this point many students give up and just ride out the semester instead of making a conscious choice to change their study behaviors. If they do not choose to find better study strategies and change their current study habits, they can fail out of college.

College Accommodations

Applying for college accommodations should take place after the student has been *accepted and made their final decision.* The university's disability/accessibility services website will have specific directions for requesting accommodations and submitting appropriate documentation. The student should complete all forms, and then send all documentation directly to the college disability/accessibility department. This can be sent through the mail, or through email. I strongly suggest a follow up call or email two to three weeks following submission, in order to inquire that the forms and documentation were received. Some families have waited months to hear approval for requested accommodations, only to learn that the documentation and forms were never received by the college disability/accessibility office. It may take four to six weeks for the college staff to process and approve the documentation. They will send a letter to the student stating the approved accommodations.

The first week of fall semester students with approved accommodations need to meet directly with the disability/accessibility staff to review their accommodations, along with their schedule, so each professor can be notified of the student's accommodations. Professors can be notified of approved classroom and testing accommodations either through email or the student can hand-deliver the letter from disability services. The student should meet with their professors within the first two weeks of each semester to discuss implementing the approved accommodations. The accommodation approval letter does not state the student's disability, only the approved classroom and testing accommodations. The student chooses whether or not to disclose their disability to professors.

Once the student has applied for and been approved for disability accommodations they need to make sure the disability accommodation letters have been sent to the professor during the first week or two of classes (if not, the student can still hand-deliver this letter). During this early part of the semester it is important for these students to meet with their professor to review their accommodations and set up extended test time; they can also take this time to discuss their learning needs. The professor will usually give the student academic guidance and will follow through with implementing approved accommodations throughout the semester. Meeting individually with each professor also sets the stage for ongoing communication and the building of a positive relationship.

If, at any time during the semester, the student feels their accommodations are not being supported by the professor they should meet with the professor, and with the disability staff to discuss and correct any concerns. The college disability/accessibility staff members are the student's advocate and will assist them with any issues or changes in accommodations as well as with faculty and housing concerns.

Accommodations should be in place the summer before fall courses begin. If families forget to send in this documentation early, they can send it in at any time throughout the semester, but the approved accommodations will not start until the request and documentation have been processed. Often students choose not to use accommodations their first semester, then find that they are struggling, and in a state of panic ask for immediate accommodations for their upcoming test or exam. Please understand that the disability/accessibility staff cannot make accommodations automatic, it may require a week or more to get the accommodation letters to professors. Students are best served by requesting accommodations early. If changes are needed during the semester the student should meet with their disability/accessibility specialist to get approval.

The Importance of Implementing Accommodations

Tanner, who had a history of a reading disability, ADHD, and experienced social anxiety, was enjoying being on his own as a college student. He met with an academic coach each week for guidance with organization, time management and tutoring, but did not want to apply for or use any accommodations. After an abysmal first semester his academic coach asked him to reconsider using accommodations. He called home and discussed applying for accommodations with his parents, who agreed that he should put these in place immediately. He spent another couple weeks contemplating this decision, but it was not until he received a D- on a history test that he decided to give college accommodations a try.

After turning in his required documentation he was approved for extended test time, testing in a separate environment, use of a computer for essay writing and tests read aloud. He took his next history test in the disability testing office with a reader. He was quite pleased when the test score improved to a B. Utilizing his accommodations, especially a reader for tests and his extended test time, helped Tanner to better read and understand the test questions, and relieved his anxiety which helped him to retrieve the information he had been studying. He realized that choosing to use accommodations was a necessity for him, and his dream of a college degree would depend on following through with approved accommodations each semester, especially with courses that required heavy reading. The academic coach also encouraged Tanner to meet with his professors by attending a first meeting with Tanner to discuss his anxiety when speaking in class; and this opened the door to better communication and discussions on how to meet course requirements that required class presentations.

There were also times that Tanner still felt overwhelmed by the course material and began struggling in courses. When this occurred, Tanner would ask his academic coach to join him in a meeting with his professor to strategize on how to manage assignments and improve his grades. In order to find academic success Tanner needed to consistently use his accommodations, receive tutoring, meet weekly with his academic coach, and keep open communication with his professors; this was his recipe for success.

When accommodations are not honored, the student can

- talk to the professor teaching the class;
- get assistance from the office of disability services;
- talk with the administrator in the department or the dean's office; or
- find out what the school's internal grievance procedure is and work with the office of disability services to follow it.

In extreme cases, and when none of the above is successful, you can file complaints with the U.S. Department of Education, Office for Civil Rights or the U.S. Department of Justice for violation of Sections 504 or the Americans with Disabilities Act (ADA).

Becoming Independent, Responsible Learners

Class attendance is completely on the student. No one is going to harass them for not attending class; they are simply marked absent, and it is entirely up to the student to contact peers for missed class information. It is important for students to learn self-discipline and to *just go to class!* Some colleges have attendance requirements, and students can be dropped from a course after five or six absences. Learning to manage their personal and academic time is the biggest challenge for college freshmen and even more stressful for students with disabilities. No one is checking over the student's shoulder to make sure they are on track with all readings and assignments, so the student needs to learn to manage their time. They should either purchase a planner or use their computer or iPad calendar to record all assignments, tests, projects and exams from their syllabi. Apple has an app called iStudiez Pro, which keeps track of course assignments on a timeline and alerts student to upcoming due dates. Students should also schedule study and tutoring times each day to read, highlight notes/text and begin long-term projects. This will keep them organized, especially before mid-terms and finals when anxiety is at its height.

October and mid-terms often bring on feelings of overwhelming stress and many students do not know how to begin to turn this around. Often students are too embarrassed to call home and tell their parents that they are experiencing difficulties with their course work. On campus they often do not know where to turn for help, or feel too embarrassed to ask for help. Asking for help can be the first step to success. Dale Carnegie once stated, "Develop success from failures. Discouragement and failure are two steps of the surest stepping stones to success" (Quotedly, 2015). Fortunately for the student, colleges have resources in place to help struggling students, such as tutors, learning centers, writing centers, academic coaches, and caring professors who will meet with and guide their students. It is imperative that the student find out where these academic resources are on campus and use them regularly. Rather than letting fear of failure keep them from achieving their goals, students should take appropriate steps to turn things around. Staff within academic or disability services, professors and counselors can direct students to the appropriate academic support and resources they may need. I also encourage students to let their parents know if they are struggling in any courses so that together they can brainstorm and discuss options for moving forward.

Another option for struggling students is to meet with the professor during their office hours. I encourage students to do this early in the semester so they can work with their professor to turn their grade around. Students will be pleasantly surprised at how comfortable a one-on-one meeting with a professor can be. This is also the time to share concerns about learning disabilities or other challenges they may be facing that interfere with academic progress in the course. The professor is often willing to give guidance and to provide names of tutors or other resources the student can tap into. This is also a good time to discuss how the approved accommodations are working out for the student, and whether these accommodations need to be adjusted.

Academic Support Services and Resources

College campuses often have some type of student learning or academic services center where tutors and staff can help guide students towards resources that will help them with their specific issues. Students can either make an appointment, or just show up at academic services to speak one-on-one with a staff member who will help them sort through their academic struggles and give them guidance towards study strategies, tutors or other appropriate resources.

Services for academic support services will vary from college to college. Most campuses do have tutors available to students; most tutors are free, but some college will charge an extra tutoring fee. Some students feel they may need tutoring but do not take the steps to request a campus tutor. Colleges often have limited tutors and their schedules may fill up fast, so it is important to request a tutor early in the semester. Some colleges will limit the number of times a student can access tutors each week, while other campuses will have unlimited tutoring available to students. Professional tutors are also available for hire in many college towns/cities. Often the disability staff or academic coaches have a list of reputable tutors that students and parents can contact for more in depth one-on-one tutoring.

College courses will be more demanding and fast-paced than what students experienced in high school and most college students feel some anxiety; the key to success is understanding how to deal with this anxiety when it hits, and knowing who to reach out to for guidance. Anxiety and stress can become overwhelming, especially for students who also struggle with learning disabilities, ADHD, Asperger's, Autism, depression, etc. Educating oneself on which resources are available to students and understanding how to access them is crucial in becoming a successful student. Time should be allotted when visiting colleges to learn about available student resources, academic support programs and assistive technology in order to choose the college that best fits the student's academic and personal needs. The student should learn ahead of time where and how to access tutors, assistive technology, counseling, and other college resources. They should also have a contact person—either a disability specialist or their advisor—to assist when anxiety or other issues arise. If the student and parent do this homework ahead of time and have these connections in place for the fall freshman semester, it will pay off immensely.

Utilizing Accommodations and Resources for Success

Paul attended a community college, and then transferred to a four-year college. Vocational rehab helped to set him up with a computer, printer, scanner and reading software for his visual disability. Paul made sure he met with the disability director in July to discuss his accommodations and walk through his schedule, making sure he could maneuver the buildings and campus, using his cane when necessary. Disability services emailed his accommodation letters to each professor before classes started so they were able to prepare handouts and a syllabus in large font, which Paul required. Paul's accommodations consisted of extended test time, testing in a separate environment, peer notes, 20-point font for handouts and tests, use of computer for essay writing and tests, access to Zoom Test, Kurzweil reading software, and Dragon Naturally Speaking, textbook in alternate format, and recording of lectures.

During the first day of classes Paul realized that two of his classes had blackboards, and even sitting front and center he was not able to read most of the notes written by the professor. He met with the DSS (disability support services) director and she was able to move his entire class to another building with a whiteboard that was more conducive to his visual disability. Paul made sure to meet with each of his professors during the first week of classes to discuss his visual disability and his approved accommodations. Paul met often with his disability specialist to discuss technology and any classroom or campus maneuverability concerns. His professors worked closely with DSS to assist Paul with any academic needs as they arose. Paul made a point to build relationships with his professors and the disability staff. This constant communication between all parties provided Paul with the assistance and resources he needed to succeed academically in college.

Learning Styles

Every student learns differently because our brains are not all wired the same; this is also why we each have strengths and weaknesses. A psychologist can administer a battery of tests to understand how the brain processes information and what the student's individual strengths and weaknesses are; this information is the basis for their high school IEP/504 plan and college accommodations. Every student has different gifts and talents, and should take time to read over their psychological report and understand how they learn, and what tools and resources they need in place to assist with their weaknesses. Neurologists have completed many studies on the brain and have a good understanding of how our brains receive store and process information.

> Neurologists have discovered that many learning disabilities are simple biological differences in the way the brain's two hemispheres connect. Dyslexics, for example, tend to have a tough time with left-brain activities, such as processing fine details and component parts as a whole. This is why dyslexics struggle with reading. Identifying the component parts (letters) and then combining them into a meaningful whole (words) is generally a left brained task. The right brain processes big-picture ideas. It is the hemisphere that helps us make connections among different ideas or items and put a thing into context. Some of the world's greatest inventors, entrepreneurs and creative people are dyslexic; their success is tied directly to the exceptional ways their brain's right hemisphere processes information [Pope, 2006, p. 22].

It is important for students to learn how their brain works so that they can explore study strategies that work best for them. They should discover whether they are right or left or whole brained, and whether they learn best through visual, auditory or kinesthetic strategies. These assessments can be easily found online, for example at http://www.web-us.com/brain/braindomin ance.htm.

They can also take a learning styles inventory, which can be easily found online. Examples can be found at http://www.educationplanner.org/students/self-assessments/learning-styles-quiz.shtml or http://www.howtolearn.com/learning-styles-quiz/ or http://www.personal.psu.edu/bxb11/LSI/LSI.htm.

After taking the self-reported assessment they will be given their preferred learning style: visual, auditory or kinesthetic, or a combination of these styles. Some students may have more than one modality of learning, so they will have a combined score. Students should review study strategies that enhance their learning style, helping them to better receive, store and retrieve information.

The chart presents specific study strategies to complement each preferred learning style and students should begin to apply these new study skills to daily study habits to see a big difference in memory recall skills. They can also try to incorporate study strategies from different learning styles to help strengthen skills in another part of the brain. Some course assignments will require students to use different strategies; for example, creating a PowerPoint or Prezi for a presentation uses visual and kinesthetic skills. "The most successful students are often the ones who can use strategies that take advantage of all the ways they learn or those who can switch styles depending on the demands of the course assignment" (Van Blerkom, 2011, p. 10). The sooner students integrate new study strategies into their daily routine and build new habits, the sooner they will see better testing results. Students who just read over their texts and class notes to prepare for tests will find that they do not perform well on tests and exams. The pace of college and depth of content requires stronger study habits in order to master the required material.

Study Strategies to Complement Each Learning Style

All students with disabilities should try to sit near the front and center of the classroom for best focusing and interaction with professors and course material.

Study Skills	Auditory Learner	Visual Learner	Kinesthetic Learner
Class note taking strategies	1. Record lectures and play them back later while you fill in class notes	1. Re-write class notes and color code topics and information	1. Use Cornell note taking method to organize notes for later study

Study Skills	Auditory Learner	Visual Learner	Kinesthetic Learner
	2. Use Block method or Cornell note taking when in class lectures 3. Participate in class discussions 4. Ask questions in class for clarification	2. Sketch or draw something on the notes to help with recall 3. Use outline or Cornell or block note taking methods	2. Actively participate in class discussions and ask questions 3. Meet with professor after class for specific clarification (or during office hours)
Reading strategies	1. Survey the chapter first, then while reading turn headings into questions, underline answers and recite the question and answer aloud, add this information to your notes or place on notecards 2. summarize information you have read 3. Survey the chapter first, read and highlight terms and main points in text, read difficult parts aloud. Place info on notecards and color code. Discuss in study group 4. Talk about what you have read within a study group	1. While reading turn headings into questions within the margins, then underline answer, place notes in book margins 2. Survey the chapter first read and highlight terms and main points then put information on notecards or add to class notes 3. Create visual maps of important terms and information, and color code 4. Label and color code diagrams and charts 5. Leave room in your notes to add drawings, diagrams, etc., for help with later recall	1. Survey the text read and highlight, then create note-cards for important information. 2. Connect the information to a specific experience or idea for recall 3. Read questions at the end of the chapter and find these answers as you read (high-light) to help with focusing on important details. Put this informa-tion on notecards (quiz self and peers weekly) 4. Label and color code diagrams and charts, review with study group 5. Use text to speech software—create notes in margins as text is read aloud to you
Test prep strategies	1. Create acronyms for steps and information and practice reciting out loud 2. Recite math steps as you work through problems 3. Create songs and rhymes to help with recall 4. Participate in study	1. Create concept maps, charts diagrams and color code 2. Create practice tests or write out exam review guides and color code concepts 3. Practice writing out essay questions—use an outline for reference	1. Create mnemonics and rhymes for content, and repeat information aloud as you study 2. Work out all steps to math and science problems several times 3. Create notecards for study content, color

Study Skills	Auditory Learner	Visual Learner	Kinesthetic Learner
	groups—teach concepts to a peer 5. Verbally explain steps to a science experiment or math problem to a peer 6. Recite information aloud while studying 7. Take online quizzes and test preps 8. Create study guides and diagrams and practice labeling 9. Create and outline for essay questions, practice writing out he essay and read aloud to self	4. Study in a quiet, least restrictive environment 5. Create plot diagrams for literature, history or religion factual content	code and quiz peers in study groups 4. Create an outline for essay questions and practice writing out the essay 5. Walk or stand while studying and repeat information aloud 6. Create models or diagrams of concepts
Test notes	Often students can study with soft music in the background—this helps with recall	Visualize the material or color coding or drawings to help with recall during tests	Try using a squeeze ball when taking a test to help with recall

Professors often place their PowerPoint presentations online where students can download and add notes and diagrams. Students who have access before the lecture can bring them to class and write on them during the lectures. Make sure to add all examples your professor goes over. Later students can transfer this information to their notebooks or create notecards for weekly study and review of material.

Online notecard tools can be found on Quizlet and Noteability.

2

What Can Be Done to Turn Around a Bad Academic Start

Will was enjoying everything about being a freshman college student. He loved living away from home, meeting new friends, and attending sporting events and classes. The reality of college hit home for Will in late September, however, once he received his first round of low test scores and he realized that he was no longer in high school; he needed to step up his game. He quickly learned that enjoying college and working at academics were two different things. He was familiar with the academic services center, so he took appropriate steps to turn things around. His first step was to meet with the academic center staff and ask for guidance with study strategies. They reviewed Will's learning style, study habits and time management skills, and then suggested some significant changes in how and when he was studying. They connected him with tutors for math and English, and suggested he meet individually with his professors. They also helped him to schedule study time daily, along with specific times to meet with tutors.

Will took their advice and began changing his habits. He made more time for studying and began using tutors to help prepare English papers and to review for his math tests and quizzes. He also spent a few hours each day in the library where he had fewer distractions than studying in a noisy dorm room. By applying better study strategies and learning how to better manage his "free time," Will was able to improve grades in each of his classes by the end of the semester, staying in good standing with the college. By creating a new study schedule Will was able to set aside study time in each day and carve out time to attend sporting events and support his college athlete peers on campus, which was a true passion for him.

Academic Interruptions

There are times when students experience injuries or other medical issues which affect their learning, throwing a curve into their academic success. Kristy started the first month of college strong. She attended classes, kept up with all assignments and was enjoying college life, until she became very sick and needed to be hospitalized. She asked her father to contact disability services so they could help her communicate with her professors and complete work from the hospital. She did not want to drop out for the semester; instead she chose to work closely with disability services and her professors while recovering. She was given peer notes to access online for her course lectures. When she returned to campus she was given tutors and peer notes to help her catch up with missed lectures. Communication was extremely helpful in helping Kristy successfully complete the semester.

Athletes in particular may find themselves injured and require surgery or a short hospital stay. These students can contact disability services and request short-term accommodations and assistance with communicating with professors to set up procedures for completing assignments and tests. Parents can also assist with contacting the disability office and sending in required medical documentation for short-term disability accommodations.

Undiagnosed Students

Some students will come to college without a diagnosis. They may have struggled in high school with test taking, focusing or storing and retrieving new information. Once these students meet with the faster pace and academic demands of college they often struggle to pass their courses. The vast amount of new information, reading and writing assignments can become overwhelming. Often they will meet with their professor to discuss their academic struggles and the professor will recommend that they meet with disability services to rule out or test for a learning disability.

Disability services will meet with students who are struggling and will review their study strategies and past academic performance. They can refer the student to a local psychologist, or the student can choose a psychologist from their hometown, who will perform a psychological evaluation to explore the possibility of a learning disability or ADHD. Some of the larger colleges will have a psychologist on staff for the testing. Most insurance plans will cover some of the testing fees. The psychologist will administer a cognitive test to determine strengths and weaknesses, with an assessment such as the

WAIS III. They will also test for academic aptitude to understand what you have previously learned, using as assessment such as the Woodcock Johnson III. The results of this testing will reveal the student's abilities along with weaknesses. Variations in the test scores will show whether the student has a learning disability. Testing can take up to one month to schedule with a professional licensed psychologist.

The student can request the psychological evaluation results be sent to the college disability director. If the student does have a diagnosed disability they can complete the forms to request accommodations. The disability director will walk the student through the steps and explain how to implement any approved accommodations. The accommodations will not be retroactive; they begin from the time the student turns in their documentation and requests them.

Discovering a Learning Disability

AJ attended college without a documented disability. She made good enough grades for admission to college because she had a good work ethic and stayed organized, but always struggled with test taking. She worked hard in each of her classes and kept up with assignments, however, she struggled to pass tests no matter how hard she prepared. After a difficult first semester of college she began working with tutors and an academic coach. They used new study strategies and worked together to prepare for tests, but she still seemed to blank out during tests. She was often unable to retrieve the information she studied. The academic coach recognized a possible processing and reading disorder and recommended that AJ meet with a local psychologist to test for a learning disability. At first AJ was upset and did not want to hear that she might have a learning disability, so she did not follow through with testing. "Nothing was wrong with me, I just needed to work on my inner strength to improve my memory." She kept up with her study habits, but had low grades at the end of the semester. AJ was frustrated because she continued to work hard without making progress. She was beginning to feel that she would never succeed at the college level.

Out of frustration, she decided to follow through with the psychological evaluation. The results showed that she had memory and processing disorders, plus a reading disability. AJ was approved for the following accommodations: extended test time, testing in a separate environment, peer notes, use of computer in class, formula card for math and science courses, and recording lectures.

Once AJ began using accommodations her grades improved. She needed the peer notes to fill in where she had gaps in her information. She used tutors regularly to help her comprehend the reading material and prepare for tests each week. In her most difficult courses she met with her tutors at least three times a week, and met with her professors for assistance and test prep. She used Quizlet to prepare notecards for each class and reviewed them daily.

AJ finally understood how her brain worked and processed information. She was relieved to know that she could work with her academic coach to improve her memory skills with new study strategies that enhanced her learning style. "At first I was embarrassed to tell my friends about my new diagnosis, but when I finally gained the courage to discuss this with them I found unconditional support. A couple of my roommates were in my classes so they formed study groups and helped me learn materials for tests and exams."

Understanding her newly diagnosed learning disability and putting new study strategies in place was the first step. She began using her approved accommodations and met with tutors consistently. AJ also realized that she could only handle three classes per semester successfully. She took a lower course load each semester and focused all her time and energy on passing these classes. "I worked even harder than ever and was able to raise my grades and GPA. I am on track to graduate on a five-year plan."

Discovering you have a learning disability or ADD while attending college can be both overwhelming and a blessing. A diagnosis shows the reason why the student is struggling and gives them support resources to put in place in order to move forward and achieve their academic goals. Struggling students should meet with the disability director and discuss their academic issues and strategies to resolve these issues.

Foreign Language Substitution

A diagnosis of dyslexia, reading disability or deafness and hearing loss may require a student to apply for a foreign language substitution. Often these students have attempted a foreign language in high school and were unsuccessful, thus the high school gave them a waiver for their foreign language requirement. Most colleges will require the student to attempt a foreign language with tutoring assistance, and if they are struggling with Ds and Fs by mid-term they can apply for the foreign language substitution. The substitution is usually a cultural course. Other colleges offer American Sign Language as a foreign language substitution. Colleges have also been offering a three-week May course in a specific country for an immersion experience into a different culture. While a few colleges will give students an accommodation for a substitution course without having to attempt the foreign language course, students should meet with the disability director of the college to determine their policy and procedure for granting substitutions.

Matt was diagnosed with a reading and writing disability in elementary school. He did attempt foreign language in high school, but even with private tutoring and extra support from his Spanish teacher he was unable to pass the course. The high school granted Matt a foreign language waiver. When applying to college he sent in a letter from his high school counselor explaining his diagnosis and exemption from a foreign language credit. The college required two years of foreign language for admissions acceptance, but they accepted his diagnosis and the letter from his high school counselor explaining his foreign language waiver.

Matt met with the college disability director to request a foreign language substitution along with his other accommodations. The college he attended required copies of his psychological report and a letter from his high school explaining his effort to learn Spanish, and which accommodations they put in place for him. The college granted Matt a foreign language waiver and he chose to take a cultural course for his substitution. A copy of the approved accommodation letter was also given to the registrar's office in order for the culture course to be counted and approved as a substitution for his core courses in order to meet his graduation requirements. The foreign language substitution gave Matt an opportunity to learn the culture of another country without having to learn the semantics of a new language. He was able to move forward with his degree plan with this accommodation.

Students who are researching good fit colleges need to inquire about the foreign language requirement for their specific degree program in order to graduate. The majority of colleges will have a foreign language requirement, while a few will not require any foreign language as part of their core curriculum for graduation. When students meet with the disability services department they should inquire about the colleges specific requirements for foreign language substitution, and whether or not they qualify for a substitution.

Building Relationships with Professors

Once students realize that they are struggling in a course they *can meet with their professors* during office hours. The professor (or their teaching assistant) may be available to advise the student on how to tackle the course

material. It is important to build a relationship with professors and is especially helpful within the major, as students may end up taking multiple
courses with the same professor. The student should take the time to share
with the professor their struggles with the course readings, bringing in specific questions to discuss. They can also get clarification on research papers
or course presentations. Once a professor learns that a student is invested in
his or her course, they will invest in the student.

College professors have spent many years in college themselves; they
love learning and nothing makes them happier than when a student expresses
interest in their course and comes to them for guidance. But *it is up to the
student* to reach out and make initial contact with each professor. Students
with learning struggles and approved college accommodations should make
sure to explain this to the professor, regardless of the nature of their disability.
They should discuss strategies that best help them succeed as a student. They
can also discuss how to use their accommodations in the course, whether it
is through peer notes, extended test times, or recording lectures.

Whenever Will began to struggle in a course he made an appointment
with his professor to discuss his academic struggles. He found that they were
very open to helping him understand the course material and often gave him
guidance with presentations and papers. Some of Will's professors were open
to meeting with him often to review and prepare for tests and exams as long
as he came prepared to discuss the material. Will learned early in his freshmen
year to keep open communication with his professors and made sure they
had a face to put with his name.

Choose to Use Accommodations

Often new college students choose not to use their approved accommodations because they want to try without them the first semester and see how
they do. These students want to be free of the labels that often accompanied
accommodations in high school. Other students do not choose to disclose
having a disability and have not even applied for accommodations. Students
with disabilities who decide on either of these routes usually have a difficult
semester.

Zack was diagnosed with dyslexia in elementary school and received
many early interventions and accommodations throughout the years. Soon
after being accepted into HPU, his mother sent in his documentation and he
was approved for appropriate accommodations. Zack chose not to use these
accommodations and did not let his parents know he was attempting courses

without them. By mid-term his grades were dismal. At this time, he admitted to his parents that he was not using any of his approved accommodations or tutoring and asked for help. His mother contacted the disability department and asked that they meet with her son and advise him of his choices. During this meeting Zack admitted that he was in over his head and felt like a failure. College was much harder than he anticipated and he realized that he could not be successful without utilizing the support that was initially put in place for him. Zack's approved accommodations were put in place immediately with each class, and he began to use them daily. Zack was uncomfortable meeting with professors alone, so he and the disability director met with each professor to discuss his learning needs and approved accommodations. His grades improved to passing for each course by the end of the semester. Zack continued to use his accommodations and tutors for the remainder of his college career.

If a student has chosen not to use approved accommodations, now would be a good time to reconsider this choice. The student has the choice whether or not to implement the approved accommodations, and should understand that these accommodations "equal the playing field" by giving them access to the material presented in class and in textbooks in a way that their brain can process. I completely understand when students share that they do not want a disability label, or want to try college without accommodations or tutors because in the past their parents always made this decision for them. College can be difficult enough for the average student; adding a disability can often raise a student's chances of failure.

The accommodations have been put in place to assist them in becoming the best student they can be. They may not need to use accommodations for all of their courses, just the ones that directly impact their disability. An example would be: if they have a reading disability, they could only use the approved peer notes, text in accessible format (or e-texts), and extended test time for courses such as history, science, economics, and religion. Then they could take their accounting, math and art courses without accommodations. They can choose when and where to apply the accommodations to impact their academic success. Many students I have worked with chose to use accommodations only to help get them through their core courses, but once they are in their major they don't seem to need all or any of their accommodations. Also, they should remember that the old labels do not exist in college. All types of students use tutors, not just students with disabilities, so they are not judged or treated differently because they use these resources. Ultimately, the choice of how, when and where to use accommodations belongs to the student; this is where self-advocacy matures.

Any time throughout the semester the student can begin implementing accommodations through disability services. The student will also need to discuss their approved testing and classroom accommodations with the professor; making sure the professor has received the accommodation letter through email or directly from the student. Each college has a test taking form and procedures that need to be completed before the student can take the tests in a separate environment, so remember to acquire this information from the disability website and staff early in the semester. A documented disability is an important part of the academic plan. Approved accommodations are put in place to help students succeed in their courses. *(See Chapter 3 for more specific information.)*

Changing Study Habits

Students should evaluate how often they are studying and which study strategies they are using, remembering that they need to set aside appropriate study hours outside of class every day for each academic course they are taking. Finding a study time in their daily schedule that works best for their learning needs is essential. If a student is failing a course their current study routine is not working, so they need to make drastic changes in order to find academic success.

Create a daily study schedule and plan time accordingly, and then follow this plan each and every day. Once up for the day, do not return to bed. Stay awake and busy! Also, evaluate what time to wake each day, making sure to get at least seven to eight hours of sleep and wake up at a consistent time each day to keep up a healthy routine.

Ryan enjoyed staying up late at night and sleeping in until his first class, then rushing across campus with no breakfast. After an unsuccessful first semester he worked with an academic coach to evaluate how he was spending his time each day. Together they completed an hourly chart and planned time for classes, studying, working out and relaxing. Ryan decided he wanted to wake up by 7:30 each morning, eat breakfast (which he had been skipping) and get organized for his day. This soon became a positive habit for Ryan and he found that when he followed the planned schedule he actually had more "free time" in his day! When mid-terms came around he found that for the first time he was not stressed out because he had been following his study plan and reviewing daily as well as keeping up with projects, readings and writing assignments, and he realized that he was well prepared for his exams.

Creating Study Time in the Day or Week

Planning and managing one's time is important to academic success. College students should plan time each day for reading, reviewing and studying their notes, as well as time for working on papers and projects. Create a weekly schedule and plan out each hour of the day, with time set aside for meals, relaxing and working out. Students who keep up with a daily schedule find that they have more time to enjoy sports, friends and exercising than when they were cramming and careless with their valuable time.

Students should find an atmosphere conducive to studying. This can be in the library, study rooms on campus, or dorm room if students can close the door and have no distractions. Study areas should be neat and organized so they can easily find and use resources. Make sure to highlight textbooks and take good class notes. If a student receives peer notes as an accommodation they should make sure to download them after each class and keep them with the class notes. Creating weekly note cards and studying them daily will make for easier retrieval. This will help prepare them for any upcoming quizzes (pop quizzes are known to happen in college!).

Make sure to study and review textbooks, online course material and notes daily to keep the information fresh in the brain. This is particularly helpful when preparing for mid-terms and finals with large amounts of information to retain and retrieve, especially when taking comprehensive exams. If a student has difficulty concentrating and studying alone, they should try to create a study group with peers from the course. Sharing notes and discussing the content will help prepare them for tests and exams.

Deanna was a focused student, but her current study skills were not helping her retrieve information for her tests and exams. Her diagnosis of dyslexia required that she spend a large amount of her time studying. In college she met with her academic coach and she took a learning styles inventory to learn how to improve her study skills. Once she learned she was a visual learner they explored techniques to help her study. She color-coded her note cards and class notes. She also wrote questions in the margins of her texts to help her focus on what information was important in the readings. She skimmed over her text before the lecture, then came back and carefully read the selection, highlighting and adding to her notes as she went. This helped her to focus better both in class and when she was studying. She also met a couple time a week with tutors and peer study groups for review, which helped her to maintain a strong GPA.

Deanna used tutors for math and English throughout high school to assist with her dyslexia, and knew that she could not be successful without this support in college. The first day of classes she met with the academic success staff and inquired about tutors. They explained how to go to the website and request a tutor. Soon she was set up with tutors for each course as well as information on how to access the writing center. Deanna used self-discipline and attended the library every afternoon to work with tutors or independently on readings and assignments. She also used RFB&D, reading with text-to-speech with each of her textbooks. She became a very strong student by utilizing all resources early in the semester.

Ryan and Deanna both learned early on that they learned best in a study group where information was discussed and shared, as opposed to studying independently. Hearing, seeing and discussing the information worked best with their learning styles and helped them to store and retrieve information from their long-term memory. They consistently seek peers to form study groups for tests and exams. Discovering one's learning style and researching which study strategies work best for their brain will help students to properly store and retrieve information for tests and exams.

Available College Resources

Tutoring—Colleges have free tutoring available to students. The tutors are often college students who have previously taken the course and received an A, as well as a recommendation from a professor, to become a tutor. These tutors attend training sessions through academic services in order to understand strategies that will assist students throughout the course. There is often an online tutor sign-up site through student services or academic services. Check this out on campus prior to beginning fall semester, to know where the tutoring is located and how to sign up for a tutor when necessary.

Colleges also have writing centers, where English majors are available to help you plan out your paper and review for grammar. They will not help write papers, but will help to correct and edit the paper or get started with a correct prompt and research, as well as give guidance with the writing process.

Student Academic Services—Colleges have trained staff to assist students with their learning needs. They will often take the time to coach students on study skills or test taking strategies as well as guide the student to appropriate tutors. The college website will have a link to their department or email addresses. It is up to the student to reach out to these departments if they want academic help.

Research Librarians—Colleges provide library staff, trained to assist students with research for papers. Often the professors communicate with the library staff on their research topics and set aside books and articles that will be beneficial to their students. Professors also specify whether the student needs to use APA, MLA, Chicago or Turabian style for their research papers. Library staff will provide information to assist the student in using the correct documentation format. The college library staff is a valuable resource that each student should tap into. College libraries are often open 24 hours a day, seven days a week. Checking out the campus library and familiarizing oneself with their posted hours of operation will serve students throughout college.

Counseling—The majority of college campuses have counseling available to students. Counselors are available to help students with stress, anxiety, eating disorders, depression, transitioning to college, homesickness and personal struggles. Counselors are advocates for the student and assist with building skills to overcome obstacles of all varieties. The student must make the appointment; parents cannot force a child to attend counseling, nor can they ask the counselor what was discussed in the sessions. The student can sign a consent form giving the counselor and parent permission to communicate, but again, the student can control what information is allowed to be shared with their parent. If the counselor has evidence indicating that the student might attempt suicide or hurt someone else, only then the counselor can reach out to the parent or college staff for emergency help without the student's consent. Otherwise, all counseling sessions are confidential, and no one else on campus needs to know that the student is attending counseling. The student can give permission for the counselor and a staff member to communicate, but the information shared with staff is regulated by the student. *(More information is provided in Chapter 11.)*

Counseling Tips

- How does a student go about requesting a counselor?
    - Students should check the college website. Most counseling contact information and guidelines are available on the college website. Some will have pictures of counselors as well as descriptions of their specialty or areas of interest.
    - Counselors will have both walk-in hours and scheduled appointments; students can either schedule a meeting online or speak with a receptionist and request a counselor and meeting time.

Counseling is available for short-term and long-term needs.
- Should students interview counselors?
    - Many students find it helpful to take time to meet the counseling

staff during a college visit, or over the summer. They should introduce themselves and ask questions regarding availability and specialty areas. Once they connect with a specific counselor, they can set up an appointment. Once the semester starts schedules become hectic and counselors may have less free time.

  ○ Familiarize oneself with resources, especially if the student has had counseling in the past, to know where to turn when issues arise.

• What if a student has an emergency or crisis during the evening or weekend?

  ○ Most colleges have counselors on call for crisis situations.

  ○ Students or other campus staff can call security or the resident director on duty. Security will call the counselor and have them speak with the student to assess the situation and determine further procedures.

  ○ Larger colleges will have a clinic on campus open 24/7. The campus website should have information on location and access of resources.

• If a student has a relationship with a counselor will they be able to reach that particular counselor during a crisis?

  ○ The on-call counselor rotates, so they may not have immediate contact with their particular counselor. The on-call person will assess the severity of the situation, find out if they are safe, calm them down and work on stabilizing the situation. The student's counselor will eventually be notified.

• What types of issues do counselors help with?

  ○ No issue is too small. Counselors are available to help students work through

    ✦ homesickness;
    ✦ roommate issues;
    ✦ time management;
    ✦ transitioning to college/independence and freedom;
    ✦ family issues;
    ✦ approaching professors/self-advocacy;
    ✦ isolation;
    ✦ balancing college and home life/friends;
    ✦ self-esteem;
    ✦ drug and alcohol issues;
    ✦ dating;
    ✦ anxiety and depression;
    ✦ grief and loss; and
    ✦ eating disorders.

• What are the confidentiality rules for college counseling?

o Both HIPPA (mental health) and FERPA (academic) laws apply to college counseling situations.

o The student must sign a HIPPA or FERPA consent form for the counselor to communicate with others, and the student approves the information shared with others.

o All counseling sessions are confidential except for the following situations:

+ if a student is threatening harm to self or others the counselor must break confidence;

+ if the student shares knowledge of *current* child or elder abuse the counselor must break confidence; or

+ if records are subpoenaed by the courts the counselor must turn over the records.

Students in Crisis

Most colleges will have established resources in place and a response plan for crisis situations. If the student knows they are in crisis they can call campus security to ask for help, and the security personnel will contact the counselor on call. Friends or parents can also contact the counseling staff or security if they recognize "red flags" or feel the student needs immediate help or is in danger.

3

Understanding Documented Disabilities and the ADA Laws for College

More students with disabilities are attending college than ever before, and educational institutions are rising to meet the challenge of creating a positive learning environment and equal access for these students. The ADA laws were created in 1973 to assist disability students in higher education. Under Section 504, Subpart E (Postsecondary Education) of the 1973 Rehabilitation Act and the Americans with Disabilities Act, "institutions of higher education must provide reasonable accommodations to a student's known disability and may not deny equal access to the institution's programs, courses and activities." The Americans with Disabilities Act, initially passed in 1990 and amended in 2008, contributed significantly to the increased growth in the number of students with disabilities attending college. Under the ADA laws, educational institutions must provide reasonable accommodations to all self-disclosed students with disabilities. Reasonable accommodations will assist the student with accessing information for their courses and in the classroom.

> Institutions are not required to provide personal devices and services such as attendants, individually prescribed devices, such as eyeglasses, readers for personal use or study, or other services of a personal nature, such as tutoring. If institutions offer tutoring to the general student population, however, they must ensure that tutoring services also are available to students with disabilities. In some instances, a state VR agency may provide auxiliary aids and services to support an individual's postsecondary education and training once that individual has been determined eligible to receive services under the VR program [U.S. Department of Education, 2015].

Once a student reaches the age of 18 years, their academic disability rights no longer follow under the IDEA laws; instead they will follow the ADA laws. These laws protect the rights of all individuals with disabilities *over the age of 18* (NC AHEAD, 2015). Students should know their rights when preparing for higher education.

The ADA Laws for college students can be found by going to http://www. 2.ed.gov/about/offices/list/ocr/transition.html.

The ADAAA is a civil rights law and was first passed in 1990 as the Americans with Disabilities Act. In 2008 it was amended and went into effect as ADAAA on January 1, 2009 (Americans with Disabilities Act Amendments Act, 2009). It provides protections for people with disabilities and prohibits discrimination against them in the workplace, school and other settings. It requires public and private institutions to make reasonable accommodations for those with disabilities but does not provide funding for services or accommodations. The ADAAA laws define a person as disabled if he or she

- has a physical or mental impairment which substantially limits one or more major life activities;
- has a record of such an impairment; or
- is regarded as having such impairment [Americans with Disabilities Act Amendments Act, 2008, §12102].

The 2008 amendment to the ADA laws outlined documentation procedures to assist students in receiving accommodations. The AHEAD (Association of Higher Education and Disability) website is an excellent source for reviewing this 2008 amendment. The updated laws state:

> With the ADA Amendments Act of 2008, Congress rejected the heightened standard for demonstrating disability that the Supreme Court articulated in a series of decisions and emphasized that it intended the protections of the ADA to be applied broadly. Revised Title I regulations state that "the primary purpose" of the ADA amendments "is to make it easier for people with disabilities to obtain protection under the ADA." Taken as a whole, the changes to the statute and regulations for Titles I, II, and III clarify (a) who has a disability entitled to protection under the ADA and Section 504, (b) who is entitled to accommodations, and (c) how those determinations are made and by whom.
>
> No legislation or regulations require that documentation be requested or obtained in order to demonstrate entitlement to legal protections because of disability and seek reasonable accommodations. The regulations acknowledge that postsecondary institutions may request a reasonable level of documentation. However, requiring extensive medical and scientific evidence perpetuates a deviance model of disability, undervalues the individual's history and experience with disability and is inappropriate and burdensome under the revised statute and regulations [AHEAD, 2015].

Colleges are required to have a DSS to assist students with setting up proper accommodations for their individual disability needs. The types of services within each college may vary, but the basic requirements to comply with the

ADA laws apply to all students with disabilities attending all types of schools from community/technical colleges and specialty colleges (like art and design) to all four-year state and private institutions.

Data recently released by the U.S. Department of Education's National Center for Education Statistics shows the distribution of types of student disabilities among college attendees:

- specific learning disabilities, 31%;
- ADD and ADHD, 18%;
- physical health conditions, 18%;
- mental or psychiatric conditions, 15%;
- difficulty hearing or seeing, 7%; and
- other, 11%.

Under the ADA laws colleges are required to provide accommodations for students who submit documentation and are given approval. Accommodations are streamlined according to each individual student's learning needs. AHEAD provides examples of possible accommodations:

Qualified interpreters, assistive listening systems, captioning, TTYs, qualified readers, audio recordings, taped texts, Braille materials, large print materials, materials on computer disk, and adapted computer terminals are examples of auxiliary aids and services that provide effective communication. Such services must be provided unless doing so would result in a fundamental alteration of the program or would result in undue financial or administrative burdens. [Note: According to a 1992 publication on the ADA and postsecondary education by the Association on Higher Education and Disability] [AHEAD, 2015].

The ADA laws require all colleges to provide reasonable accommodations to students who self-disclose their disability:

Given legal mandates under the ADA, postsecondary institutions must make reasonable accommodations in order to provide students with disabilities an equal opportunity to participate in courses, programs, and activities. This includes extracurricular activities. These accommodations can be in the form of academic adjustments or modifications such as extended time for test taking or completing course work; substitution of specific courses to meet degree requirements; modification of test taking or performance evaluations so as not to discriminate against a person's sensory, speaking or motor impairments, unless that is what is being tested. Accommodations can also take the shape of auxiliary aids and services such as qualified sign language interpreters, note takers, readers, braille, large print, and electronic formats of print materials, and adaptive equipment.

The laws further state:

Colleges and universities do not have to provide accommodations that would "fundamentally alter" the educational program or academic requirements that are essential to a program of study or to fulfill licensing requirements. The determination of what is a fundamental alteration, however, is one which requires specific steps and a reasoned, determinative process on the part of the campus community, and necessitates that colleges and universities question their notions of what is truly fundamental and provide for alternate methods of achieving the results intended by the educational program [American Psychological Association, 2015].

A college student who is 18 years old or older and has a documented disability is responsible for making decisions regarding their academic accommodations. They are not required to disclose their disability, but if they are seeking accommodations related to their disability they will need to contact the disability/accessibility department of the college and complete the appropriate paperwork. Most forms and procedures can be found on the college disability website. Under the IDEA laws the high school student had an IEP or a 504 plan; these accommodation plans are not used on the college level, but most colleges will view these plans to help aid in understanding the student's disability and learn which accommodations worked for them in high school. The student can also write a personal statement sharing how their disability impacts their learning and which accommodations worked best for them in past educational settings. Colleges may also want to meet individually with the student and parents to better understand their learning needs. Many colleges will ask for a personal impact statement in order to give them more knowledge of the student's strengths and weaknesses, and to learn which accommodations have been used successfully in the past. If the college does not ask for a personal impact statement, I suggest that the student write one anyway and turn it in with their psychological report, so the college has a more complete picture of the student.

Successes and challenges in high school will also help the student in deciding the type of support they may need at college. Remember, there are no IEP's in college. Different legislation, Section 504 of the Rehabilitation Act of 1973, will now provide access but this is very different from what students may be used to in high school. Degree programs and course requirements will not be modified to fit them; students need to find the program into which they will fit. The only way to know that is to know more about oneself, and attempting a challenging curriculum in high school is one way to do that (Planning for College Success, 2014). College accommodations may differ considerably than high school accommodations, so it is important that students and their parents understand these differences.

High School	*College*
• *School is responsible to identify students, test, plan and implement programs to maximize student potential*	• *Student must self-identify* • *Primary responsibility for accommodations belongs to the student—student-initiated!*

High School	College
• *School bears primary responsibility for accommodations/no cost to parent*	• *No parental involvement unless student signs FERPA*
• *Identify/evaluate and plan*	• *Colleges DO NOT modify curriculum or assignments*
• *IEP/504 plan required and reviewed each year*	• *Documentation needed to approve accommodations*
• *Modifications can be made to curriculum and assignments*	• *Student should choose a college that provides specialized services*
• *Parents are actively involved in the entire process*	• *Student chooses to use accommodations*
	• *Assessments paid for by parents*
	• *SERVICES VARY from college to college*

Disability Documentation

All colleges will require documentation regarding the student's disability. The parameters regarding this documentation may differ a bit from each academic institution of higher learning, but they basically follow similar guidelines and procedures that are reasonable and comply with section 504 and Title II ADA laws.

> Institutions of postsecondary education are not required to conduct or pay for an evaluation to document a student's disability and need for an academic adjustment, although some institutions do so. If a student with a disability is eligible for services through the state VR services program, he or she may qualify for an evaluation at no cost. High school educators can assist students with disabilities in locating their state VR agency at http://rsa.ed.gov (click on "Info about RSA," then "Resources," then "State and Local Government Employment Resources," then "Vocational Rehabilitation Offices"). If students with disabilities are unable to find other funding sources to pay for necessary evaluation or testing for postsecondary education, they are responsible for paying for it themselves [U. S. Department of Education, 2015].

The college disability website will have specific guidelines and procedures for each disability category. Psychological tests, such as the Woodcock Johnson III and the Wechsler Adult Intelligence Scale, are helpful in determining the student's need for accommodations. The psychologist will determine which assessment tools to use for each individual student. The documentation must be provided by a licensed or appropriately credentialed professional.

The following are some basic guidelines for appropriate disability documentation. Please make sure to check out the disability web page at the college of choice for the institution's specific set of requirements.

• *ADHD/ADD Documentation*—Most institutions of higher learning will require a psychological report, no less than five years old. Test scores should include the child's cognitive scores, plus their academic abilities, such as reading, writing, math, processing speed, and memory scores. These scores will show the student's strengths and weaknesses, and guide the disability department in approving the appropriate accommodations "to provide equal access" while the student attends college (including graduate school). Students should have a complete psychological report completed during their sophomore or junior year of high school.

• *Medications for ADHD*—If the student takes prescription medications for their ADHD, they will need a letter from their doctor stating their diagnosis, which medication they have been prescribed, and the recommended doses. Some colleges request that a copy of this letter be filed with the health center on campus. A local pharmacy can refill prescriptions. Some college health centers may also be able to refill prescriptions. Students may want to purchase a small safe to keep all medications locked up in their dorm room.

• *Learning Disabilities*—Required documentation for a student with learning disabilities is a psychological report, usually no less than three years old, although some colleges will accept a report up to five years old. This documentation needs to have the student's cognitive abilities as well as their academic abilities. The scores will show the student's strengths and weaknesses, and should have a stated diagnosis with recommended accommodations. This test should be completed by a certified psychologist. Students should have a complete psychological report completed during their sophomore or junior year of high school. Some examples of learning disabilities are: dyslexia, dyscalculia, Autism/Asperger's, reading/writing/math disabilities, memory, and processing disorders.

• *Medical Disabilities*—Students attending college with a medical disability will need a letter from their current doctor stating the diagnosis and dates when the student was diagnosed. The letter should also state how this medical condition will impact the student academically, and have suggestions for possible accommodations, including housing accommodations. If the student's condition changes during the semester, the doctor should submit a new letter stating how the medical changes are currently impacting the student. A new letter will be required at the beginning of each new academic year in order to continue accommodations. Examples of some medical disabilities are: hearing impairment, visual impairment, Crohn's Disease, IBS, allergies, epilepsy, MS, cancer, paralysis, HIV, Tourette's, etc. Short-term medical disabilities can include: concussion, broken arm or leg, injuries from playing sports, etc.

• *Psychological Disabilities*—Students with a diagnosed psychological disorder will need to have a letter from a licensed psychiatrist, or psychologist. Documentation must state their diagnosis, dates diagnosed, medications and possible academic or housing accommodations. The letter must have a statement describing how the documented disability impacts the student's learning needs. Most colleges will require a new letter at the beginning of each academic year, especially if the diagnosis has changed within the past year. Some examples of psychological disorders are: OCD, anxiety, depression, bi- polar, eating disorders, PTSD, schizophrenia, etc.

College approved accommodations may be different than the 504 or IEP accommodations from high school. It is important that *the student attend their IEP/504 meetings throughout high school* so they have a good understanding of how their disability impacts their academic studies. Attending these meetings with parents and educators enable the student to ask questions about and contribute to the discussion regarding their disability, strengths and weaknesses, and appropriate accommodations. They should leave high school with a solid understanding of their academic strengths and weaknesses, as well as how their ability to function as a student is limited as a result of their disability (U. S. Department of Education, 2015). Psychologists should also take time to discuss which accommodations the student will need on the college academic level, as these will differ from the high school accommodations. This should be part of the transition plan. It is very important for students to understand that in college, "degree programs, course requirements and due dates will not be modified to fit the student; the student needs to find the program to which they will fit" (NCLD.org, 2015). This is why it is important for the student to meet early with the DSS department on campus and set up the appropriate accommodations so that they will be in place in time for the student's first semester of college.

College Accommodations

Students with documented disabilities and ADD/ADHD have a variety of resources and programs available to them on the college level. The ADA laws state that colleges must provide accommodations to students with documented disabilities. It is important that students with disabilities register with the department for disability support services. The parents and student should contact DSS soon after sending in their commitment deposit. It may take four to six weeks to process the needed documentation and approve specific accommodations for the student. Students need to go to their college disability/accessibility services website in order to research the appropriate documentation they need in order to register and qualify for specific accommodations. Once they have turned in their documentation and completed the appropriate disability intake forms, they should discuss their accommodation requests with the disability/accessibility services department in person or by phone. Once the accommodations are approved the student will receive a letter explaining which approved accommodations they will receive, both in the classroom and for testing, as well as any specific housing needs. These accommodations will stay with the student throughout their undergraduate degree.

At the beginning of each semester, the student must go to the DSS department and ask for new accommodations letters to be written, then either emailed or hand-delivered to their professors. It is then up to the student to meet with each professor during the first couple weeks of classes to discuss the approved accommodations for the course and how to implement testing and classroom accommodations. The student must initiate contact with the professor. Even though a letter may have been emailed to the professors from the disability department, the student has to initiate the process by requesting testing accommodations and peer notes, etc. The sooner the student meets with the professor, the more the professor will understand their academic needs and follow through with accommodations, and confusion over follow-through with testing accommodations can be avoided.

Sometimes the student may experience changes regarding their disability; if this happens they can apply for additional accommodations or changes to their accommodations. If approved accommodations are not working the student should meet with the disability staff to make appropriate changes as soon as possible. It is up to the student to follow through with implementing these accommodations each semester. It is important to remember that accommodations *are not retroactive*; the accommodations start once the student requests and implements them.

If the student encounters a professor who is not willing to honor the approved accommodations the student can ask the disability staff to intercede for them and clarify any misunderstanding. The disability staff will become advocates for the student and their disability needs at the college. It will be beneficial for the student to meet with the DSS staff each semester and more often as needed throughout the semester. The better the DSS staff knows them as a student and understands their disability needs, the more insight they will have in giving guidance, support and advocacy.

Some resources available on college campuses include

- disability/accessibility services center;
- academic services center (tutoring resources);
- counseling center;
- writing center;

- math labs or tutoring centers;
- peer mentoring (through student life or counseling center); and
- technology resources (adaptive technology).
- fee-based academic support programs.
- campus health center.

Here are some tips for using your college disability resources:

- Contact the office of disability services when visiting potential colleges. Find out what documentation they accept, and their procedures to apply for and receive accommodations.

- Make sure (you) the student picks up his/her accommodation letters at the beginning of each semester, as students must give these letters to each professor, unless the specific college emails the letters to each professor through the disability department. The student will need to meet individually with the professor during their office hours to discuss implementing the accommodations.

- The student is responsible for informing the professor of their learning needs/challenges. The more the professor knows about the student the better they can help guide them through their course. Take time to build a relationship with your professors to assist with issues or illnesses throughout the semester.

- Do yourself a favor and *use* your accommodations; don't wait until you are failing a course to put your accommodation in place. These accommodations "level the playing field" for you, and they are not meant to give you an advantage. There is no need to be embarrassed or shy about using accommodations. Approximately 10 to 15 percent of the college population uses accommodations, so you are not alone; and colleges take care to keep your anonymity. These accommodations are in place to help you succeed in a very challenging academic environment.

- Students may not need accommodations for all of their courses, so they can choose to use the accommodations only for the courses that do impact their disability. Example: if you have a reading disability you may not need accommodations for math-related courses, so instead use the accommodations for history, English, religion, ethics, science, etc. as needed.

As students research colleges, they should also spend time researching and reading to gain a better understanding the ADA laws and how they will impact them as they transition into a college student. Plan to meet with the disability services office at each college to make sure they have the resources and accommodations necessary in order to become a successful student. Planning early to make this a crucial part of the college search will save students frustration and disappointment in the future.

4

Physical Disabilities
Student Testimonies—
Collin and Chase

As students with physical disabilities begin to prepare for a career, many are looking into postsecondary institutions and preparing for this transition by taking rigorous high school courses to meet the admission requirements of the college of their choice. Choosing a college and career path will require preparing a transition plan, setting educational career goals for their field of study, exploring assistive technology, and investigating overall campus and dorm accessibility. Accessibility expectations are especially important for students with physical disabilities. These students will have to become more independent than they were in high school and develop self-advocacy skills. Students should begin working with their transition specialist starting in ninth grade in order to successfully prepare for their college transition through their IEP or 504 plans. Once the student turns 17½, they can also contact vocational rehabilitation services for further transition assistance.

The ADA/ADAA Laws for College Students
with Disabilities

Once a student reaches the age of 18, they are no longer governed under the IDEA laws; instead they are served under the ADA laws. These laws provide students with disabilities access to accommodations to assist with college and career success. The student must self-advocate by requesting accommodations and housing needs, because the parent is no longer legally their advocate. Parents play a lesser role once their child reaches 18 years of age. College accommodations may differ from high school accommodations, so make sure to meet with the disability office early to review which accommodations they can approve and put in place to meet any specific needs. The disability director will review the student's current IEP to learn which accommodations worked best for them in high school, and they will ask them to complete a personal statement to better understand their strengths and weaknesses and which accommodations have been successful in the past. Physically disabled students should also take an active role in their high school IEP meeting and transition planning to partake in making decisions regarding their academic goals and enhance their advocacy skills as they move towards more independence on the college level.

Finding the Right College Fit

Finding the right college fit with sufficient mobility access is a priority for students with physical disabilities. Each student's physical and academic needs will vary greatly lending to a variety of possible college fits across the country. "Students with physical disabilities can have very different types and combinations of impairments. There is no one size fits all recommendation, and students will need to select their college and their services with their own specific needs in mind" (Tiedemann, 2012, p. 3). The student must decide first whether they want to start at a two-year college or a four-year college, and then look into the physical setting for accessibility and accommodations to meet their needs. Some students consider two-year colleges to start off with, and have a plan to transfer to a four-year college as they become more comfortable with their growing independence. "Two-year colleges are considered a good option for students with physical disabilities because they offer the opportunity to become accustomed to college level academics while still residing at home, where personal care services and other types of assistance are available" (Tiedemann, 2012). Another option is to consider a four-year college within driving distance to home so the student can still have the college experience yet maintain access to personal care assistants. Many colleges are also offering online degree or certification programs, which also allow the student to live at home while attaining their career goals. For those who choose to move out, the geographic location—specifically, proximity to home—is important to consider when deciding on a college choice. Many students with physical disabilities want to be close enough to come home for doctor visits and other medical providers. If students choose to live on campus farther from home, they should make sure to look into transportation options in the area to fit their physical needs.

Diligently researching potential good fit colleges should start during the freshman and sophomore year of high school for students with physical/ mobility disabilities. Along with finding the right major and location for college the student needs to take extra time to visit each college and explore the campus to ensure mobility, building, and classroom and dorm accessibility. Colleges are required, by the ADA laws of 1990, the Higher Education Act of 2008, and the Veterans Educational Assistance Act of 2008 (a post–9/11 bill) to make it possible for all students to maneuver the campus and access buildings, parking, elevators, etc. The student and their family should visit potential colleges and meet with the disability/accessibility staff to discuss their specific accommodation needs.

Students and their families should take time to "walk the potential campus" to ensure that they have

- accessible buildings with automatic access;
- accessible classroom furniture;
- handicapped restrooms with grab bars;
- plenty of handicapped parking available;
- curb cut-outs located around campus to easily maneuver sidewalks and roads;
- ramps leading to buildings and sidewalks;
- elevators large enough to carry a wheelchair;
- shuttle transportation; and
- handicapped dorms with accessible showers, closets, kitchens, beds, etc.

Students should take the time to visit the colleges they are seriously interested in attending. While on the campus tour they should make sure there are enough curb cut-outs to easily maneuver campus from building to building. Is the terrain easy to maneuver in a wheelchair or on crutches? Make sure the buildings are in good repair, especially elevators and building access. Take time to explore and use building ramps for handicapped access; where are they located? How accessible is the campus during bad weather, such as rain, snow and ice?

Buildings that were erected before the ADA laws were passed have been grandfathered in and are not legally bound by the law. If the student does choose a college with many older buildings they can meet with disability/ accessibility services to discuss whether some classes can be moved to a more accessible building. Many colleges have renovated these older buildings to make them accessible, so make sure to take time to tour all academic and dorm buildings during the college visit. In addition, students should take time during their visit to discuss emergency evacuation policies for students in wheelchairs and look into accessible public transportation. Students can also take advantage of this visit to look into adaptive sports programs, clubs and support groups available on campus.

Campus Residential Living

If the student chooses to live in a residential dorm building on campus they will need to meet with the housing staff about six months before they move in. This will give the housing staff time to properly equip the dorm room with special door access and shower facilities, as well as to adjust closet organization for accessibility depending on the student's individual physical needs. The disability staff will meet with students to approve any housing accommodations and will assist with communicating with the student life/housing department to ensure that all housing needs are being met. The campus security staff will also assist with putting an emergency evacuation plan in place for fires, tornadoes, or other dorm/campus related emergences. Make sure to meet with the security staff before classes begin to arrange any specific emergency needs.

Assistive Technology

Technology is constantly improving and providing students with immediate access to their world. Reading, writing and recording software are paving the road to more student success than ever before. Smartphones give access to family, friends, email, internet resources, FaceTime conversations, photo and videos. They have become a valuable resource to physically disabled students by creating accessible communication, independence and security. Speech activated software assists with opening and responding to texts/emails and conducting internet research. Students have access to computers with text to speech software, dictation software like Dragon Naturally Speaking (for assistance with writing), along with keyboard and pointing devices, to name a few. Vocational rehabilitation services are an excellent resource to begin exploring appropriate technology while still in high school. College disability services departments also have technology experts and assistive technology available to students, but services vary greatly, so make sure to check this out thoroughly on college visits. Make sure to meet with the disability office at the college of choice *more than once* to explore and set up any specific assistive technology needs. Having the right technology resources in place can make the difference between success and failure. *(Chapter 17 has more specific technology information.)*

Requesting Accommodations

Make sure to arrange a visit with the disability/accessibility department while on college tours. Students should share current high school IEP or 504 plans with them to discuss the accommodations they currently receive, what has worked best for them in the past and which accommodations they are eligible to receive for college under the ADA laws. They can ask about accessible technology, transportation, accessible buildings and any dorm accommodations they may require, and visit the cafeteria to make sure they will have assistance getting food, and that the seating is wheelchair accessible.

Once a student has made the final decision on their college choice, they should send in documentation and formally request all academic and housing accommodations. Each college has a disability website that identifies the required documentation to support accommodation requests and forms to be completed by the student. It may take three to six weeks for the accommodation approval process. An accommodation letter will be sent to the student via email or to the home address stating all approved accommodations and instructions for following through with all accommodations.

The approved accommodation letter does not state the disability, only classroom and testing accommodations. The student should meet with each professor during the first week of classes to deliver the letter and review all approved accommodations and discuss procedures for implementing them; this is especially important for testing accommodations. Also, meet with the disability staff to review approved accommodations for assistive technology. They will make sure the software is loaded onto computers and other devices and instruct the student on how to properly use the software programs or other adaptive technology. Requests for tutoring can also be set up at this time.

Personal Care Assistants

Under the ADA laws colleges are not required to provide a personal aid for students. Once the child leaves high school and attends any type of college the student and family are responsible for creating a personal care plan and to hire and train a personal assistant to help with daily living. Inquire with the disability/accessibility office for referrals of local agencies and types of assistance programs in the area. The disability/accessibility office should have a list of contacts for these services in their community. Some students will need minimal care, while others will require extensive care. The college health care services can be another resource to aid in finding personal care assistants.

Vocational rehab also assists with setting up personal care assistants for students. Make sure to meet with this department during the senior year of high school to get the necessary requests in place. They are another resource for finding quality personal care for the student, and they may help with the cost. While this is certainly possible, colleges do not generally supply personal aids to assist with the student's physical needs. A few colleges do provide personal care assistants, but this is usually a separate fee-based program. Keep in mind that special identification cards and parking passes will be required of these aids, and the college security office will need to assist with putting these items in place.

The one million plus undergraduate students with physical disabilities can successfully complete their goal of getting a college education; whether at a technical college, art college or a two-year or four-year college program, as long as they have all the physical and academic accommodations in place. Students should work with their high school disability specialist and Vocational Rehab specialist to create a transition plan and a personal care plan. Taking time to explore technology early and practice using the assistive technology software and devices so the students will have one less learning curve to overcome once they are attending college is advised. The student should decide whether living closer to home or farther away with support systems in place will be best to care for all of their personal and academic needs.

Collin

Collin was an avid sports fan and spent most of his spare time following his favorite sports teams. He proudly wore his USC Gamecocks, and HPU Panthers team shirts, and would often razz his fellow college students about scores of the latest games. As a high school teenager he was a great athlete, playing basketball, baseball and football, and excelling in each. In order to play Collin had to keep up his grades, so he worked on his academics in order to keep his place on the team. Collin was also a very social person in high school. He had many friends and stayed very active. Academics were not the highest priority for Collin; his focus was sports and he looked forward to playing college athletics one day.

All of this changed on August 16, 2005, when Collin was 15 years old. One Friday night he was riding around in a car with a few other football players when they were in a freak accident. The driver of the car Collin was riding in crossed the center line on a two-lane road, overcorrected, bounced off a large grass plant and eventually ran into a tree. They were not speeding, and no drugs or alcohol were involved. Each of the boys in the car were injured, leaving Collin and another boy both quadriplegics. At first Collin and his family did not know how badly he was injured. At the scene of the accident he was aware and talking, but had no idea the extent of his injuries. He didn't even remember the actual accident; his only memory of the accident was just seeing the other car's headlights coming at them. Immediately following the accident, he knew his body was "messed up," but did not know how badly he was injured. After being in the hospital a few weeks, he learned the extent of his injuries when the physical therapist came to tell him and his parents that he would never walk again. Collin was devastated, especially since he would never again be able to play sports, which was his passion in life. He always thought he would eventually become a professional athlete, but first he looked forward to playing college sports. Learning that he was now a quadriplegic was confusing for Collin; sports family and church were everything to him, but after receiving this devastating news he felt that he had lost his identity.

A few weeks after the accident Collin had a better understanding of his physical limitations and was overwhelmed with what he could not do. He had extremely limited use of his hands and could not write or dress himself. He needed help with everyday personal and physical activities, from getting out of bed to bathing, dressing, eating, writing, etc. He was especially distraught about not being able to play sports, being able to help his younger sister practice her sports, or help his parents around the house. "Everything I ever thought of doing was gone." In a matter of a few precious minutes his life had forever changed. The realization that he had severe limitations was overwhelming and frustrating, especially since he was cut off from all physical activities.

Collin was transferred to a rehab center in Atlanta. At this center he was taught how to use adaptive equipment in order to regain some independence. This was a very frustrating time for him, but he was constantly encouraged by the physical therapists and fellow paraplegics who were also learning how to adapt to their body's limitations. Collin eventually learned to maneuver his wheelchair and he gained upper body strength. He was taught how to use phones, computers, and a hand device, which helped him turn pages in a book. He was also given a special tool to assist with writing. The rehab center became his new home. Collin was very comfortable here because he was learning how to adjust to his limitations and there were many others like him or worse off than he was. He had accepted his physical limitations and was learning to adapt, with the help of the rehab staff.

After three and a half months at the rehab center it was time to go back home and finish high school. Collin found it very difficult to adjust to life outside of the rehab center. At the center he was one of many experiencing similar situations, but once he was home he was "different" from everyone. Collin felt very fortunate to have a close community within his church that gave tremendous support. "My parents and our church members were there for me 100 percent," Collin said.

Collin's immediate family was his biggest supporter; they believed in him and never gave up, no matter how dire the circumstances. Collin felt that he had to succeed because he did not want to let them down. "My family has been extremely supportive of me and my academics. My mom even substitutes for my college driver and scribe, Earnest, when he cannot be here in college classes with me. If I ask for help studying they drop everything and help me out." Collin continues to support his younger sister with her athletic dreams. "My little sister hopes to play basketball for High Point University one day. I can't play basketball with her anymore, because my fingers don't open so I can't hold a ball in my hands, but I am hoping she will have the college experience I never had and I will be on the sidelines cheering her on the entire time."

With Collin's return to his high school he was surprised and saddened to find that he was judged and separated from many of his former friends. He was physically different and could no longer be the "cool" athlete. Most of his old friends ignored him; they did not seem to know how to interact with this new Collin. He had to face a depleted social life as well as dealing with the physical struggles of being a paraplegic student. It took him a while to emotionally come to terms with his new life. Collin learned that he had to refocus his goals. Before the accident, he was not on a college academic track, but he quickly learned that academics was the one area of his life where he still had control, so he decided to make this his new focus. He could no longer be an athlete, but he knew that if he worked hard he could become a better high school student and eventually get into college.

During his remaining two years of high school he was given a personal tutor who stayed with him the entire day. The scribe would write for him because he had very limited use of his hands, and could only do so with a special device. He took tests orally and the scribe would write the responses for him. Former friends did not know how to relate to him, and some didn't even speak to him. A few stepped up and revealed themselves as *true* friends, but nothing was the same. "It was a bit awkward getting used to the wheelchair and crowded hallways, etc. I could never again be the person they knew me as." Collin had to figure out who he was and where his intelligence and physical limitations could take him.

"After recovering from the accident and going back to high school I found that I also had to focus harder on academics. Academics was now the only thing I had control over in my life, so I decided to focus on school and make sure I have a career, so that I would not be financially dependent on my parents for the rest of my life. This became my first priority. I stayed somewhat involved in sports by watching them on TV, and it took at least a year to gather up the courage to actually attend one of our high school games. I was kind of running away from it because it hurt to think about being on the sidelines and not in the game with my friends. In my heart I really just wanted to be on the team again with them, but I knew that ship had forever sailed. I just kept my focus on school academics, because I still wanted to get to college and there would not be an athletic scholarship to help pave the way financially."

College Becomes a Reality

"I applied to High Point University," Collin explains, "because I knew I met their admissions requirements. I also felt that this was where God wanted me to be. HPU was close enough, 45 minutes from home, so I could commute each day. My mother had met the disability director at a college fair; she was the disability coordinator for the university. After discussing my academic needs in depth my mother felt she was amazing and HPU would be the right fit for me."

"The disability director understood my physical disabilities and what accommodations needed to be in place in order for me to be a successful student. She also met me and seemed to care about me as a person, not just another student. Since I had such severe physical limitations, and needed a personal care aid to help dress and bathe and help with my personal needs I knew that I would not be able to live in a dorm. I am a very social person and the thought of not being able to live on campus with my peers was another devastating hurdle I had to overcome."

"It was difficult to attend HPU as a freshman and not be a part of the social activities on campus. I could not attend dances, fraternity parties or clubs because I had to go home after classes each day and do my required physical therapy. I am a real people person and I don't like to miss out on social activities, so not being able to attend on campus activities was very difficult for me. Each year I set a goal to actually live on campus, hoping that this would help me participate in social clubs, activities and sporting events more often." Collin worked hard to attempt to live on campus as a student, but was unable to fulfill this goal. He completed four years of college, living at home and commuting daily.

Collin has a personal assistant named Ernest who is a retired engineer. Soon after Collin's accident, Ernest, a fellow church member who had never met Collin before, made the decision to become Collin's personal assistant because he felt God was calling him to do this. Ernest went through training to become a personal health care aid. As soon as he was certified he spent five days a week taking care of Collin's personal needs. Collin explained, "Ernest attends classes with me, drives me back and forth from home to campus; he attends all my classes and takes class notes, helps with meals, and my daily exercises and all my personal needs. I have found that having Ernest with me every day has been really helpful, and he takes interest in my classes and will offer to study with me. Ernest has been a blessing each and every day. Even though he is retired, he is once again enjoying the academics of college life."

"My mother and I attended an admissions open house during my junior year, and I fell in love with the campus and people and knew that this was where I wanted to attend college. The summer before attending HPU I met with their disability support staff and they set up approved accommodations for me. I needed a personal scribe in class with me each day, so Earnest volunteered to do this since he was already pushing my wheelchair to and from classes, so he eagerly agreed to sit next to me during classes as my personal note taker."

Earnest arrived at Collin's home around 5:30 each morning to assist with his personal care needs and his daily physical therapy. He transported Collin to campus, pushed his wheelchair across campus and sat next to Collin as a personal note taker during classes. Earnest took a personal interest in Collin and his college career, and he encouraged him to meet with the disability director and ask for help when he began struggling in courses. The extra support and care Earnest offered made all the difference for Collin throughout his college years.

Collin's Approved College Accommodations

Classroom Accommodations:

- use of a class scribe/note taker and scribes for tests;
- books in an alternate format;
- Kurzweil 3000, a speech-to-text software program; and
- Dragon Naturally Speaking, to assist with writing papers.

"These accommodations help me to succeed with the physical aspects of being a college student," Collin says, "by allowing me to access the academic information so I can do the required assignments, papers, presentations and exams."

Testing Accommodations:

- 50% extended test time;
- testing in a separate environment;
- use of a laptop and use of speech to text software;
- a scribe for tests when needed; and
- no use of scantrons.

Unlike many others in his situation, Collin did not use housing accommodations. Instead, he lived at home with his parents because this was best for his physical therapy and personal care needs. Earnest drove him the 45 minutes to and from college each day, as well as took care of his personal needs.

Academic Struggles

Collin quickly found that college classes are more difficult and faster-paced than in high school. Much more is expected of a college student. "I was very fortunate in that my professors at HPU are really nice and extremely helpful; I enjoy being around their brilliant minds. As a college student I quickly found that I was not prepared for the pace of college. I enjoy having more free time in college than in high school. Unfortunately, like many freshmen I abused that time at first, because I didn't know how to manage my time. Fall of my freshmen year I did not read much outside of class and often procrastinated with all of my papers and assignments. During mid-terms and finals, I would feel overwhelmed and stressed, interfering with my concentration during tests. I met with the disability director and asked for help with study strategies and time management. I had to learn to do course work when I wasn't in classes, and to also use tutors when I needed them. I learned that I had to stay on top of course work daily, and I had to do more independent work. So, free time wasn't really free, it was time to work on long-term assignments, study, read and meet with professors and utilize tutors weekly. To be successful as a student I learned to set aside time in my day to study and keep up with reading textbooks; there wasn't a lot of time for slacking off!"

Collin enjoyed his courses (his favorites were history and sports management), but academically he found college to be much more challenging than high school. The work came faster and he needed to be more independent with his studies. Collin found himself enjoying the information presented in his courses and the classroom discussions and group activities, but often procrastinated when it came time to read course materials and write papers. Consequently, he would often cram the few days before a paper was due, often starting his work at 9:00 p.m. As a freshman he would look over his notes and read the chapters a few days before the exam, cramming all this information into his brain, but not really "learning" it. It took him a while to learn to manage his time better and stay on top of assignment due dates.

He found that if he met with math or English tutors each week he was better prepared for his tests and papers. He also realized that he could not start a paper, especially when research was required, the night before it was due and expect it to be college quality work! After struggling with writing his first couple papers Collin learned new writing strategies, including organizing his research, breaking the assignment down, working with his tutor and starting the paper early.

Collin met with his English professor to get feedback and guidance before completing and turning the paper in. He began meeting with this professor weekly for extra support and guidance with his papers. He began to build excellent relationships with each of his professors, because they saw that he was committed to their class. Collin took the opportunity to visit them during office hours or after class. "The professors make a huge difference in whether I like the classes or not," says Collin. "My professors made themselves available during office hours and other times as needed. I found that when my grades were suffering my professors would actually approach me and ask what was going on, or give me a name of a good tutor to contact. I have been fortunate to have some great professors here at HPU." Professors would look over his papers and give him feedback before he turned in the final copy; this feedback helped Collin become a better student.

Personal Struggles

Collin's biggest obstacles in college were making new friends and learning how to maneuver a new terrain/campus: "I am in a wheelchair, and needed to learn how to get around campus using the handicapped ramps and curb cut outs. No one else from my high school came to HPU, so I did not know another person on campus. It was extremely difficult to make new friends since I did not live in the dorms, and many students were hesitant to talk with me. I had Earnest drive me to and from home each day, plus he pushed my wheelchair and accompanied me to all my classes and helped me with my lunch and personal care needs. Other students did not come to sit with me or talk to me much. It was pretty difficult the first semester to meet people and make friends. I usually don't get to come back for many evening activities because I live 40 minutes away and need to pre-plan transportation for any evening activities, as I am dependent on my parents or Earnest for this. I cannot dedicate myself to any clubs or campus activities, because I am dependent on others to transport me around campus and to and from home. Vocational rehab is working with me on getting certified to drive my own vehicle with hand controls. I am hoping this happens in the future."

Collin shared that he also went through some personal internal struggles when first attending college. After the accident he did not see himself as being on the same playing field as his peers, both physically *and* academically, so he had to work hard to mentally overcome this attitude. He slowly began to meet students in classes because they were required to participate in many group activities within his major. This gives students an opportunity to really get to know each other; friendships often bloom from these experiences. "Once I started making friends and succeeding in classes I felt like a true college student. I would love to go to all the sporting events, unfortunately that is not possible because I live at home, which is a 45-minute drive to campus," Collin says. His family does bring him back for games and activities when they can. "I haven't been able to meet a lot of people because I don't live on campus, so I have to initiate any conversations or relationships. I have had to learn to put myself out there and meet my peers! Most people see the wheelchair before they see me, the person. I've accepted this, it has taught me to be more accepting of others. I feel I would at least say hello to someone in my situation, although most people at HPU at least say hello to me. I have found that most of the athletes, soccer and basketball players, are really nice to me. They know how much I enjoy sports, so they engage with me more often than most students. I met a couple of female soccer players, now they all talk to me often and I go to the games and watch them play when I can."

Internal Motivation

Collin keeps himself academically motivated because he understands the importance of completing his degree. "Jobs for people with physical disabilities are very limited, so I need this degree to take care of myself in the future. Less than ten percent of paraplegics go to college, less than one percent actually graduates college. I want to be in that one percent and be able to take care of myself in the future and live on my own someday. I will probably never be able to live completely on my own, as I will need a health care person to assist with my daily physical needs. I do plan to move out of my parents' home, once I have a job, with the help of an assistant and health aid of course!" Collin hopes to find a job in radio or TV sports announcing. He still has a passion for sports and since he can no longer play the games he hopes to report on others playing these exciting games.

While Collin attended High Point University, one of his professors, Dr. Ellenburg, encouraged Collin to assist with the men's basketball team. Since sports were Collin's passion, his was an excited "yes" response, and it gave him hands on experience with college athletes and coaches. Collin spent the 2012–13 season being an aid to the team and traveling to a few games on the team bus. This was a dream come true for Collin and an experience he will never forget. After graduation Collin continued to assist with the basketball team during the 2014 and 2015 seasons.

Graduation Success

Collin graduated HPU in May of 2013, with a degree in mediated communications and a minor in sports management and officiating. Graduation day was exciting for Collin, his family and his professors. Many hurdles had been overcome to get to that day. Collin arrived at HPU very unsure of himself, and four years later came out a mature, confident young man with a degree and options for a very successful future!

Graduation day held another big surprise for Collin and Earnest. President Qubein was aware of Earnest and his great contributions to Collin's success as a student and gave him an honorary degree from High Point University! Collin and Earnest made history together and the crowd cried and cheered at this beautiful accomplishment.

Completing a degree within four years is the goal for most students, and can be especially challenging for students with physical disabilities. Vocational rehab will help pay for some of this college education, as long as the student's GPA stays above a 2.0. Utilizing all college resources, such as tutoring, counseling, meeting with professors, and math and writing labs, will all help with academic success. Making sure you are a strong self-advocate, who is willing to ask for help and guidance, explain maneuverability issues, ask for assistance with study skills, and learn to use appropriate technology resources will make the difference between success and failure.

Chase

Chase was born with osteogenesis imperfecta, a genetic disorder that affects the bones, which causes him to have some physical limitations and requires him to use a power chair to get around. He has a passion for computer programming and decided to transfer to HPU after attending a larger state college. His passion for gaming led him to major in interactive game design, within the school of communication, with a minor in business. Chase set career goals to achieve a master's degree, and possibly a doctorate in his field.

Under an IEP for elementary school, Chase was given special accommodations; he had a personal assistant, an extra set of books for home use, a special/separate bathroom to accommodate his wheelchair and stature, and special transportation on a bus with a wheelchair lift. Chase has always been a strong student, so he progressed through school without academic difficulties. His biggest hurdles were physical. He continued under an IEP and 504 plan throughout high school. During his junior and senior years of high school Chase, along with his mother, counselor, specialist and vocational rehabilitation counselor, put together a plan to transition to college. Vocational rehab also gave him $6,000 per year towards his college tuition, as long as he kept grades at or above a 2.0 GPA.

Making Right Fit Choices

Chase originally wanted to major in computer programming, and knew that he needed to live at home for the first year or so, because the transition to living on a college campus was huge due to his physical limitations. He knew that he needed time to first adjust to college academic life; then he would focus on actually living on campus. He initially attended a large state college near his home and applied for accommodations. Overall he had a good experience here, both academically and maneuvering about campus.

Buildings were far apart, so he needed to create a schedule that gave him enough time to get to each building. He attended all classes, met with his professors to ensure accommodation implementation and received assistance from professors as needed.

During his sophomore year he learned about the new interactive game design degree at High Point University and applied to the college to pursue this degree, which was a passion of his. He visited the campus and found easily accessible buildings and was able to successfully maneuver through campus. He was admitted and soon met with disability services to request accommodations. His documentation consisted of medical information, a vocational rehab report, and his accommodation letter from the state university. Due to his small stature, most accommodations were to help him access classroom desks; he also needed the use of a small computer for note taking and writing.

Chase's Approved College Accommodations

Classroom Accommodations:

- the ability to type tests as needed;
- special desks in classrooms as needed;
- all classes on the first floor of buildings;
- textbooks in alternate format;
- priority registration; and
- all classes on the ground floor for easy access and emergency evacuations.

Testing accommodations:

- 50% extended test time;
- testing in a separate environment; and
- the ability to type essay tests.

Housing Accommodations:

- disability accessible dorm room close to center of campus at no extra cost;
- bathroom modifications, including special faucets, grab bars in shower and next to toilet, bench for transfer;
- modified bed;
- modified closets; and
- automatic door opener.

Chase met with each of his professors during the first day of classes in order to go over his accommodation list and make sure the classroom desks fit his needs. He built good relationships with his professors and often met with them outside of class. Chase found them to be very compassionate and helpful. "They didn't always know what I needed, so I usually came to them with concerns or asking for help," he said. Chase built excellent relationships with his professors, and met with them as needed throughout the semester.

During his first semester at HPU Chase lived at home again, in order to adjust to the campus first, and then he looked into campus housing. He excelled in his new classes and enjoyed the intimacy of smaller class sizes and great access to professors. He easily made friends with his classmates, and one of them decided to room with Chase the following semester, helping him to an easier transition to independence and living away from home for the first time.

Chase and his mother met with housing staff to explore residential living on campus. He would need a first floor handicapped accessible dorm room, for easier emergency exit. A handicapped dorm suite with two bedrooms, a bath, living area and kitchen was available, but modifications would need to be made in order for Chase to maneuver successfully each day, and become as independent as possible. This dorm was situated near the cafeteria, a couple of restaurants and the school of communication building, where most of his classes would be held. The resident director was located across the hall in case of emergencies.

The housing staff set up bathroom modifications to accommodate his needs. They placed extra faucets within easy reach for Chase, both in the shower and on the right side of the sink. They added a new shower head to accommodate his small stature, and put in a transfer bench, so he could easily maneuver himself into the shower without needing a health assistant. They also placed handicapped bars where he could easily access them. The shower doors were replaced with a shower curtain for easy access. The transfer bench could be easily lifted up to sit along the shower wall so his roommate would not be disturbed with it while showering.

The dorm kitchen had a cutout under the sink for wheelchair access, and a new microwave was put in where Chase could easily reach it from his wheelchair. His bedroom also needed accommodations. The bars in the clothes closet were lowered so he could reach in to get his clothing; they also built drawers into the closet for him. They built a new lower base for his bed so that he could get up close with his wheelchair and be level with the bed for easier self-transferring. They placed a special table in his dorm room, instead of the typical desk, so his wheelchair would easily fit. The hallway door was fitted with automatic doors and a remote door opener so Chase could easily open and close the door. Now he was ready to move in with his roommate and be on his own for the first time in his life!

Chase found that some older buildings on campus had access ramps on the side or the back of the building, so he needed to plan his time to accommodate going around the building to gain access. Each building had electronic access when using your student badge, the height of which, while up to code, were sometimes a little high for Chase and his smaller stature. Often his peers would open doors for him and assist him with entering buildings and elevators. Overall he was able to successfully manage his day, maneuvering from building to building, even shopping at the food store on campus. Living on a smaller campus gave him the security he needed to venture out on his own, gaining more independence.

Building Relationships

Chase made friends easily within his major and eventually joined a fraternity on campus, "Kappa Sig." He was able to attend all events and kept his above the required GPA. He made lasting friendships and memories while attending classes, and is thankful to the many campus staff who worked with him to live in the dorms successfully. Chase also became very active in the gaming club and made strong friendships with his peers, which have lasted outside of college.

Gaining Independence

Eventually Chase also gained a service dog that lived with him on campus for assistance with independence, and quickly won over the hearts of all students in his dorm. Vocational rehab services assisted Chase with his wheelchair and computer, working simultaneously with the disability and housing staff to help meet all his needs. Chase went to VR and asked for their assistance in gaining more independence by learning to drive a specialized handicapped car that would fit his body, and have controls where he could manipulate them. Vocational rehab aided him in this process.

Chase not only successfully completed his bachelor's degree in interactive gaming (and a minor in business); he also went on to complete an MBA degree from High Point University. His love of learning has him considering a possible Ph.D. at some point in the future! Success came to Chase by diligently using all resources available to him, asking for assistance as needed and working hard to make his academic dreams come true.

Chase has some advice for college students with physical disabilities:

- Be sure to advocate for yourself. If you don't no one will do it for you.
- Make sure you know what you need to be successful in the classroom and living on campus, and find someone to work with within the different campus departments to figure out your needs.
- If you encounter any barriers to living on campus talk to the housing staff and disability services to discuss possible solutions. Housing staff and campus enhancement made it possible for me to fulfill my dream of independently living on campus.
- Don't be too stubborn to accept or ask for help from both peers and adults. I had trouble with this at first because I pride myself on being independent, but asking for help is not a weakness, it helps you move forward with your goals.

Procedures for All Students with Physical Disabilities Who Require Accommodations

REQUESTING ACCOMMODATIONS

Students need to self-identify their disability and request appropriate accommodations. The college disability services will not make contact with you until you first self-identify. Make sure to visit with the disability/accessibility department while on your college tours. Share your current high school IEP or 504 Plan with them and discuss the accommodations you currently receive, what has worked best for you in the past and explore which accommodations you are eligible to receive under the ADA laws. Ask about accessible technology, transportation, accessible buildings and any dorm accommodations you may require. Visit the cafeteria to make sure you will have assistance getting your food, and that the seating is wheelchair accessible.

Once you have made a commitment to the college of your choice, contact disability/accessibility services and find out what documentation they require for your physical disability. You can email or use the U.S. postal services to send in documentation directly to the disability director of the college. Make sure to either meet with them in person or have an in-depth Skype or Face-Time conversation about your accommodation needs, and to review all policies and procedures for implementing your approved accommodations. The earlier you follow through with requesting accommodations, the more time the college has to prepare properly for your needs, especially with housing and classroom equipment. I had a student who needed an adaptive microscope for her science labs, and this took a few weeks to order and process, then another couple weeks for delivery. So please give disability services plenty of time to approve your accommodation requests and to order all approved classroom and housing accommodations.

Meet with disability services again once you arrive to campus to have a final review of your accommodations, assistive technology and housing needs. The disability staff will become your advocate while you are attending college. Remember to meet with them regarding any problems with implementing accommodations or tweaking accommodations as needed. I recommend that students set up a few appointments for the first month of college to just meet and discuss your progress and any concerns with accommodations. Students can meet with the disability staff any time throughout their college career. If accommodations are not being met by professors the disability staff will assist you with setting up a meeting with your professor and assist with problem solving.

MEETING WITH PROFESSORS

During the first week of classes (or earlier, if possible) meet individually with each professor to share your approved accommodation letter and review your approved accommodations for classroom and testing. Discuss the policy for testing in a separate environment to have this in place for your first tests. If there are any issues regarding your classroom accommodations, meet with disability services immediately to resolve these issues. Keep open communication with your professors throughout the semester; this is especially helpful when you encounter emergencies and health issues arise, or you need to miss class for important doctor's appointments. Most professors are familiar with the ADA laws and will work with you to accommodate your needs.

Colleges have support systems in place for all students with disabilities. If you have grievances please take them up with the disability department, and if they cannot help you resolve the issue you can contact the Office of Civil Rights (OCR) and complete a form to file a formal complaint.

Possible Accommodation Requests

Classroom Accommodations:

- peer notes;
- use of laptop for essay writing;

- textbooks in alternate format (many textbooks can be ordered as e-books, or on CD for computer and software access);
- reading and/or writing software;
- specialized seating or desk/table;
- request to move classroom to an accessible building;
- priority registration; and
- reduced coarse load.

Testing Accommodations:

- 50% extended test time;
- testing in a separate environment;
- use of laptop/computer for essay writing;
- use of reading or writing software for tests/exams;
- scribe for tests/exams; and
- reader for tests.

Housing Accommodations:

- priority housing;
- modifications to dorm room to meet the student's physical needs; and
- modifications to bathroom and shower.

Students and their families need to set up their own personal care assistant.

The numbers of students with physical disabilities are increasing on college campuses and these students are successfully utilizing accommodations and other resources to achieve their academic and career goals. Make sure to start with the right college fit, and then meet with disability services to request accommodations to meet your specific needs, and use them! Try to make relationships with your advisor and professors, who will be happy to assist you as any issues arise. Build your self-advocacy skills in order to seek guidance and help when needs arise. Most staff, students and professors on campus will be happy to help you. Those of you who plan to leave home and live on campus will have many experiences that will help you gain independence as you transition further into the adult world. Get involved in clubs and activities, and attend sporting events as well as theatre and music performances as often as possible to have a positive overall college experience.

5

Medical Disabilities
Student Testimony—Kristy

Medical situations can occur at any time during a student's college career. Some students will enter college with a diagnosed illness or medical condition. Other students may have an accident while playing a sport, driving in a car, or exercising, and require temporary medical accommodations until their injury heals. Students with medical conditions can apply for both academic and housing accommodations, depending on their medical situation.

Some medical impairments may include cystic fibrosis, epilepsy, diabetes, cancer, severe allergies, deaf and hearing impaired, blind, low vision, kidney disease, liver disease, HIV infection, irritable bowel syndrome, just to name a few. The law states that in order to receive services from a university for a medical condition the student will need to disclose their disability by submitting appropriate documentation from their medical doctor. A medical disability will require a letter from the student's doctor, stating the disability and how it will impact the student's learning. "The documentation should be submitted by a professional who is licensed/certified in the area for which the diagnosis is made and who is not related to the student. The report must be presented on a practice letterhead and signed by the examiner" (UNC Chapel Hill, 2015). If the student do not have a copy of the documentation and needs to request it from their medical provider, they will need to obtain a release of information form, and fax it to their doctor. Most colleges will have this form on their website; if not, they can request this form from their doctor.

A new letter will be required at the beginning of each academic year to update information on the medical disability and change or add accommodations as needed. If any changes occur during the semester the student can request to add any appropriate accommodations at any time, as long as a documented letter from the medical doctor supports the request. Short-term medical issues, such as when an athlete breaks a leg, or a student has surgery during the semester and may need the use of a wheel chair, can also require accommodations. A student whose arm is in a cast may request peer notes until they heal and can resume their usual activities. The student or their parent can contact disability/accessibility services and request accommodations as long as they send in the appropriate documentation.

Required documentations consists of a letter from a certified licensed physician who is currently treating the student. The disability staff may contact the doctor to verify or clarify the needed accommodations during the approval process. The accommodations are usually approved within a few days in order to best assist the student.

HIPPA Release

The student will need to sign off on the HIPPA form, giving permission for the parents/guardian, doctor and disability director permission to speak about the student and share pertinent medical information. The student, being 18 years of age, has the right to privacy regarding their medical diagnosis. The student can choose to give permission to the disability director to share a limited amount of information to the professors and staff as needed.

Kristy

Imagine it is May of your senior year of high school. You are eagerly looking forward to prom, graduation, and all of the award ceremonies and events surrounding graduation. You have finally achieved the academic milestone you have been working towards for years, and you're looking forward to the next stage of your life as you anxiously dream of heading off to college in the fall to start a new academic endeavor.

Then a medical emergency has you in the emergency room, where a few days later a visit from your doctor quickly shatters all of your dreams. You have just been diagnosed with a bone cancer, which was not operable at the initial diagnosis, and would immediately need months of chemo followed by radiation treatments. In a matter of days your life has changed drastically. You are now a cancer patient, living at the hospital and receiving numerous chemo drugs that are making you terribly sick. The shock of the diagnosis is overpowered by the immediate medical attention you need, and processing what is going on with your body is overwhelming. Graduation celebrations and dreams of attending college in the fall are quickly becoming non-existent. This happened to Kristy.

At age 18, Kristy looked forward to celebrating the end of her senior year of high school, and attending college in the fall to begin her studies in interior design; but a constant progressive pain in her back sent her to the emergency room weekly for six months. She had been feeling very sick for months and had been to the emergency room multiple times, but was never diagnosed. Her father finally demanded that the doctors do an MRI to get a clear picture of the painful area. After meeting with multiple doctors, Kristy learned she had a large tumor located on her spine which needed to be removed immediately. Within three days she was in surgery. Soon after surgery she began intense chemo. Doctors told her they hoped the surgery and chemo would work, but there were no guarantees. After one year of chemo treatments she would have to endure radiation treatments.

Kristy spent the next thirty days in the hospital, yet she still held hopes of attending her high school prom and graduation. She had a positive attitude and plenty of support from family and friends, although no one could help her deal with the reality of this catastrophic event. She felt she no longer had control of her life, instead her body and her doctors controlled everything. Her doctors did allow her to attend prom, which was quite a unique experience. Kristy felt exquisite in her beautiful gown, with a handsome date on her arm. But her energy levels were low, so she had to rest often. As if she wasn't dealing with enough already, on this day, of all days, her hair started falling out from the chemo treatments. By the end of the evening she looked quite different than when she started out earlier that day. Being Kristy, she took this all in stride and chose to enjoy her evening!

Kristy spent the summer in chemo treatment and worried about not being able to attend High Point University in the fall, where she had been accepted. Her doctors urged her to put college on hold, but a part of her wanted to move forward with her life. This first summer was extremely difficult, both physically and mentally. There were days she feared that she would not be able to fight this cancer. She also feared that staying home would add to the distress of being a cancer patient, whereas focusing on college gave her a distraction and motivation to fight the cancer. Understanding how to manage all of this while still being so sick was a constant worry. Her father told her he would support her decision, whatever it might be.

Soon Kristy met Laura, who was also attending High Point University in the fall as a freshman. They found each other on social media, and discovered they lived within an hour's distance. Through emails and phone conversations they quickly became friends. Laura shared that she also had a bout with cancer while in high school and was in remission for the past year, which further cemented their friendship. Laura visited Kristy throughout the summer and constantly urged her to attend college. This gave Kristy the security and support she needed to move forward with her college plans, and once Kristy made this decision there was no stopping her. She and Laura decided to room together and soon began making plans for their new dorm room. Kristy, her father, and her doctors made plans to continue her treatment through the Duke Cancer Center, which was closer to the university.

Kristy's father contacted DSS at High Point University and explained his daughter's medical complications and Kristy's desire to attend college while undergoing her cancer treatments. Together they began the process of preparing documentation and approving her accommodations. Letters from her doctor stated her medical disability and the accommodations she would need. She would continue to have chemo treatments throughout the semester, which meant five days of chemo and three weeks off.

Kristy's Approved College Accommodations:

Classroom Accommodations:
- copy of peer notes;
- priority registration; and
- excused absences when needed for treatment.
  Testing Accommodations:
- extended test time; and
- testing in a separate environment.
  Housing Accommodations:
- dorm room with kitchen (Kristy was not allowed to eat cafeteria food due to bacteria, and would need to make her own meals);
- dorm room with separate bedroom; and
- dorm close to health center.

Kristy was also given housing accommodations. She requested a two-bedroom suite with a kitchen since she was not allowed to eat cafeteria food and would have to make many of her own meals. She also met with her advisor over the summer to explain her medical circumstances. During this meeting they made adjustments to her schedule to accommodate her treatments. Her advisor suggested she drop the interior design courses for the first semester, as these would require a great amount of out of class work, and he wanted her to feel physically stronger when taking these demanding courses. Kristy's father also hired a student, Whitney, to help Kristy with shopping, laundry, and other physical needs she would have while her back was healing and while she was going through chemo treatments.

With all of these resources in place, she was ready to begin her freshman year. Arriving on campus wearing her beautiful head scarf was both exciting and overwhelming, but Laura and Whitney were there to help with the transition. Kristy and Laura were soon settled into their new dorm room and ready to begin classes.

The disability services director contacted each of Kristy's professors through email, explaining her medical condition, future treatments and accommodations; this began a relationship that would be vital to Kristy's success. Outside of being extremely tired, the first month of college went smoothly, until Kristy began suffering from an infection and ended up in the hospital for a couple weeks, where she could be found trying to complete course assignments from her hospital bed. She asked disability services to let her professors know of her setback, and asked for assistance with setting up new due dates for assignments. Kristy was very weak, but she continued working on assignments and kept up with readings when she could. She remained in contact with professors and emailed them with questions and assignments. When Kristy returned to campus she worked with tutors and professors to catch up, especially in math. She completed missed work in chunks until she was able to catch up completely. All the while she had DSS helping her communicate with professors.

Many days were a struggle, both emotionally and physically. The monthly cancer treatments drained her energy, brought on bouts of nausea and interfered with her short-term memory. Most young college students would choose to take a medical leave, but Kristy's strong spirit kept her focused on academics and motivated her to accomplish what she could in order to attain the goal of a college education. She did not have much of a social life because classes and assignments took all of her energy. Fortunately, Laura was very social and brought friends over for movie nights or hanging out, which helped Kristy to feel more like a college student. They soon formed a small group of friends who eventually become a strong support system for her throughout college. Kristy got through the semester week by week and kept her sights on receiving her degree, which kept her motivated. She kept in close contact with DSS, informing them of her physical and academic needs.

Eating the right foods was another issue for Kristy. She was not allowed to eat cafeteria food because of possible micro bacteria and low blood counts, so she requested housing to place her in a dorm with a kitchen. She had Whitney shop for her groceries when she was unable to get out, and she did most of her own cooking, when she could physically eat. She was often unable to eat much, so her energy levels were very low and she slept whenever she could. Completing course work became a monumental task. She would start assignments and papers early, but her body and brain fatigue from the chemo drugs caused her to shut down and sleep often. She often worked on assignments in small segments until completed, and there were times she would ask professors for extensions on her due dates. When she was too sick to attend classes she would email her professors. Most of her professors were empathetic and worked closely with her needs, but a couple expected her to complete assignments on time; which caused extra stress. Kristy worked through many difficult days while battling fatigue and nausea.

Attending college without hair could have been a monumental setback for most young women, but Kristy also took this in stride. She purchased many colorful scarves and was always well coordinated. She also ordered a wig to wear, especially when she went out to social activities. She wanted people to see her as just another college student, not "the girl with cancer," as she was often referred to. Even though Kristy had confidence about herself, she did find that some of her peers were uncomfortable with her medical disability. Often she noticed other students and some of her professors did not come up to speak with her directly. Instead they would ask her roommate or friends how she was doing, or ask them for information about her type of cancer.

Kristy never complained about the stress of having cancer and attending classes, even when managing the most unbearable days. She faced each day with a positive attitude and reached out for help through friends, academic services and disability support as she needed it. She took a full course load, but ended up dropping a math course because it was difficult to keep up with the daily assignments when she missed classes. She successfully completed the course the following semester.

Scheduling courses for spring semester brought on some new challenges. Kristy would need to have radiation treatments each day for eight weeks. Disability services gave her priority registration and helped her to find courses that would fit her medical schedule. Her advisor helped her to choose courses that also fit her time frame and were not as taxing on her time.

January of her freshman year found Kristy back in the hospital with another infection from the chemo treatments. Once again she asked disability services to help her connect with professors and communicate assignments. Professors worked closely to assist her through this illness, as well as during the next few months of radiation treatments. Kristy worked closely with her advisor to plan classes around her daily radiation treatments. She was not as sick during these treatments, and was better able to keep up with her coursework throughout the semester, but she still battled physical and mental fatigue daily. Kristy focused on getting through this year as best she could, without stressing to achieve As. She focused on completing the coursework and moving forward in her major. Having a student undergoing cancer treatment was new territory for many of her professors, and some were not comfortable speaking with her; they were more comfortable using disability services to communicate with Kristy. Others emailed her directly and kept easy and open communication. Kristy also made an effort to meet one-on-one with her professors when she was physically able to do so, both to give personal updates and to receive assistance in their course.

Kristy came to High Point University with plans to major in interior design, which is a challenging major for any student. Many students in this major put in long hours and spend many late nights completing projects for presentations. Kristy worked hard to keep up with all of her assignments, and met with professors or asked the disability staff to create open communication when she had medical setbacks. Her love of art and design kept her focused and involved with her courses, and professors found she had a natural talent for design. Kristy also had a couple of close friends in her major who assisted with explaining the design projects, and at times delivering handouts and forms to and from professors.

Chemo drugs kill many cells in your body, both good and bad. This meant that not only did Kristy have to deal with the cancer treatments themselves, but also many side effects or even just getting sick more often than other students because her immune system was compromised. She would often push herself through constant fatigue and nausea while attending classes and studying. She learned to take small naps throughout the day to keep going. Kristy mustered up her strength and kept focused on her academics, even when just looking at the computer made her nauseated. She set a goal to graduate from college and would not let anything, even cancer, deter her from this.

Kristy progressed well with her health and her courses until the spring of her junior year. She had been in remission for two years at that point, but a visit to the emergency room over spring break to address severe pain in her lower back revealed that her cancer had returned. Once again she would require surgery and chemotherapy. Much of what the doctors were proposing was experimental, so there were no guarantees. This was a devastating setback for Kristy, but her family, friends and boyfriend rallied around with support. Surgery was very difficult, but she took comfort in having her boyfriend by her side, along with her father. Kristy had been dating her boyfriend for a year and a half, and he gave her unconditional love and support throughout her entire treatment program. He kept in close contact with Kristy's father, his parents and their college friends; drawing strength from each other and surrounding Kristy with the love and support she would need to get her through surgery and another round of chemo treatments. Once again, her roommate Laura actively supported Kristy by attending doctor's appointments with her and organizing support and communication with family and friends. Kristy's father, her boyfriend and his mother stayed with Kristy through her surgery and helped with her transition back to college with chemo treatments.

Kristy was well into her major by now, which meant she knew her professors well and they knew her and respected her strong work ethic. She needed the support of her professors and her classmates in order to finish her classes. Her friend Caroline was in all her courses. She shared her class notes with Kristy and helped relay information on projects. Caroline also helped her stay organized with class notes and coursework. Professors and classmates were all extremely supportive with her for the next eight weeks. The initial surgery and chemo wiped Kristy out for the first couple weeks, so she relied on disability services to forward her emails to professors and communicate her medical progress. The positive support from her professors was a saving grace at this point. Kristy was a very independent student, and as she got stronger she wanted to do things on her own. She was too invested in her major and did not want to drop any of her classes, so she powered forward, met with her professors, and set up timelines for projects so she could progress to her senior year.

Learning to prioritize her coursework for each class was essential. She knew that she did not have the energy to complete everything, but she could focus on the most important items. She also knew that she had to focus her energy on getting better and had to give up any social aspects of her personal life. It was physically impossible to push herself too much, so she accomplished what she could because she was determined to graduate the following May.

Of the many difficult decisions Kristy had to make, one was giving up the internship she had in place for the summer before her senior year. She continued chemo treatments throughout the summer and was able to return for her senior year fall semester with a renewed energy. Completing her senior year was a triumph for Kristy. Her determined attitude and support of her boyfriend, father, friends, family, professors, and disability services helped her meet her goals. Everyone was there to cheer her on during graduation ceremonies.

Kristy's enthusiasm and strength was evident from the fact that even though she found out two weeks before graduation that the cancer had returned a third time, she still celebrated her accomplishment in great style. At the writing of this book she is once again undergoing surgery and chemo in hopes of beating this cancer.

Kristy has some encouraging advice for her peers who plan to attend college while undergoing cancer treatments or suffering through other medical issues:

• Find someone you can trust who can be your advocate on campus, and who will take care of things when you can't. (For Kristy this was the disability services coordinator and two of her peers, Laura and Caroline.)

• You will need support from others, both physical and emotional. Having the right support system in place when medical emergencies arise is most important. These people will need to communicate information when you are not physically able to do so. It is also important to have these people around to talk to when you have physical discomfort, terrible pain, or emotional anxiety. Rely on your family and good friends; do not be afraid to reach out to them.

• Rank what is most important to you and begin prioritizing. Understand that you will not get everything done anymore. Accept that your energy needs to focus on physical healing, so you may need to give up other aspects of your life. Drop a course or two if needed to get rid of undue stress.

Support from Disability Services

Students with medical disabilities can face numerous issues that range from unpredicted flare-ups to class absences, hospital confinement, access to professors, and keeping up with coursework and exams. The student and their parents need to have a good relationship with the disability department and the professors, and communicate regularly. Disability services will be able to ensure the credibility of illness complications as well as assisting with setting up reasonable deadlines for completion of courses. Some ways disability services can help include the following:

• There may be instances where a student decides to take an incomplete for the course and complete the course requirements at a later date when their health improves. This completion date is set by the professor. Disability services can proctor the tests and exams as requested by the professor. Once the coursework is completed the incomplete grade with be changed.

• Medical situations can occur at any time throughout the semester. If this happens the parents should contact the college disability office and share the student's medical situation. The disability service department will guide the parents through the documentation process and set the approved accommodations in place.

• When a medical condition or flare-up arises, the disability services staff will contact the student's professors to get the accommodations in place as soon as possible.

Medical Accommodations

College students with medical issues will need to have a letter from their doctor stating their diagnosis and how it will affect their academics, housing, and food services. The doctor should also state any possible accommodations the student may require for the academic year. A new letter will need to be provided each year in order to set up or keep accommodations. The diagnosis may change throughout the college years, so this communication with the parents and doctors is vital to the student's progress.

Some possible medical accommodations to request are:

• 50% extended test time;
• testing in a separate environment;
• peer notes;
• excused absences when related to the medical condition;
• special housing needs (this will vary depending on the student's needs);
• priority registration; and
• use of assistive technology (as needed).

Some possible medical conditions that need special accommodations can be Crohn's disease, cystic fibrosis, seizures, severe food allergies, irritable bowel syndrome, cerebral palsy, multiple sclerosis, muscular dystrophy, and cancer, just to name a few. Students with these types of medical diagnosis may need to miss classes, attend doctor's appointments, attend physical therapy or have a restricted diet.

Short-Term Medical Disabilities

Short-term medical disabilities fall into a separate category, but disability services can help set up temporary accommodations. Following are some examples:

- If a student is in a car accident and suffers injuries or broken bones, they can be granted temporary accommodations until their body heals. Each case will be unique, so contact the college disability office for the required documentation.
- Concussions often occur, and the severity may require accommodations until the doctor clears the student. A letter from the doctor is required to set up accommodations and also to release the student from accommodations.
- Athletes may experience sports-related injuries, which can be temporary. Once again, disability services will work with the student and their doctor to set up temporary accommodations until they heal. The doctor will need to send a letter documenting the injury and how it will impact the student. Once the student heals the doctor will send another letter clearing the student of medical issues.
- Medical leave—students can choose to take a medical leave during a semester. They can withdraw from classes without affecting their GPA. Students should contact the college if the medical leave needs to last longer than a semester.

The student's approved accommodation letter will NOT state the medical condition. It will only share the approved classroom and testing accommodations. The student can choose to share more personal information with each professor during a scheduled private meeting if they feel this will help the professor understand them better. It can be helpful to share some medical history with professors so they will be better prepared and more understanding when medical flare ups occur, or hospital stays are required. Good communication between students, professors, parents, and disability services will be critical at these times.

Dietary Needs

Students who have a severe food allergy or have specific dietary needs should meet with the disability services and the food staff manager to discuss their special dietary needs. Often these students need a dorm room with a small kitchen in order to make their own meals, and to store foods in a refrigerator. The meeting with the food manager should take place during the summer, at least a month prior to the first freshmen semester in order to give the staff time to arrange for the dietary needs.

Other students may need meals prepared especially for their dietary needs, and will need to meet with the head of food services to discuss their specific diet. Most colleges will prepare and store separate meals for these students, but all of this must be arranged ahead of time. I encourage students in this situation to meet or have a phone conference with the food staff at least a month ahead of time to arrange for these special services.

Each student with a medical disability is unique and will require the disability staff to help advocate for their needs and accommodations. The medical documentation should be up to date yearly, and any changes in the diagnosis and accommodation needs should be brought to the attention of the disability staff as soon as possible.

6

Dyslexia

Student Testimonies—
Zack and Deanna

A growing number of students with dyslexia are graduating college and have found that colleges across the country have effective resources and support services in place to address their learning needs. The majority of these students were identified as dyslexic in grade school, and were given academic support and accommodations under IEP or 504 plans, which helped them to successfully complete their education and receive their high school diploma. Students diagnosed with dyslexia are often bright; with average to above average intelligence, but their brain has difficulty learning and processing language, which can manifest itself in any of the following skills: reading, writing, spelling, math, handwriting, etc. Most students have been diagnosed in elementary school, but a few are not diagnosed until college or even as an adult.

A high school student with a dyslexic diagnosis will have an Individual Education Plan (IEP) in place or a 504 plan and a transition plan, which outlines the services they have received throughout high school. Colleges will look over the IEP or 504 plans to understand the student's progression, as well as which accommodations and resources have helped the student. Colleges and universities will not implement these plans. Instead the college requires a current psychological report with a diagnosis. Therefore, it is helpful to have the student's skills re-evaluated by a licensed psychologist in their junior or senior year of high school for the most current cognitive and achievement scores. Colleges and universities provide accommodations under the American with Disabilities Act and Section 504 of the 1973 Rehabilitation Act. The college disability staff will review the documentation and approve appropriate accommodations. Sometimes the accommodations approved in high school will not be approved for the college setting.

Students with dyslexia often have strong work ethics, formed early on as they persisted through reading programs such as the very successful Orton-Gillingham method of teaching them to read and write. These students learned how to store, transmit and retrieve information through re-routing the information through the brain. As these students prepare to transition to college it will become important to understand the ADA laws and to find the right college fit with appropriate resources, such as: smaller class sizes, technology resources, individual tutoring, academic support programs and a strong disability services department. These resources can make the difference between success and failure for the dyslexic student at the college level. According to the College Board students with disabilities should start off with requesting accommodations for the SAT and ACT college placement tests, as students who have used accommodations improved their scores.

Basics of Dyslexia

Over the years these students have learned to persevere by accessing special programs, tutors and technology to help them learn. Students with dyslexia often have high IQ's however struggle with reading, writing and spelling tasks. The International Dyslexic Association offers a thorough definition: "Dyslexia is a specific learning disability that is neurobiological in origin. It is characterized by difficulties with accurate and/or fluent word recognition and by poor spelling and decoding abilities. These difficulties typically result from a deficit in the phonological component of language that is often unexpected in relation to other cognitive abilities and the provision of effective classroom instruction. Secondary consequences may include problems in reading comprehension and reduced reading experience that can impede growth of vocabulary and background knowledge" (International Dyslexic Association, 2015).

Eventually, dyslexic students can learn to read and write, but their reading is often slow and laborious and they struggle with spelling and grammar skills. Fortunately technology has worked in their favor by providing them access to text to speech software, assisting them with reading textbooks. Exploring the disability/accessibility services department during campus visits will help students to discover appropriate accommodations, including the availability of tutors and technology. Students should look for colleges with accessible support staff, assistive technology, and trained tutors to assist with coursework and test preparation. Dyslexic students may also need an extra academic support program. A few colleges have this available free to a limited number of students; other colleges will have a fee-based program which offers extra supports, such as an academic coach, assistance with time management and organizational skills, help with study skills, professional individual tutors, and communication with professors and parents. Participating in a program like this, especially during the first year of college, will help these students get off to a strong start with solid support systems and good study strategies in place.

The majority of dyslexic students will also require tutoring in many of their core classes. Find a college with a strong tutoring program with both individual and group tutors and unlimited tutoring hours. All colleges offer free tutoring available to students, but services can vary. Dyslexic students should look for a college with individual tutoring, a writing center and a math center to assist them through many of their core courses. Many colleges also have trained student instructors (SI) in core classes to assist the professor with helping students succeed. The SI is often a peer note taker and is available for group and individual tutoring, and will also help prepare students for exams.

Assistive Technology

The world of technology is rapidly changing and software programs and devices to assist dyslexic students with reading and writing continually emerge, opening doors to successful learning. Text to speech and speech to text software has allowed these students to read and write at a faster pace, keeping up with the demands of college academics. Software programs such as Kurzweil 3000, Natural Reader, RFB&D, and Read and Write Gold have been assisting dyslexic students to successfully access reading materials and keep up with the academic pace of college. Dragon Speak allows these students to write using diction software programs, while spell-check assists with spelling and grammar. SMART Pens and other recording devices will record lectures so students can listen to the lecture again while going over and filling in their class notes. The majority of this software is compatible with computers, tablets, and iPhone. Many colleges have assistive technology available to these students as they tackle their academic courses, but available technology will differ from college to college. The right technology to assist with reading and highlighting textbooks, note taking, recording lectures, writing papers, and creating presentations will help pave a road to academic success.

Having the right tools in place from the beginning will make all the difference in creating a successful academic year and assistive technology needs to be part of the plan. Colleges such as Landmark College in Vermont has an excellent program for students with dyslexia, where each student is taught to use appropriate technology such as Kurzweil 3000 and Dragon Naturally Speaking to assist with their learning needs in each class. Their professors and staff are also trained to use and integrate the technology in their classrooms. Lynn University in Florida also has excellent technology resources available to students, and they have trained students and professors to universally use the iPad for all courses.

Requesting Accommodations

During college visits plan to also visit the disability/accessibility services and academic support programs at each college. Meet with the disability staff and go over the student's disability documentation to discuss appropriate accommodations available to them.

Possible accommodations to consider are

- priority registration;
- foreign language substitution;
- textbooks in alternate format;
- peer notes;
- recorded lectures;
- priority registration;
- use of assistive technology for reading, writing and recording lectures;
- use of laptop for essay writing; and
- use of calculator for math problems.

Possible testing accommodations are

- extended test time (50% or 100%, depending on the students processing speed and memory skills);
- testing in a separate environment;
- use of laptop for essay writing;
- reader for tests;
- scribe for tests;
- no use of scantrons; and
- use of calculator.

Completing foreign language requirements is often an obstacle for students with dyslexia. Many high schools give these students a foreign language waiver due to their disability. Two to three years of high school foreign language is often a college admissions requirement. I encourage dyslexic students to write a letter with their application explaining their documented disability and high school foreign language waiver. Colleges often approve an accommodation for a foreign language substitution course or a waiver for this core requirement for students with diagnosed dyslexia. Students can also choose to look into colleges that do not require a foreign language as part of their core curriculum.

Math requirements may also be an obstacle for some dyslexic students. Some colleges will offer a math substitution, but the course is rarely waived completely for students. Some of the arts colleges do not have a math requirement, so it will benefit the student to look into majors that do not require a high level math course in the degree program. I have had students with a math disability choose to take the math course during a summer session, with tutoring support. Taking the course alone allows the student time to focus on just this course, with support from a tutor to help get them through the course. Students can use their approved accommodations during the summer. I encourage students to have accommodations and tutoring in place and use them each day to help understand the course material. Achieving a C- or D- in the class is required to pass the course and move forward with their degree.

Finding the Right College Fit

Dyslexic students usually have very strong right brained skills and are often creative out of the box thinkers; once they find the right career path to enhance their strengths they are very successful. I encourage these students to take a career inventory test and explore careers that complement their strengths.

Take time to also check the college websites for the course curriculum in the degree you are seeking to make sure you are in a good career fit that will not create frustration and anxiety due to your dyslexia.

Dyslexic students should also look into academic support programs that have extra support in place, such as an academic coaching, unlimited tutoring. Review some of the college options I have researched in Chapter 17 to give you some guidance with tutoring and other academic support programs offered.

Once these students complete college they make excellent employees, and many become entrepreneurs because they have dedication, creativity and an excellent work ethic.

Zack

Academics were an uphill struggle for Zack, beginning with kindergarten. Zack was born two months premature, at two pounds, 14 ounces. Developmental delays followed him throughout each stage of his young life. When Zack began kindergarten it was evident that he was academically behind his peers. His teacher suggested he repeat kindergarten, where he progressed well and went on to first grade.

First grade seemed to also be a struggle for Zack. He hated going to school and became more frustrated each month. He was often very slow in completing his schoolwork and was made to stay inside during recess to catch up with assignments. He was very embarrassed to find that he fell behind his peers with reading and writing and math, and most days he came home from school angry and frustrated. Daily his mother assisted with homework and noticed that he easily "read" to her the required reading assignment, but could not read a single *new* word in his new library books. She realized that he was memorizing the story which was read aloud in class, and could not recognize or sound out new words presented to him. Zack was obviously a strong auditory learner but was having trouble mastering the reading skills; it was apparent that he needed to be tested for possible learning disabilities.

The public school psychological testing results showed a learning disability, and the school put some extra tutoring in place for Zack. The tutoring was helpful, but did not make a dent in the large learning gap he had already suffered. Zack's mother impulsively picked up a book about children with dyslexia at the library and read it through in one weekend. She realized that her son had many similarities to the dyslexic children in this book. She decided to get further testing done on her son and hired a private psychologist. Once this thorough testing was completed, Zack was given a diagnosis of dyslexia. The challenge now was finding the best academic program to meet his learning needs.

Zack had dyslexia and would need a specialized reading program, and extra tutoring. His parents placed him in a private school which taught him the Orton-Gillingham reading strategies, and for the first time Zack was reading and writing. He became excited about attending school each morning. Class sizes were smaller and he was receiving the extra academic support he needed. He would need this support throughout his education, so his mother convinced her father to donate some land in order to build a special school for students with learning disabilities. His mother, Sherry, along with other community members and a handful of educators spearheaded the building of a new private school for students with learning disabilities. Zack stayed in this school and had access to resources and a specialized disability program through eighth grade, where he made steady progress, learned to understand his disability, and made use of tutors and resources to assist his learning.

High school posed some new academic challenges for Zack. His current struggles with word recognition and reading fluency were once again holding him back. His parents began researching to find a high school with technology that would assist Zack with these skills and help prepare him for college. He was placed in a private high school program where he received assistive technology, tutoring, resource classrooms and academic coaching. Technology such as Smart Pens, tablets, and use of laptop computers with reading and writing software assisted Zack with his disability, allowing him to progress academically. Teachers also worked to improve his organizational and study skills, preparing him for college. The use of technology kept Zack on a successful academic path. Zack stayed motivated and focused throughout high school. He enjoyed his teachers, and most of all he enjoyed learning! His grades began to soar and he eventually was inducted into the National Honor Society. Having the right tools in place, with supportive teachers made all the difference in Zack's education.

Transitioning to College

Zack explored different colleges his junior and senior year of high school, looking for assistive technology, an academic coaching program with strong tutoring support, a good disability program and smaller class sizes. He was given a new battery of psychological tests to update his psychological report, which were required in order to apply for college accommodations. He finally chose High Point University, located within an hour from his home. Vocational rehab provided a portion of Zack's tuition, and he applied for scholarships to help with more of the private school tuition. He was ready and excited to begin this new chapter of his life.

During spring of his senior year of high school Zack and his mother met with the college disability coordinator and discussed his successes with assistive technology and the accommodation he had in place during his high school years. He was pleased to find the same resources in place at this institution.

The college disability team reviewed his updated documentation and approved accommodations.

Zack's Approved College Accommodations:

- 50% extended test time;
- testing in a separate environment;
- use of laptop for essay tests and exams;
- peer notes;
- reader for tests;
- use of Kurzweil and Dragon Speak software; and
- reduced course load (12 hours or less each semester).

Another resource that was available at the college was a freshman summer experience program, which an introductory program, taken in the month of July that helps freshmen transition to the demands of college academics. Zack's mother encouraged him to attend this program for freshmen, where he would receive eight college credits, live on campus and use accommodations and tutoring. This was not how Zack envisioned his summer; reluctantly, though, he agreed to attend the program. He attended classes for five hours each day and studied at least six hours a day in the library utilizing tutors and other resources. Zack was also enrolled in the learning excellence program where he had access to professional tutors and an academic coach. The course work was challenging, but Zack liked his professors and the college experience over-all. Zack worked hard and excelled in this academic environment where he learned to use the college resources and maneuver the campus. He even formed some lasting friendships! He was ready to conquer fall semester.

Fall semester proved to be more challenging than Zack anticipated. He took English, history, game design, and a presidential seminar. He enrolled in 12 credit hours because this was the most he could handle each semester. He was also enrolled in a fee-based academic support program with tutoring, technology resources, required study hall hours and communication with professors. Being a full-time college student was more challenging than Zack had ever envisioned. Zack began struggling in each of his courses but did not reach out for help. His accommodations were in place, but he chose not to use them and never gave the accommodation letters to his professors. He had difficulty taking notes in class, but never requested his accommodation of peer notes. Years of being labeled with a disability created embarrassment for Zack, so he wanted to try the semester without the use of accommodations. These first six weeks of college were extremely frustrating, and Zack was quickly becoming discouraged. His planned strategy of attempting college without accommodations was creating a lot of stress and anxiety, but he was not sure how to go about fixing the situation.

Family weekend was a turning point for Zack. His mother, Sherry, met with each of his professors, where she quickly learned that he was performing poorly in each class. His history professor asked why he never brought his textbook to class, and Zack explained that his textbooks were on a CD in order to be compatible with the Kurzweil reading software that assisted his reading disability. His mother provided background information on Zack's learning struggles and the professor quickly became very supportive. A new and caring relationship formed between student and professor, and Zack began to realize that hiding his disability was not helping him succeed. Together they shared his learning struggles and his accommodation letter with each professor. Zack began to feel more comfortable sharing his disability, especially seeing how caring and supportive his professors became. He and his mother proceeded to meet with the disability staff to get further supports in place.

With the help of the disability coordinator, Zack shared his learning diagnosis with each professor and discussed putting his accommodations in place, along with academic tutors. He began taking tests in academic services with extended time and tests read aloud. He began to actively use tutors and the software programs. He took class notes, but also had access to peer notes. Writing tutors helped him organize his papers, assisting with grammar checks and breaking the assignments into more manageable parts. Once he accepted his academic struggles and accessed his approved accommodations he saw vast improvements in his grades. He learned to work closely with his tutors/professors, and met often with the disability staff for further support.

Moving forward Zack and his mother drafted a letter describing his dyslexia and how it impacts his learning. Zack gave this letter, along with his accommodation letter provided by disability services, to each professor at the beginning of each semester. This helped Zack and his professors to communicate well at the very beginning of each semester. Zack and his mother made a point to continue meeting with each professor during family weekends to discuss how things were going; Zack could then make any necessary adjustments that his professors may recommend based on their insights during the first half of the semester.

The following is an example of the letter Zack shared with each of his professors at the beginning of the semester, so they could better understand his learning disabilities.

August 19, 2013

Dear Professor Piperato,

I am looking forward to being in your class this semester. I am writing with the help of my mom to let you know that I am severely dyslexic and ADD. I was born prematurely, weighing less than 3 pounds. As a result and despite significant special schooling and training since 2nd grade, I still struggle with reading, spelling and writing.

My last Psychological Evaluation during my high school senior year notes an average IQ, but my raw grade equivalency (GE) *without accommodations* in basic reading skills was 6.0 and written expression was 5.1. Dr. William Sloan noted in his recommendations on his evaluation:

> *"It seems very clear from the present results—considered in the context of Zack's previous test results and his history of considerable academic interventions and support systems—that he will continue to need substantial accommodations if he is to be successful in college. It is not that Zack cannot learn—he can clearly comprehend what is being said to him at least at an average level. Rather, he cannot quickly comprehend what is text-based, or indicate his level of knowledge through writing, at the level one would expect of someone with average intelligence."*

However, with a GE of 13 in comprehension, substantial academic accommodations and the support of my teachers, I was able to graduate from my college prep high school with honors and complete my junior year at HPU with a 2.70 GPA.

I work very closely with the Coordinator of Disability Support and tutors who have all contributed to my success here at HPU. I use Kurzweil, which reads text books to me. I utilize note takers. I write with a program called Correct English. I am always eager to learn. I am happy to meet with you if you would like more information or you feel that it would be beneficial to have a face-to-face meeting.

I wanted to share this information with you as I would welcome any ideas or suggestions both now and throughout the semester that you may have that would help me to be successful in your class.

Sincerely,

Zack H.

Zack was also enrolled in the learning excellence program (a fee-based comprehensive academic support program). At first Zack did not take advantage of what this program had to offer because he did not want to be different, he wanted to do it on his own. He felt that his entire academic life he had to carry these dyslexic and disability labels and now he could choose to no longer carry them. After almost failing the first six weeks of college he learned that his academic struggles were part of who he was, and pretending they no longer existed was holding him back. Zack now decided to accept his disability and use all accommodations, tutors and all other resources he could in order to succeed. From the beginning of the semester Zack attended the mandatory study hall hours, but did not work productively, but after family weekend he became a better student. He worked hard utilizing all his resources and was practically living at the library. His new attitude and use of resources helped to improve his GPA to a 2.4 by the end of the semester.

Once Zack chose to accept his disability, use all available resources and build a strong relationship with each professor he was able to successfully complete his courses.

Zack came to the realization that in college *everyone* uses tutors, not just students with learning disabilities. During high school he thought that only "struggling students" used tutors. He learned to let go of that false perception. Many students taking calculus, history, biology and English used tutors to prepare for tests, get help with research papers, or just improve their overall grade to a B or an A. Zack learned that many of his peers and friends attended group tutoring support, making him feel like a regular college student. Tutors in college are usually fellow students who have previously taken the course, understood the professor's expectations, received an A and have gone through tutor training. These peer tutors were a huge help to Zack. Immediately his grades showed improvement and his comprehension of the material was solid. Zack also learned to use the professional tutors within the learning excellence program. Zack learned that pretending he did not have a learning disability was detrimental to his success. Once he accepted that he not only had a disability, but had to use the approved accommodations and communicate his learning needs to his professors, he could actually be more successful as a college student.

Zack also learned his limits. He found that he could only take twelve credits each semester, and he had to space out the courses that required more reading and writing assignments. Taking fewer credits each semester would not allow him to graduate on time, so he committed to taking at least two courses (eight credits) each summer in order earn enough credits to graduate within a four year time frame. He would often save his most difficult courses for summer so he could spend more time focusing on the course content with the help of tutors.

Most students with dyslexia struggle with learning a foreign language, and Zack was no different. His freshman year he attempted to take Spanish, but this proved to be extremely difficult for him. He dropped the course, and applied for a foreign language substitution with disability services. Based on his disability documentation he was granted the foreign language substitution and took a global studies course in its place.

Zack understood that he needed to put in extra study hours each day, along with meeting with tutors and professors on a constant basis. He has also learned that he needs plenty of sleep, at least seven hours each night; and studying until the wee hours of the morning did not work for him. He made time in his day for breakfast, lunch and dinner, eating especially healthy during finals week for brain power. He found that many of his friends frequented the library often, and they would study together and encourage one another; even quizzing one another for test prep, making the library a very positive place to be.

His academic coach helped Zack learn which study strategies worked best with is learning disability. A combination of auditory and kinesthetic study strategies works best for him because he an auditory and a hands-on learner. He learned to highlight his textbooks on CD using the tools in Kurzweil; he always makes notecards and uses tutors for all of his core classes. He consistently uses a writing tutor and a software program to assist with grammar and spelling when writing papers and essays. He found he was no longer embarrassed to have a learning disability.

A good relationship with his professors and disability services helped Zack build trust, making it easier to ask for help and guidance when needed. He also learned to advocate for himself by meeting individually with each professor and sharing, on a personal level, information he felt his professors needed to know regarding his dyslexia. His attitude became very positive, and he knew who to contact on campus for additional support, such as career services, counseling and club coordinators.

Zack had a very successful college career, completing a graphic design and digital media degree, with a minor in communications, earning a cumulative 3.0 GPA. He is a true success story. His perseverance and positive attitude have brought him where he is today, and will continue to be his best asset as a young adult in the work force!

Deanna

Learning to use your accommodations from day one as you enter college will help students with dyslexia find success. Deanna knew that without accommodations she would easily fail out of college, so she researched small colleges with strong support programs and a good disability department. She, like Zack, chose High Point University. When touring the campus she also met with the disability department and the Learning Excellence Director to research their programs and make sure they were a good fit for her learning needs.

Deanna struggled with learning to read and write since she began kindergarten. She would spend hours completing her homework and studying for tests in elementary school, but had very low recall of subject matter. She worked hard to earn better grades, but to no avail. She was not diagnosed with dyslexia until fifth grade, where her teacher realized that she was a few grades below her peers in her reading skills. Once she was tested by a psychologist, she was given a diagnosis of dyslexia, and low memory skills; an IEP was created and accommodations were put in place immediately. She was assigned to a learning specialist who taught her new reading strategies, and read all of her tests aloud. She signed up for RFB&D (Reading for the Blind and Dyslexic) and ordered all of her textbooks through them. Deanna and her tutor also worked on improving her short and long-term memory skills with visual memory strategies to help her retain information for test recall. Deanna continued to work with her tutor and was rewarded with better grades each year.

Throughout high school she continued to work with her learning specialist who taught Deanna time management and organizational skills, along with study strategies that supported her visual learning style for each new course. She learned to color code her notes for easier retrieval, along with constantly reviewing them to store the information in her long-term memory. She had to study constantly to keep up with her courses. She was given the following high school accommodations:

- 50% extended test time;
- testing in a separate environment;
- copy of peer notes or teacher notes;
- tests read aloud; and
- books on tape through (RFB&D).

Deanna attended regular classes, but also attended the resource room for extra tutoring and academic support each day. Study strategies and organizational skills were reinforced constantly to help prepare Deanna for college. Her grades were all As and Bs; she excelled in competitive swimming and kept active high school clubs and community services. She was well prepared to send in strong college applications.

Accommodations were also used for the College Board ACT. She was approved for extended time (the ACT test was given over a three-day period), testing in a separate environment and tests read aloud. Her first attempt with the ACT was taken without accommodations, and she earned a total score of 21. During her second attempt with ACT testing she chose to use her accommodations and earned a total score of 29, which earned her a partial college scholarship! This was an outstanding reward, and showed the accomplished efforts Deanna put into studying over the years! She had learned how to learn, how to study, and was rewarded with success. She was proud of her GPA and test scores, and felt as academically accomplished as her siblings who did not have learning disabilities.

Deanna enjoyed the feeling of academic success and wanted to continue using her accommodations, tutoring and organizational support during college. She researched colleges in the southeast that fit her intended major, and had extra support programs in place to assist with her learning needs. During her college visits she explored academic support programs and met with the disability staff to learn what supports they could put in place for her. Deanna made her decision to attend High Point University, where she would study home furnishings. She immediately enrolled in the learning excellence academic support program and applied for accommodations. She was approved for the following college accommodations: 50 percent extended test time, testing in a separate environment, use of computer for essay writing, copy of peer notes, tests read aloud, record lectures, textbooks in alternate format.

All of the appropriate tools were in place and fall classes began. Deanna dove into college with positive energy and high expectations for herself. Deanna soon learned that it was harder to keep up with the fast pace of college courses. She also found it difficult to pay attention in classes that lasted 90 minutes. During high school she was used to 45 minute classes, so this was a challenge for her. She had trouble focusing and taking notes for these long classes. While taking notes, she would over-focus on spelling names and terms correctly and would miss large amounts of oral information. She found that her peer notes were a great help. She was able to go over the peer notes and fill in her notes with information she missed when she had trouble focusing. Regularly she would re-write her notes and color code information for easier study and retrieval. The constant repetition of writing, speaking and seeing her notes helped improve her memory of the information. When studying for tests and exams she would re-write her notes or the study guide five or six times in order to store the information in her memory. She used her strong visual skills to help with retaining information within the colored notes, which allowed her to easily retrieve the information during tests.

Anxiety was another issue that plagued Deanna during college. She would constantly worry about her grades and strived for all As. She soon found this an overwhelming task and was so frustrated that her anxiety kept her from moving forward. She began attending counseling with a campus counselor to help her work through her anxiety. This was an excellent resource for Deanna. She loved her counselor and met with her throughout her college career.

Deana also has an oral sensory disorder which keeps her from eating many different types of foods. She discussed this condition with her counselor, who helped to find a nutritionist to assist Deanna with eating healthy.

Deanna works together with nutritionist to find foods she can tolerate and still give her the nutrition her body needs.

Throughout college Deanna made an effort to build a relationship with her professors each semester. She would meet with them during the first week of classes to review her accommodation letter with them and ask questions about testing procedures. This gave the professors a face to go with the name on the accommodation letter, and opened the door for easy communication throughout the semester. She made a habit of meeting with her professors often to ask for clarification on lectures, assignments or papers. Taking tests was always hard for her, especially tests with multiple choice and true and false questions because they always made her second guess herself. She much preferred to take essay tests or write a research paper She would often bring her study guide to her professor to inquire whether she had all the material she needed for review. They would give guidance and suggestions to help her best prepare for tests and exams.

Core courses were the biggest academic struggle for Deanna and created the most stress. She appreciated when these professors put their PowerPoints presentations on Blackboard because she would print these off before class and add her notes during the lectures. If these PowerPoint presentations weren't available before the class lecture she would print them afterward and still add her notes to these printouts. She would also use these to create her study guides for tests. She set up appointments to meet with campus tutors, who would help her understand course material and review for exams. The learning excellence program helped her to organize her time, planning out research papers and projects so she was able to meet the deadlines with ease.

Consistently using each of these tools helped her keep up a strong GPA. She learned that she did not need all As to be a successful student. She learned to do her best in each course and use tutors and other resources as needed. Deanna has a positive attitude and keeps open communication with her academic coach and parents. She is majoring in home furnishings, with a double minor in marketing and communications.

Deanna shares advice with students in similar situations:

- Definitely use accommodations from day one.
- Don't stress out about grades as much as real world networking and how you present yourself.
- Make study guides at least five days before a test. Go over it with your professor to make sure you are covering all the major points.
- Meet with professors often to build a positive relationship. Meet with

them early in the semester so they can put a face with the name on an accommodation letter.

Zack and Deanna both used resources, technology and tutoring to help them succeed in college. They never let their dyslexia diagnosis keep them from attaining their academic goals. During times where they struggled, both students were able to reach out to staff and professors for the help they needed to move forward. College success came to them with hard work and staying motivated. They believed in themselves, and with the support of family and friends both Zack and Deanna have earned college degrees.

Students attending graduate school can also use their psychological report and the approved accommodation documentation to apply for accommodations at their graduate school. The student will need to meet with the disability staff and follow their guidelines (usually posted on the college website) in order to apply for accommodations. Further documentation may be required. Students with Dyslexia planning to attend graduate school can apply for special accommodations for the graduate exams. Information and guidelines will be on each individual college website.

Graduate tests include GRE, GRS, MCAT, LSAT, and DAT.

7

Reading and Writing Disabilities

Student Testimonies— Ryan and Dee

Diverse learning challenges in reading and writing are fairly common and the majority of these students receive assistance for their learning disability under an IEP throughout elementary, middle and high school. Once these students attend college they are asked to read and write at a faster pace and their disability can become debilitating. In order to keep up with extensive reading assignments it will be important for the student to carve out time in each day to read and highlight their text. Reading software programs are available to assist students with their reading; these programs have tools for highlighting and note taking within the text. Learning how to manage daily reading and writing assignments will be crucial to earning a college degree. The mere thought of reading 50 pages each night is overwhelming for students with reading disabilities and can often cause them to procrastinate, which eventually causes even more stress and anxiety. Using good time management skills and study strategies that complement their learning style, along with assistive technology, will lessen stress and keep the student moving forward in their college courses.

Requesting Documentation

Students with a documented learning disability in reading, writing or math often receive academic support through an IEP throughout their childhood education. Upon entering college, however, these students fall under the ADA laws and they will need to request accommodations to assist with their learning disability. The student must first self-disclose to the university, then send in the required documentation that supports their disability and apply for new college accommodations. The documentation usually consists of a current (no less than five years old) psychological report with test scores and recommendations for accommodations. It is helpful if the student is re-tested during their sophomore or junior year of high school so that the test scores reflect their current ability levels. The approved college accommodations may be different than their high school accommodations, but will give them the academic support they need to level the playing field in higher education. Students with learning disabilities will face new academic challenges during their college journey, and need to understand which resources are available to them. These students have an average to above average IQ but may struggle with writing skills, reading comprehension, memory skills, math calculations, and processing skills, to name a few. The National Center for Learning Disabilities website states, "Colleges will require more independent reading and writing, which will challenge your learning disability. You will have to work longer hours and harder than your peers to achieve success." College students will be expected to complete the same course and major requirements as all other students. The professors are not required to change course requirements or due dates. The student must use their accommodations and seek out tutors or other support services as needed to successfully complete their curriculum. All students should make a point of meeting independently with their professors at the beginning of each semester to discuss their approved classroom and testing accommodations, and continue with open communication throughout the semester.

Students with learning disabilities need to explore their learning style to understand how they learn, then research study skills that complement their learning style. I recommend that students take a learning styles inventory. "These are informal inventories with self-report questionnaires that can provide you with information about your preferred learning modality (learning through your senses). After taking these inventories student often learn that they have some characteristics from each style" (Van Blerkom, 2011). These can be found online, or in any college study skills book. The college academic center or disability/accessibility center should also have these informal assessments available to students. The results of the learning style inventory will clarify the preferred learning style for learning new information (Van Blerkom, 2011). Follow up with study strategies that work best for the specific learning style. Students may be auditory, visual, or kinesthetic learners, which mean they will benefit from using study strategies that enforce their particular learning style by strengthening how the student stores and retrieves important information for tests and exams.

The following active study strategies have been helpful to students with reading and writing disabilities (Van Blerkom, 2011):

• Record course lectures and replay these while filling in their lecture notes to reinforce important information.

• Study with peers or a group tutoring session and verbally explain the steps to math problems, steps in a science lab, major points for psychology, science, historic battles, etc.

• Use acronyms or catchwords and recite these aloud to help retrieve information for tests and exams.

• Take course lecture notes using the Cornell note taking method, then cover over the information side of notes and verbally recite the information under each term or heading.

• While reading texts, turn headings into questions by writing the question in the margin and read to find the important information to answer the question; make sure to highlight this information.

• Create notecards using important terms, dates, people, events, etc. (Color coding topics on notecards is also helpful.)

• Create notecards each day from course lecture notes then take time to review these notecards daily to help prepare for tests and exams. This technique helps students' retrieval during tests because the constant reviews help the student to over learn the material.

Students who take the time to learn helpful study strategies and use them daily have improved their test scores. College level courses are more challenging than high school courses and require students to step up their study time and use different auditory, visual and kinesthetic study strategies. Students who work with individual tutors have found it helpful to share their learning style with the tutor, who can adjust their teaching style to complement the student's learning style.

Ryan

Ryan was an avid outdoorsman. He enjoyed hiking, kayaking, bike riding, and keeping active. He looked forward to attending college and participating in club sports and activities. He was diagnosed with a learning disability in grade school and worked closely with teachers who provided extra help and accommodations, and his parents provided private tutors until graduation. Ryan spent years working with tutors and receiving assistance with his reading and writing skills to successfully earn a strong GPA and his high school diploma. After years of having support services in place, Ryan felt he was ready to handle college without academic support. He learned study strategies in high school and stayed organized and responsible. He wanted to try college without any extra support services because he was certain that all the study strategies he used for high school would work for his college courses, and he wanted free time to explore activities and clubs and not be tied down with evening tutoring.

Ryan and his parents explored different sizes of colleges—large, medium, and small—in a few different states within driving distance from home. He originally wanted to major in business, and each college he visited had a strong program. Ryan chose to start his freshman year at a large state college. He wanted to attend the same college as a couple of his friends because he had severe anxiety, which he believed would intensify if he attended a college completely on his own. Once he made his college decision and knew he would be rooming with a couple of high school friends, he was excited to begin his new college adventures.

His first semester was much more difficult than he anticipated. Ryan had trouble maneuvering the large campus, especially finding offices and academic resources. He did not know who his advisor was or where she was located, and was too shy to seek her out. This large university did not have a strict attendance policy, so Ryan would often skip a class or two each week. Since many of his classes had two to three hundred students, he felt the professors would not miss him. He felt he was capable of keeping up with the readings and assignments on his own and decided not to access any tutors. Mid-terms proved to be extremely stressful. Ryan used his high school study strategies, but still felt unprepared for his exams. He did not have access to tutors, but he did try to study with friends when he could. He was struggling and did not know who to turn to for help.

Anxiety started to set in early; Ryan was overwhelmed with the large campus and class sizes. He had not built relationships with professors or his advisor and did not feel comfortable approaching them regarding his academic struggles. He was shy and did not make a lot of new friends and often kept to himself or stayed in his dorm room and just hung out with his roommates. Ryan's shyness and social anxiety kept him from reaching out to disability services, so while he now realized he certainly needed accommodations, he did not know who to ask or how to begin to request accommodations. He was embarrassed to tell his parents that he was struggling in his classes, and instead kept all this frustration inside, which created even more anxiety.

Ryan spent most of his free time with his roommates and high school friends on campus. College provided many types of distractions and Ryan found that his original academic motivations dwindled quickly. He no longer had the self-discipline to study daily and began procrastinating. He did not feel good about himself or the semester and did not know how to turn this around. He received a letter in December stating he was on academic probation and needed to meet with his advisor. This was the first communication he had with her and their meeting was not very helpful. She encouraged Ryan to begin using tutors but she did not help him to set this up and Ryan was too shy to follow through. After a second unsuccessful semester, he realized that drastic changes were necessary.

Ryan now understood that this large university setting was not a good fit for him. He was in the wrong college and the wrong major. He began to communicate more with his parents and shared his academic frustrations. He found his parents were very understanding and supportive and were willing to help him look into other colleges and resources to turn his academics around. Over the summer he and his father discussed their options and looked at colleges with the support services Ryan needed, and decided to take another look at a smaller college that was on his original college list. After taking a second tour of this college and discovering excellent tutoring, a fee-based academic support program, and accommodations that could be put in place to assist him, Ryan decided to make the change.

Ryan applied to this smaller private college that had rolling admission still open. Ryan was accepted on the condition that he take their college study skills course and start over as a freshman, since his previous grades were not strong enough to transfer. He was admitted as a conditional student for one semester. He immediately enrolled in a fee-based program that offered an academic coach and weekly tutors to assist with his coursework. Ryan also changed his major from business administration to sports medicine; his career goal was to work with sports teams as their athletic trainer. He was feeling good about the move to a smaller college and soon made friends with a group of boys that enjoyed working out and participating in outdoor sport activities with him. The new college had a strict attendance policy, so he had to attend classes regularly. Ryan paid attention, took notes, and kept up with assignments. He had a much better semester. Ryan also took a college study skills course, where he learned about his particular learning style, which was visual. He applied study strategies that worked with his learning style, such as creating note cards, highlighting main points in his textbook and creating acronyms to connect information, which greatly improved his comprehension of the course material. He also took the time to take the online quizzes that correlated with his textbook and wrote out steps and procedures for math, science and psychology courses, which helped him to store and retrieve information for tests. Even though he had positive semester, his GPA was still lower than he wanted and he felt he was not working to his full potential. Ryan was struggling with learning the course material in the health science courses and decided that the sports medicine major was not the best fit. He and his advisor explored his strengths and he chose to switch his major to graphic design. Ryan had a natural talent for art and photography and soon felt very comfortable with the coursework in his new major and became excited about learning again. He had no trouble paying attention in class because he could easily connect with the information and assignments. He started enjoying his classes and, for the first time, began to build relationships with his professors. His professors constantly gave him positive feedback and guidance with his projects and papers. He looked forward to attending classes and took pride in his creative projects. Ryan knew that he was finally on the right career track.

The following semester he was assigned a new academic coach who took the time to ask him about his academic struggles, learning disability, and the types of accommodations he had in place for high school. After a couple of lengthy discussions exploring his high school support systems and his academic roller coaster Ryan decided to apply for college accommodations to assist with his academic progress. He was no longer reluctant to come forward and discuss his learning disability. He was enjoying college for the first time and wanted to become a stronger student. Ryan's parents sent his psychological report to disability services and Ryan met with the director to discuss academic accommodations for his disabilities in reading/writing and test anxiety

Ryan's Approved College Accommodations

Classroom Accommodations:

- peer notes; and
- textbooks in alternate format (used with reading software).

Testing Accommodations:

- 50% extended test time; and
- testing in a separate environment.

With these accommodations in place, Ryan worked even harder to learn the course material and raise his grades. The extended test time helped to reduce his anxiety and he was able to successfully retrieve the test material, which produced improved grades! The peer notes filled in where some of his class notes were lacking, giving him the appropriate information he needed to prepare for tests. Reading course texts had felt somewhat overwhelming, so he now used the reading software on his computer to listen to and highlight his texts, saving him time and reading frustration. He no longer labored over reading assignments, which used to zap much of his energy and motivation. Finally Ryan was feeling like a successful college student. He set a goal to earn a 3.0 GPA for the semester, and stayed focused and determined to make this happen. This successful semester earned Ryan a 2.7 GPA, and even though he was happy to have achieved this, he kept himself motivated by setting another goal to earn a 3.0 GPA or higher the following semester, which he accomplished. His parents were thrilled to see the motivation and confidence return in their son.

Ryan also began working closer with his academic coach on both study skills and time management. He understood that he needed all resources from his academic coach, tutors and the fee-based support program to succeed, especially in his core courses. He met with his academic coach each week to improve his organizational and study skills. He kept track of all assignments and activities on a weekly schedule and a semester calendar. Ryan also made the choice to change his current eating, sleeping and study habits. He realized that it was important to wake up early each day and not sleep in until his first class. He began to exercise and work out in the early morning on his busiest class days in order to have more energy for academics. He carefully planned out his day for class, study, tutoring, and working on projects.

Organizing large papers and projects was often challenging, so he met with his academic coach, to examined his large research projects and created a plan to break them into smaller tasks with earlier due dates. He learned how to highlight and organize his research so he could easily adapt it to his papers. These new skills helped build his confidence as he became a more productive student. Ryan always thought he was organized but learning solid time management skills made all the difference for him. He made sure to study first, and then add in the extra-curricular activities. Using this formula, he found that he actually had more free time than in the past. He was also less stressed during mid-terms and exams because he began preparing for tests at least five to eight days ahead instead of cramming at the last minute, and he kept up with a weekly review of his course materials.

Approaching professors during office hours or after class had always made Ryan extremely nervous. His academic coach encouraged him to meet with his professors after class to get clarification on his projects. He also began meeting with them during office hours to get extra support in preparing for tests and exams. Once he began building a relationship with his professors, his anxiety decreased and he became comfortable approaching them as needed throughout the semester. They understood his learning needs and how to best support and encourage his many talents.

Asking for help with research papers was another big step for Ryan. This was an area where he usually procrastinated because he was overwhelmed with the writing process. He was shown how to break the large assignment down into smaller steps. He would do research, create an outline, then begin writing the paper. Previously he would just start writing, without a definite direction. He left plenty of time for a writing tutor to edit his work, or he would meet with his professor to get input. Once he learned some good research skills he was able to complete a large paper. He learned to start early and pace himself. He became excited about learning his topic instead of feeling overburdened with the paper itself. He looks forward to research and keeps the attitude "I am ready for the next paper and look forward to learning something new."

Having all these tools in place helped Ryan keep his grades up, but each winter he began to lose his motivation and focus. He was encouraged to look into the trigger for this setback and discovered that he had seasonal depression. This insight helped Ryan to learn how to identify the signs and deal with the depression before it impacted his grades. With some guidance he soon understood the importance of keeping with a daily routine and challenging himself to get up early and stay motivated by attending classes and tutoring. He makes a point to study with his peers often and keeps open communication with his family.

The graphic design major proved to be a perfect fit for Ryan's natural talents. Ryan felt that "each course has been challenging yet exciting." From digital photography to art history to graphic design studio, Ryan's skills have improved and he has built an impressive resume. Through exploring his career options, he gravitated towards his strengths and talents; he now feels confident in his skills and is ready for his future career.

Ryan says that attending a smaller private college "molded me into the better person I am today. I have become a more responsible student and have learned better organizational skills. I know that my professors care about me as a person. If I miss a couple of classes they send me a caring email encouraging me to attend and keep up with the assignments. Participating in the Learning Excellence program and working with an academic coach helped to keep me on track with assignments and due dates, especially for large research assignments. I felt that everyone I worked with from professors, to tutors, coaches, advisors and housing staff cared about me and wanted to help me succeed."

Ryan made the effort to turn around a bad start; instead of dropping out of college he chose to change his habits, ask for help and put resources in place. His parents were always a solid support system for him, helping him succeed by listening, staying positive and encouraging him to switch to a smaller college and use the fee-based learning support program. They also encouraged Ryan to use his accommodations. Once he had accommodations and support services in place his learning disabilities no longer blocked his path to learning. He explored majors until he found the right fit, where he excelled. Ryan learned that in order to be academically successful he needed to use his accommodations and to rely on his academic coach for support with time management and organization. He also made a point of meeting independently with his professors to get guidance with his many projects. He worked hard each semester to keep his grades above a 3.0. His passion for his major in graphic design grew with each course, and his interest in photography guided him to add this as a minor. He graduated with a strong GPA, self-confidence, and excellent graphic design and photography skills to bring into the work force.

Ryan was not alone in believing that he could complete college courses without using accommodations to support his learning disability. Many students no longer want the disability label and choose not to disclose their disability once they reach the college level. Other students want to begin college completely independent of tutors or accommodations, because they feel they have a handle on their disability needs and can be successful without relying on accommodations or tutoring. Unfortunately, many of these students find themselves struggling in classes before mid-terms during their first semester of college. I encourage students to start off strong by requesting and using all accommodations to help them successfully complete classes. Once they have a strong GPA they may be able to choose which classes for which to apply for accommodations.

Dee

Dee's high school years were filled with soccer games and travels to many sporting events. She was a good athlete and stayed active and involved in clubs and activities. She held a dream of attending college and one day teaching children with learning disabilities. She spent her summers working at a camp for handicapped students and knew that this was her life's passion. Unfortunately, she had a few hurdles to overcome before she could make this dream a reality. During Dee's preschool years she was diagnosed with a language disability and received speech and language therapy. She was later diagnosed with a reading and writing disability and Attention Deficit Disorder (ADD). She continued to receive academic support through an IEP during her elementary, middle and high school years. She was placed in resource classrooms and received tutoring.

After many years of receiving academic support services, Dee felt she was well prepared for college. Throughout high school she was given the following IEP accommodations:

- extended test time;
- testing in a separate environment;
- reader for tests; and
- use of a computer for essay writing.

Dee attended regular classes, and had an inclusion teacher to access when she needed extra academic support. She also attended a resource room one period each day for assistance with her writing assignments and preparing for tests. When it came time for her college search she researched small colleges with extra academic support programs and easy access to professors. She decided on High Point University. "My older brother attended HPU and was a very good student, so I thought I could be just like him and I wanted to do it on my own." Dee had a strong connection with her brother and his friends, building an immediate support system. Dee's mother encouraged her to participate in the summer experience program, which was a college transition program for freshmen students. She attended this program in July and received good grades. She also signed up for the learning excellence program, which was a fee-based program with extra support services. With this in place, Dee was excited to start her college career.

Fall semester came quickly and Dee easily settled into college life. She attended classes regularly and met with her learning excellence coach weekly. One of Dee's strengths was in organizational skills, so she reviewed her syllabi and kept all assignments, tests, and projects in her planner, staying on top of assignments. Dee's mother encouraged her to also apply for and use accommodations in her courses, but Dee convinced her mother that she was well prepared for college and would do fine on her own; she knew that she *should* apply for accommodations, but chose not to. "I wanted to try by myself to see what I could do," Dee said. "I was in the learning excellence program, and thought that would give me all the support I would need." She also felt that her first year courses would be a review of high school, so she did not foresee any problems.

Her first month of college went well, until she had her first test. She did not do well; she had no accommodations and her anxiety level went through the roof. She saw her peers finishing their tests and turning them in, so she rushed to finish, with very poor results. When it came time to study for tests, Dee would complete the review guide a couple of days ahead, and feel she was prepared. While taking the test, however, her anxiety kicked in and she could not retrieve any information from her memory. Each test and exam became more frustrating for her, but she still did not apply for accommodations. Dee kept up with all assignments and papers, but did not meet with professors or ask for help. Her first semester grades were low, but she passed all her courses.

During freshman year Dee noticed that she was extremely tired and began taking naps between classes, and she began rushing through her work to get the sleep she needed. She went home over the Christmas break and met with her doctor, who performed blood work and allergy tests. These results showed that Dee had an underactive thyroid. She was placed on medication and this made a big difference in her energy levels. The allergy testing showed that she was allergic to wheat, so she began watching her diet, and eliminating wheat foods whenever possible. Reducing her wheat intake also improved her energy levels. Once these medical issues were addressed, Dee had more energy and time to focus on her academics, making a difference in her overall grades.

Dee was majoring in special education and loved the courses in her major. She stayed motivated and worked at building relationships with her professors. She still struggled with her core classes and limped along in these courses, which pulled down her cumulative GPA. During her sophomore year Dee realized that her GPA was not high enough to stay in the education program, so she had to switch majors. This was a difficult decision for Dee, since she had always wanted to be a special education teacher, and even spent her summers working at a camp for children with disabilities.

With the help of a new academic coach Dee explored different majors and their curriculum requirements. She finally chose to major in criminal justice, with the hope of working with children in this field. Once immersed in her new major she began to excel in her courses, which improved her GPA. This was a smaller major, so her professors knew her well and often reached out to her. They were available for support with papers and exam reviews.

Dee made a couple other changes her sophomore year. She requested a different Learning Excellence coach, and also had a separate academic coach.

Both coaches worked together and made a positive impact on her academics. The Learning Excellence coach helped her with organizing her time and assignments and set up tutoring. Both coaches helped her to improve her study strategies, gave assistance with writing papers and reviewed for tests with her. The academic coach encouraged her to apply for accommodations, and took the time to review her disability and learning style, explaining how accommodations would give her the tools she needed to be successful in the classroom and reduce anxiety when test taking.

Dee's Approved College Accommodations

Testing accommodations:

- 50% extended test time;
- testing in a separate environment; and
- reader for tests.

Classroom accommodations:

- copy of peer notes and textbooks in alternate format.

Dee immediately began using the peer notes accommodations. She still took notes in class, and each day she would look over the peer notes and re-write her notes, adding any information she missed. Dee added: "The peer notes reinforced my notes, and I would compare the peer notes to my class notes and see whether I missed important information, then I would add this to my notes. I also took time to re-write my notes each day, because I am a visual learner, and this would help me study. I also color-coded my notes. I wrote everything out by chapter, and proceeded to color code each chapter to keep the information organized. The colors made it easier for me to study for tests. During tests I would visualize the 'blue' key word, and then be able to retrieve the rest of the information around the word from my long-term memory."

During high school Dee learned how her brain worked at receiving and storing information. She took a learning style inventory and discovered that she was a visual learner. Once she started using study strategies for her visual learning style she was able to better prepare for tests and retrieve important information during the tests. She consistently created notecards with color-coding, rewrote her notes for review and highlighted her text with color coding.

Testing accommodations also made a difference in her grades. She began using her 50 percent extended test time and took the tests in a separate environment read aloud by a reader. Dee was amazed at how these accommodations reduced her anxiety and allowed her brain to successfully retrieve the information she had been studying. Her test grades improved dramatically and Dee soon became a more confident student with a strong GPA.

Dee still had one more hurdle to address. She had ADHD and had never tried using medications to help her focus. Her academic coach took time to discuss the possible benefits of ADHD medications with her and Dee decided to meet with her doctor at home and see whether she was a candidate for ADHD meds. After her doctor completed the testing Dee learned that she should definitely be on medication. Her doctor gave her a prescription for Focalin, which Dee began using right away. She made sure to use the medications when studying and when taking tests and exams.

With the help of her academic coaches and parents, Dee finally addressed all areas that affected her learning and test taking. She appropriately uses her accommodations, tutors, coaches and medications. She makes time to meet with her professors often and values the importance of these relationships. Her daily/weekly planner is color coded to assist with her organization. With all of these tools in place, Dee found that she was able to excel as a college student. Dee maintains, "I wish I had done all of this when I first arrived at college, it would have saved me so much stress and time. Before I began using my accommodations I put in so many extra hours on my coursework, studying and trying to do well, but I couldn't move forward. If I had to do it all over again, I would listen to my mom, because mom is always right! She wanted me to get the help and support from the beginning, but I was stubborn and wanted to do it my way. Unfortunately my way was definitely harder, and I should have used my accommodations from the beginning, and not waited until I was struggling."

Dee's has advice for students facing similar situations.

• Don't be afraid to use your accommodations. In college no one will make fun of you for having a disability; if anything your peers may be jealous that you do get the support.

• Listen to your parents! I wish I had used my accommodations from the start, and I wish my parents had been more forceful in making me apply for accommodations from the beginning.

• Don't take your accommodations for granted; *use* them, *don't abuse* them!

• Take the time to build relationships with your professors. They are there to help you, and they want you to do well. You can go to your professor with any issues, even personal ones. They respect you as a person.

Ryan and Dee both learned through trial and error which tools they needed in place in order to become a successful college student. They would be the first to tell you to have all accommodations and support services in place from your first day of college, instead of waiting until you are failing courses to reach out for help and support. Months of frustration and self-doubt can be avoided by choosing to accept your specific disability and exploring resources within the college.

Some Possible Accommodations for Students with Reading and Writing Disabilities

Classroom Accommodations:

- peer notes;
- textbook in alternate format;
- use of laptop for essay writing; and
- record lectures.

Testing Accommodations:

- tests read aloud;
- extended test time; and
- testing in a separate environment.

Assistive Technology:

- Kurzweil 3000 reading software;
- Smart Pens (Live Scribe Pulse Smart Pens, or Echo Smart Pens);
- Dragon Naturally Speaking;
- Noteability or Study Blue apps from Apple; and
- iStudiez Pro (calendar for assignments links to iphone and computer).

Apple constantly launches new educational apps for all students. Please check out this website for their innovative and ever changing technology resources: https://www.apple.com/education/ipad/.

Steps to Assist with the Writing Process

- Choose your topic (meet with your professor for specific guidelines and citation styles).
- Research articles, journals and books on your topic.
- Go through each resource and highlight relevant information.
- Create an outline with three to five important ideas for your research.

- Create a thesis statement.
- Brainstorm ideas and free write.
- Meet with professor to review outline ideas and get feedback.
- Begin writing each section ... rewrite and rewrite (work with the writing tutor at least twice a week).
- Make sure to cite all sources.
- Meet with a writing tutor for assistance with grammar, punctuation and flow.
- Meet with a tutor and the professor to get additional feedback and to polish the paper.
- Meet with a writing tutor to go over grammar and punctuation and use spellcheck.

Also meet with the professor and writing tutor each week for support.

Writing assignments can become extremely daunting without support in place. Do not be afraid to ask for help; that is why colleges have writing centers and professors hold office hours. Attempting to research and write papers on one's own can quickly become frustrating and at times overwhelming. A tutor at the writing center will assist students in breaking the assignment into smaller, more manageable parts. They will assist with brainstorming ideas, creating a thesis and preparing an outline; once these tools are in place the student can begin to create the paper. Students should make sure to get clarification from the professor and topic approval early in the project, and then meet with them a few more times to make sure they are on the right track with both research and writing; then remember to use the writing tutors as often as possible to assist with grammar and punctuation. After each successful paper, students gain confidence, improve their writing skills and often improve the quality of their work.

Students who use the support services along with technology reading and writing software (Dragon Naturally Speaking and Kurzweil 3000) and tutors have successfully completed their courses. Their learning disability is supported with these resources and does not become a burden. Knowing which tools to have in place for specific learning needs in individual courses will keep students on the path of academic success as they complete their college degree.

Math Disabilities

A specific learning disability in math is often labeled as dyscalculia, and is noted as a cognitive impairment in mathematical ability. Students with a math disability often have difficulty identifying math terms, symbols, signs and math rules. Each student will vary in their ability level. Often students who struggle with algebra will perform better in geometry. In order for a student to progress in math they need to master terms, symbols, calculations, understand math calculations and process formulas. The deficit in these cognitive abilities within the left hemisphere of the brain interrupts this learning process.

Throughout elementary, middle and the high school years the students diagnosed with a math disability have received support services and accommodations to help them progress. Once these students reach college they will also need to request accommodations under the ADA laws. The student must meet the requirements of their degree, which may include a math course. Sometimes the college will grant a substitution for a lower level math course, depending on the degree track the student is perusing. There are college accommodations for students with math disabilities:

Classroom Accommodations:

- copy of peer notes; and
- use of calculator.

Testing Accommodations:

- extended test time (50% or 100%);
- testing in a separate environment (although most students want to be with their professor in case they have questions during the exam);
- use of a note card with formulas;
- use of graph paper to help organize problems on a page; and
- use of calculator for tests.

Students with math disabilities often take longer to master the skills required in the math course. They will benefit from working with a tutor who is trained to work with students with math disabilities. They will need repetition of the major points from the course material and recent lecture and repeated practice with new formulas. The tutor should also give the student practice test problems to work out independently and then review with the tutor.

Many math professors will also meet individually to tutor students and help them prepare of tests and exams, as long as the student has prepared practice problems.

The following are tips the students can put into place in order to progress in the math course:

- Keep a well-organized notebook with
  - formulas;
  - practice problems;
  - terms;
  - symbols; and
  - illustrations.
- Create notecards with new formulas and terms.
- Meet two to three times each week with a math tutor.
- Meet at least once a week with your professor or grad assistant.
- Meet with a study group and practice teaching a specific math skill or problem set to the other students—explain steps, create drawings, label diagrams.
- Color code our notes for help with memory retrieval.
- Practice, practice, practice those math problems to help with your memory retrieval skills on test day.
- Take your test with extended time with your professor for extra support (your professor can provide a quiet, less distracting environment for the testing session).

Take your math course when you do not have a heavy academic semester. Some students choose to take the math course during the summer when they have only this course to focus on. Utilize tutors and meet with your professor often. Other students have taken their required math course at a local community college near their home over the summer and transfer the credit to their college. (Students must earn a C or above for the transfer credit to count.)

Other students have taken their required math course more than once in order to pass the course. If you fail the course you can retake it another semester, and the new course grade will wipe out the original grade, but your transcript does show that you attempted the course twice. Make sure to use tutors, peer notes and meet with your professor weekly so they know who you are and how dedicated you are to learning the material in their course.

8

Experiencing College
with ADHD/ADD

Student Testimony—Tanner

Attention deficit hyperactivity disorder (ADHD) is a neurocognitive behavioral developmental disorder most commonly seen in childhood and adolescence, but which often extends into the adult years (Antshel et al., 2008). As students diagnosed with ADHD/ADD get ready to attend college their disability can present new challenges to their academic success. Attention deficit is a neurological disorder and comes in different forms. "People with ADHD are usually described as having one of three types of attention difficulties: predominantly inattentive, predominantly hyperactive and impulsive, or combined inattentive/hyperactive" (Costello et al., 2011). Symptoms of ADD/ADHD are "impulsivity, hyperactivity, mood swings, low frustration tolerance, difficulty falling asleep, and difficulty completing tasks, disorganization and difficulty concentrating" (Quinn, 2001, p. 14).

Twenty-five percent of students with disabilities report having significant levels of ADHD (DuPaul, 2011). Often students with ADHD/ADD have been very successful in high school, but may become overwhelmed with the demands of this new academic environment, especially with time management and organizational skills. Other students may be diagnosed with ADD for the first time during college. College courses require larger amounts of reading and independent learning, along with better organization of time and assignments, causing extra stress for students already struggling with focus and concentration. A majority of students with ADD procrastinate because they often have trouble prioritizing assignments, so they put things off, and then try to rush through assignments in order to meet deadlines. These students need to manage their ADD/ADHD symptoms and attend colleges with academic support resources. Colleges have effective resources in place to assist students with ADHD/ADD as they pursue their academic goals.

Learning to manage free time and keeping up with long-term assignments often becomes an uphill struggle. "ADD affects the frontal lobes of the brain. These lobes are responsible for the executive functions, performing tasks like those of a corporate executive- transmitting information, planning ahead, learning from errors, keeping emotions at an even keel, determining the length of time for a task, creating motivation, and knowing the appropriate thing to say" (Sarkis, 2008, p. 8). Students in college with ADD often struggle with getting to classes on time, managing multiple assignments, procrastination, following through with tutoring appointments, decreased motivation, and taking the time to access available resources. Motivation is often a big hurdle to overcome: "It is difficult for your brain to motivate itself to start a task" (Sarkis, 2008, p. 9). Without motivation these students often procrastinate, then try to cram for tests, or write a paper the night before a due date. Students have been known to fall asleep during an exam because they stayed up all night cramming and their brains were too exhausted to stay awake and focus on the exam.

Students with attention deficit disorder usually have poor executive functioning skills, which interfere with college success, and need to work hard to improve these skills. High school teachers who take the time to teach these skills are giving these students excellent support skills for college survival. The ADD student needs to take an active role in their high school IEP so they have a solid understanding of their strengths and weaknesses, and know which resources to put in place during college. Students with ADHD need to have good study strategies and time management skills in place, or utilize a coach to help them learn these skills, as they can make a positive impact on the overall outcome for these college students. Students who take the time to find the right college fit, manage their symptoms, put appropriate resources in place and utilize accommodations are setting themselves up for success.

New Challenges

College students are required to become independent, responsible learners. Parents are no longer hovering around to help with organizing study time, getting students to school on time, or making sure they get to bed at a decent hour and take their medications at the appropriate time each morning. The student needs to learn to manage their life so they can get to class on time, meet deadlines and complete reading and writing assignments promptly. This can become a daunting and frustrating task for many ADD students. Fortunately colleges do have resources in place to assist these students.

The following are some steps ADD students can take to set themselves up for success:

- Students can apply for academic accommodations, such as extended test time and copies of peer notes to help them address their focus issues.
- They should work consistently with tutors who will help them organize course assignments and review notes and reading material to prepare for tests and exams.
- Most colleges will offer a college study skills course, which will help them understand how they learn and equip them with appropriate study and test taking strategies.
- Many fee-based programs offer an academic coach to work independently with the student to help with time management/organizational skills, arrange tutoring and reinforce study strategies. The academic coaches also help students learn good self-advocacy skills and encourage them to initiate contact with their professors and counselors.

Investing in these types of resources, especially during the freshman year, will help the ADD student get off to a good start and build healthy study and life skills.

Medications can often control some symptoms of ADHD, but students will need more resources in place to help improve social, academic and executive functioning skills. "Most patients show residual disabilities in several areas, including executive functioning, deficient emotional self-regulation, and 'real-world' functioning in school or employment, or in maintaining relationships. Some have suggested that ADHD is a disorder of performance, not knowledge. Thus, despite reduced ADHD symptoms and knowing how best to manage their affairs, residual impulsivity often continues to negatively affect functioning. For this reason, establishing reasonable expectations with patients and parents may be crucial for the success and continuity of the treatment" (Antshel et al., 2008).

Resources such as counseling, tutoring and academic coaching have been used successfully for many of these college students, especially assisting with procrastination, executive functioning skills and keeping up with weekly assignments.

It is amazing how many freshmen students with ADHD/ADD are able to convince their parents that they do not need college accommodations, stating, "I want to try the first semester without any accommodations; I want to do it on my own." Unfortunately the outcome is often the same: failing classes, inability to keep up with assignments and papers, and students left feeling overwhelmed and frustrated by mid-term, often turning to a social life to boost their self-esteem. Years of having a diagnosis of ADHD, having to take medications on a regular basis and use academic accommodations like extended test time, peer notes, and receiving extra tutoring have left the student feeling inferior to their peers, so they want to dump the label and all resources that go with it. These students feel that college is a fresh start and want to be as successful as their peers without being labeled or using accommodations. Others feel that the years of tutoring and accommodations have taught them enough study strategies that they will be able to handle college academics on their own; usually neither of these scenarios works out for the student, and instead puts them at risk for failure.

Attention deficit is a neurological disorder and comes in different forms. Whether the student is predominantly inattentive, predominantly hyperactive and impulsive, or combined inattentive/hyperactive (Costello et al., 2011), the diagnosis impacts a student's executive functioning skills with planning, organizing and carrying out tasks. It also affects their ability to pay attention during lectures and take good notes at the same time. A large majority of college classes are taught lecture-style, often putting these students at a disadvantage; this is where having appropriate accommodations (such as peer notes or recording lectures) in place to assist the student with this deficit helps them succeed. Using approved accommodations, utilizing tutors, applying new study strategies and using prescribed medications appropriately are all steps the ADHD student should consider as a college student.

Disability Disclosure

College students have the choice whether to disclose their disability and apply for accommodations or not. Required documentation should be on the college disability website. Most colleges request a psychological evaluation with intellectual functioning and academic scores with strengths and weaknesses. The Wechsler Adult Intelligence Test (WAIS) and Woodcock Johnson III test are acceptable evaluations, along with recommended accommodations. Testing should include an ADHD checklist, such as the Conner's Rating scale. The psychological evaluation should be completed by a qualified professional. The student should also submit a letter disclosing their disability and accommodations that worked best in the past. The high school IEP or 504 plans can be presented as a resource to help the Disability Specialist understand resources that have been effective in high school.

Students with ADHD who choose to disclose and use accommodations give themselves a fighting chance for academic success. "If a student chooses not to self-disclose their disability, it often remains hidden. This can be detrimental to their learning experience because many students with ADD and LD struggle in college and often struggle on their own" (Costello et al., 2011). Professors who are unaware of an ADHD/ADD diagnosis often view these students as being disengaged or unmotivated in their classroom. Their disability is hidden, and without support systems in place these students will struggle with the transition to college. They can become easily overwhelmed with assigned readings, note taking, study strategies, along with sustaining attention during classroom lectures. "Students with ADHD/LD frequently have lower grade point averages, more academic problems and are more likely to face the possibility of academic probation than other college students. In addition they are less organized and have fewer study skills than their peers" (Weyandt & Dupaul, 2008; Costello et al., 2011). Choosing not to use accommodations and available campus resources is often a recipe for failure; however, students who choose to use accommodations along with other academic resources usually have better grades and stay on track for graduation.

College Accommodations

Students with documented attention deficit disorders can disclose their disability by sending in their documentation to the college disability services director and completing the required online forms. The documentation should include a current psychological report, a letter disclosing the disability and the current impact it has on the student's academics. Students should also share which accommodations have worked for them in the past. If they have a high school IEP or 504 plans they can share these with college. Although these plans are not appropriate for college accommodations, students can use them as a guide for accommodations and resources that worked previously. Approved accommodations are effective from the date of request, but are not retroactive.

Classroom Accommodations:

- peer notes;
- record lectures; and
- textbooks in alternate format—use with reading software (assists with reading comprehension and focusing issues).

Testing Accommodations:

- 50% extended test time; and
- testing in a separate (less distracting) environment.

Some colleges offer their disability students the option for priority registration. This allows the student to work with their advisor to create a schedule that works with their brain and allows them maximum time to focus best while on their ADD medications. Students should let their advisor know that they have the ADD/ADHD diagnosis and they will assist the student with scheduling and finding professors who work best with their learning style.

There will be times when the student has to take a more challenging course that may tax their focusing and organizational skills. I recommend that when taking these types of courses they work closely with a tutor from the beginning, join study groups, stay current with assignments and readings, and meet with their professor often for review and clarification of the course material. It will take planning and effort, but ADHD students can pass these courses.

Managing Medications

Medication can be beneficial for most ADHD college students, and should only be taken as prescribed by their doctor. Sarkis (2008) suggests that if a student used ADHD medications in high school, they will usually need medication to assist with their ADHD in college. "When you have ADD your brain produces a low level of the neurotransmitter dopamine. When you take the ADD medication as prescribed, the level of dopamine in your brain goes up to a normal level" (Sarkis, 2008, p. 108). Students who do not take medications find that they have lost gaps of information from both lectures and reading materials, thus putting them at a disadvantage when studying for tests and exams. Sarkis states that the medications help increase attention, but the student still needs to use appropriate study strategies to help store the information properly in memory for retrieval.

Side effects can occur with these stimulant medications, so students need to discuss any concerns with appetite, difficulty sleeping, and headaches with their doctor. Remember to take *any* side effects seriously and report them to the doctor. Students should also follow up with yearly or regular check-ups with their doctors. According to research completed by Antshel, et al., "most patients show residual disabilities in several areas, including executive functioning, deficient emotional self-regulation, and 'real-world' functioning in school or employment, or in maintaining relationships. Some have suggested that ADHD is a disorder of performance, not knowledge. Thus, despite reduced ADHD symptoms and knowing how best to manage their affairs, residual impulsivity often continues to negatively affect functioning. For this reason, establishing reasonable expectations with patients and parents may be crucial for the success and continuity of the treatment" (2008).

Campus health services can usually assist with prescription needs. Call or meet individually with health services staff to learn their specific policies and procedures. Federal law states that all prescription medications should be kept in their original container and labeled with the student's name and the name/dose of the medication. "Don't self-medicate. Many students have a mistaken notion that, if one pill works well, two will work even better. While that may be true for other medications, that is not the case with stimulants. A specific amount of medication fits for each person's brain chemistry, which is why you should work with a medical provider to periodically reassess whether your dosage is working for you" (Quinn, 1998).

Procrastination and Prioritizing

It is easy for the average student to become overwhelmed with course assignments, papers and presentations, and often the result of this is procrastination. Students with ADHD face even bigger challenges with these assignments and often feel they have plenty of time, so they put off beginning projects and papers, even if they do keep up with course readings and reviewing for tests. Other students procrastinate because they do not completely understand the directions for a project or paper, and feel uncomfortable staying after class or attending professor office hours to get clarification. Good executive functioning skills help students to prioritize and stay organized with these types of assignments, but ADHD students are at a disadvantage because these skills do not come naturally for them.

I suggest working with a tutor or academic coach to schedule daily time and weekly assignments, and planning to begin research projects and presentations early so students are not rushing and cramming at the last minute, (which often produces lower quality work). The student should let the advisor know that they have the ADD/ADHD diagnosis and they will assist with scheduling and finding professors who work best with their learning style. Their advisor will help them create a schedule that works with their best "learning and alertness" times of the day. Classes too early in the day or too late in the evening may not work for them.

Make sure to discuss online classes with the advisor before signing up for them. Some students with ADD find that they can manage these courses because they can complete the work whenever they want, as long as they meet the deadlines. The assignments are usually laid out on Blackboard along with tests and projects, but students usually will not be given access to the course material until each specific week. Keeping up with due dates is critical for online classes, as once the submission date and time passes the portal is usually closed.

Technology Resources

Assistive technology can help students with ADHD manage their course material and class lectures, along with organizing assignments, papers and projects.

Examples of these resources include:

• SMART Pens—Records lectures while student takes notes during lecture. Then students can send notes to a computer for review and study.

• Organizational apps (Study Blue from Apple)—Assist students with keeping track of assignments on course syllabi, appointments and calendar reminders for meeting and when to start long-term projects and assignment due dates

• Reading software (Kurzweil 3000, Natural Reader, Read and Write Gold)—Assists students with the large quantity of reading material required for many college courses. Text-to-speech software highlights the text on the computer screen while reading it aloud to the student. Students can also highlight and create marginal notes with this software.

Finding the Right College Fit

The majority of students create a list of requirements when researching possible college fits, such as distance from home, cost, choice of majors, class size, division I sports, clubs and activities, size of city or town, fraternities or sororities, etc. Students with an ADHD/ADD diagnosis also need to consider available resources to help them succeed. Some college resources to consider are the availability of unlimited tutoring access, academic coaches, executive functioning coaches, writing centers, math labs, and accessible professors. Another consideration is the student-teacher ratio. Smaller class sizes help with focusing issues, and professors may be more accessible.

When making college visits students should thoroughly check out the academic resources center, tutoring center, writing center and disability services center. Even though many students check out these resources online, it is best to visit them in person to feel out the staff, technology and tutoring resources. Speak with other students in these resource rooms and ask them about accessibility and the level of service and dedication of support staff. They will be the best judge of these resources.

Many students with ADHD/ADD are not mature enough to attend college right out of high school. They may need a "gap year" to explore their interests, volunteer abroad, or partake in an internship within a field of study they are interested in exploring. For example, I had a student apply for an internship with the ASPCA because she wanted to study nonprofit leadership and she had a passion for helping animals. Another student spent six months interning for a political candidate, assisting with their political campaign. This gave him some experience and knowledge about the political science degree he was interested in pursuing.

Tanner

Tanner always enjoyed learning and grew up in a household with good support and plenty of structure. He was required to complete homework after school, eat healthy and go to bed at a regular time each day, which created good study and personal habits for him. He began struggling with learning in middle school and his teachers recommended that his parents have him tested for a possible learning disability. He was diagnosed with ADD, an auditory processing disorder and a reading disability. His doctor placed him on Adderall medication to help with his ADD symptoms. The medication did improve Tanner's focus right away, but he began to suffer from side effects. The side effects he experienced were poor appetite and weight loss, mood swings, and low energy levels in the late afternoon. As soon as he went off the Adderall medications, however, his grades dropped. The doctor decided to change his medications and put Tanner on Vyvanse. This ADD medication worked very well, with no side effects. Tanner continued to take this medication throughout high school with very good results. Tanner was also given accommodations for his auditory processing; these included testing in a separate environment and copies of class notes, which he used consistently.

Tanner looked forward to moving on to college and gaining his new independence. He chose a college within four hours driving distance from his home, and planned to major in international business with an entrepreneurship focus. Tanner made the decision to try college without using accommodations and medications. He felt successful with his high school education and the study skills and time management strategies he learned, and felt confident that he would be successful in college.

Unfortunately this was not the case. Tanner tried to keep up with his course work the first semester, but found that he was struggling in two of his courses, and barely keeping up with the others. He also began to enjoy his freedom, opting for an active social life over studying. He was no longer in a school program that monitored his daily homework, and did not have his parents monitoring his medications and social choices. He began staying up late and hanging out with his new friends, and was often exhausted in the mornings, so he began missing some classes. This proved to be a recipe for disaster. He ended up failing two courses and received low Cs in the other two. He was placed on academic probation and required to take a college study skills course.

During the second semester of his freshman year, Tanner made a better attempt to attend classes and keep up with course assignments. He still chose not to use accommodations or ADD medications, thinking he could turn this bad start around on his own. Consequently, he still struggled with time management and getting assignments completed and turned in on time. He also crammed for tests, with poor results. The college study skills course taught him some good time management and study skills, but Tanner rarely used them, instead he fell back to his old ways of studying and was constantly scrambling to keep up with last minute assignments. He would procrastinate with assignments, and then stay up late trying to complete them, which resulted in poor grades. He missed many appointments with tutors because he let other things take priority. He passed all of his classes, but his grade point average was very low. He needed to attend summer school in order to bring up his grades.

Tanner and his parents utilized new resources his second year of college. Tanner enrolled in a fee-based academic support program. He met with an academic coach each week and she helped him use time management skills to organize and keep up with his coursework, papers and presentations. She also set him up with weekly tutors. He realized that he needed the structure provided within the fee-based program, which he could not provide on his own. Tanner started his sophomore fall semester much stronger, but still struggled with passing tests and managing his study time. He worked harder this semester, but he still struggled academically. Procrastination and time management skills still challenged him.

The following spring semester Tanner began working with a second academic coach who helped him request disability accommodations, set up a meeting with a college counselor and discussed looking into using ADD medications. Tanner followed through with requesting and using accommodations and experienced some immediate improvements. He was approved for extended test time (50 percent), testing in a separate environment, copy of peer notes, textbooks in alternate format and tests read aloud. The first test he had read aloud improved his test grade from a D to a B. He was amazed at how much his comprehension improved with this accommodation. He attended counseling a couple of times, but did not feel a connection with the counselor, so did not pursue this further. Once again he chose not to use the ADD meds. His grades improved this semester and he felt he once again had a handle on everything.

The following fall semester was not as successful. Tanner was again feeling overwhelmed with his classes and coursework, and he was having some personal issues that took precedence over his academics. He lost his confidence and motivation. His parents and academic coach encouraged him to take a withdrawal for the semester. Tanner needed a break from school and time to get his head together. He enrolled in an outward bound program in South America that taught leadership skills along with decision making, maturity and teamwork. Tanner had a very positive experience, and felt renewed by the end of the program. He learned to make responsible choices and gained confidence and leadership skills.

When Tanner returned to classes for spring semester, he came with a new attitude and motivation. He decided to meet with his doctor and began taking his Vyvanse medication again to help him focus on his academics. He used all of his accommodations responsibly and met with tutors and his academic coach weekly, especially when studying for tests. Having all three of these resources in place made a huge difference in his academic progress. His confidence grew with each good test grade. He learned to use his calendar daily, weekly and monthly to stay on top of assignments, papers and preparing for tests. He learned to meet individually with his professors and share his academic struggles. They worked closely with him and even did some individual tutoring before exams. Tanner learned that he needed to have external structure, such as tutoring, the fee-based academic support, and time management support in place because he could not function successfully without it. He needed the same structure his parents provided growing up, which helped him to manage his ADD symptoms successfully.

Tanner was struggling with a few courses in his major, especially the higher level Spanish courses and the accounting courses, and realized that this was not the best major for him. He met with his advisor and decided to look into a major that better fit his interests and abilities. He selected nonprofit studies as his new major and found an immediate connection with the course material and his professors, which kept him interested and focused during class. Tanner experienced a very successful academic year, achieving a 3.0 GPA.

In order to stay on track for graduation Tanner took summer courses, either at the college or online. He realized that he could keep up with the online courses if he set time aside each day to work on the assignments. He also held down a summer job while taking these courses and was very successful at both. His last two years of college he chose to live in an off-campus apartment. His parents let him manage his money and pay rent, food, and utilities each month. The first two months were the most difficult because he thought he had a lot of spending money, so treated himself to a few things. Later that month he had little money for groceries, so he learned to budget a small amount after setting aside money for rent, food and utilities. He enjoyed handling his own money and felt a new sense of maturity with this responsibility.

Tanner finally had the right major, stayed on his medication for ADD and used academic resources to stay on a successful academic path. He had all the right resources in place to manage his ADD and successfully complete his courses in order to meet his career goals. Tanner has tips to share for students with ADD/ADHD.

• Use your accommodations consistently. This made all the difference in my courses. I didn't want to use them at first because I did not want to explain to classmates why I was not in class for test days. I quickly learned that this did not matter, and I cared more about my grades than what others thought.

• Use your medications. They helped me to focus in class and during tests and exams.

• Understand how you learn and use good study strategies daily. You will be amazed how prepared you will be for tests.

• Use a planner and calendar; sync this to your phone for daily and weekly reminders. I learned to use all time management strategies, and they are now a good habit that I will take into the job force with me.

• Exercise regularly—this helped me manage my stress and kept me motivated.

• Eat healthy and get enough sleep. This helped me to follow through with daily assignments and appointments.

• I never mixed alcohol and my ADD meds. This is a very bad combination.

• I took a break from ADD meds over relaxing weekends and during vacations.

- A new semester can be a fresh start, just put resources and accommodations in place.
- Do not register for early classes; 8:00 and 8:30 classes are difficult to attend and focus on.

Attention Deficit Disorder does not have to negatively impact a student's college success. The right resources and accommodations need to be in place from the beginning in order to manage ADD/ADHD effectively. Putting resources in place from the beginning will make the difference between success and failure for students with ADHD/ADD. I urge students to disclose their disability, use all approved accommodations, and do not let their disability remain hidden. Meet with each professor at the beginning of the semester, so they are aware of any academic struggles, and discuss classroom and testing accommodations. Instead of waiting to see whether a student can achieve good grades on your own, I advise them to start off fully in charge of their academic future; do not leave it to chance. They should take control of their disability and accommodations by applying them to courses from the start. Knowing which resources they need for each particular course will put them in the driver's seat and give them control over their education.

9

Deaf and Hearing Loss Students

Student Testimony— Michael

Students who are deaf or have a hearing loss have been successfully completing college for many years, but they do require special accommodations to assist them with accessing all information. Attending college as a student who is deaf or has a hearing loss will require some extra planning during the year prior to the first college semester. The college needs to create equal access to academics, services, programs and activities by providing interpreters/transliterators, auxiliary aids and technology. U.S. Department of Justice guidelines state that colleges must provide "an interpreter who is able to interpret effectively, accurately and impartially both receptively and expressively, using any necessary specialized vocabulary" (F.R. § 35.104. See generally, Patrick, 7 NDLR 470 [1995]).

The deaf and hearing loss student should first research carefully to find the right college and career fit, and then proceed to requesting accommodations. *College accommodations do not alter the academic requirements, they give student access to academic materials*; students must complete the same academic requirements as their peers in order to earn an equivalent degree.

Research from the University of Tennessee's Center on Deafness found that "involved parents were ascertained to be instrumental in fostering the career development and enhancing readiness for post-high school education for their deaf offspring. The combination of knowing personal preferences and accepting hearing loss strongly influenced forming a realistic career choice" (Watson et al., 2007). Once the student has chosen their preferred college and major, they should contact the disability services or Accessible Services department on campus. The college will need access to the student's medical diagnosis and recent audiological report in order to both set up accommodations for the classroom and to have enough time to hire an interpreter or transliterator for the classroom. Services and technology will be put into place to meet each individual student's needs. It is imperative that the college create comprehensive support services for their communication and accessibility needs both academic and interpersonal. Students should meet early and communicate often with Disability/Accessibility Services to ensure that they have enough resources in place to succeed. The first year of the college transition is a vulnerable time for these students, and they need access to support services in order to successfully adjust to the new academic and social demands of college life. Having these resources in place from day one will also reduce the amount of stress they will experience in this new environment. Most hard of hearing or deaf students do not want to be labeled as "disabled "or "hearing impaired"; instead they prefer their deafness to be labeled a "communication loss" (Watson, et al. 2007). These students have worked very hard throughout their prior education to learn how to communicate and access information. They have grown strong and confident in their abilities and want a chance to be a "normal" college student. Having appropriate accommodation in place will allow them to have a positive academic experience.

Some colleges have more experience and technology resources in place to assist the deaf and hearing impaired students to succeed with their academic goals. Colleges with strong services in place may be found online at http://www.collegexpress.com/lists/list/colleges-with-accommodations-and-services-for-the-hearing-impaired-student/405/.

College scholarships are also available to this specific community. A website that gives students a good start in their scholarship research is http://www.listeningandspokenlanguage.org/document.aspx?id=286. Some of these scholarships include

- the Sertoma Scholarship for the Deaf and Hard of Hearing;
- the Alexander Graham Bell Association's AG Bell Scholarships;
- the Minnie Pearl Scholarship;
- the Cochlear Implant Scholarship (for Nucleus Cochlear Implants and Baha implant recipients); and
- the National Cued Speech Association.

Deaf and hard of hearing students will also experience new and diverse college settings, such as dorm living, larger classrooms, cafeteria noises, group conversations with strangers, and accessing new technology or assistive listening devices. Adjusting to many new situations at once can become over stimulating to these students and cause stress. Students with strong assertiveness will be able to adjust to these new social and academic settings. Being confident in asking for clarification/directions, asking peers to look directly at them when speaking, meeting individually with professors, and communicating with resident dorm staff and housing staff will ease some of these new stresses.

The student should also meet with the housing staff to arrange for emergency notification of fire drills, tornado and other emergency situations. It will be important to visit colleges early in the junior year in order to make an informed choice, and set up needed accommodations prior to the first semester. Once the student decides on their college of choice, the student and parents should meet with the disability and housing staff to put all needed accommodation in place. If the student plans to live on campus they should meet or contact the housing staff in May, in order to give them enough time to set up emergency dorm lights or other needs. Housing accommodations should include an emergency flashing light installed in the dorm room to alert the student of fire alarms or other building or campus emergencies. Many deaf students also require a bed alarm that is connected to the emergency light alarm to shake them awake in case of an emergency, because the flashing light alone does not always wake them up. The student should also become acquainted with the dorm staff (resident assistants) as soon as they arrive on campus, because these staff members will also check to make sure the student is safely out of harm's way in case of an emergency. Assistance dogs are allowed to live on campus with the student.

Moving on to campus is a big weekend for most freshmen students and their families. During orientation week it will be important for the student to walk the campus, finding all classrooms as well as the disability/accessibility office and advisor's office before all the students arrive on campus, to give them confidence maneuvering the busy campus before the crowds of students arrive. All disability accommodations should be in place before the student attends classes. At least three months ahead of the first semester the student should have requested accommodations, including a transliterator for cued speech students, an ASL translator for student who use American Sign Language, and CART or G-Chat services as needed for lectures. Peer notes along with the translator or G-Chat will be necessary in order for the student to gain access to all course lecture material. It is difficult for the deaf/hard of hearing student to watch the transliterator or translator and the professor while taking notes at the same time. They can often miss a lot of important information, especially since most college core classes are 90 percent lecture based. I encourage these students to ask for peer notes along with the translator or remote note taker. Gaining access to all of the course material is the goal for these students and having the right resource accommodation in place is the first step to success, along with the student being persistent in utilizing all the resources available to them. The disability/accessibility staff will assist the student in setting up these needed accommodations.

Communicating with the disability/accessibility staff in late spring to begin setting up appropriate accommodations is ideal. The student and their family can meet individually with the appropriate staff members or communicate through emails in order to send in the appropriate documentation needed to approve accommodations and to sign the disability paperwork. The student is now an adult and their own advocate, so they are ultimately responsible for requesting any accommodations, signing paperwork and making sure that their approved accommodations are being properly implemented. Parents are welcome to contact the campus support services to send in documentation and get clarification on procedures if there is a concern that is not being addressed or an emergency situation regarding the student.

Michael

Michael was born deaf. His mother realized that he could not hear when, as an infant, he did not respond to her voice or sounds around him. At age five he had surgery for a cochlear implant, and soon after he began learning cued speech. He had never heard voices or sounds before, so it was very difficult for him to adapt. At first he found this to be very distracting, but slowly he learned to adjust to this new sense. He began to attend Camp Cheerio (a camp for deaf and hearing loss children and their families) in North Carolina each summer, where Michael and his family enhanced their cueing skills each year. He also learned to read lips and strengthen his verbal skills. During this weekend experience Michael and his family were immersed into cued speech with a trained transliterator and exposed to new information and technologies, all while building long lasting friendships with other deaf families.

When Michael started elementary school he was mainly placed in special education classes, where he received specific support with his hearing loss and language skills. Michael constantly found the noises around him very distracting, which interfered with his learning process causing him to score low grades throughout much of elementary school. He was placed on ADD medication at age eight, which helped with constant distractions, and his grades began improving. Later, when he was in fourth and fifth grades, teachers began mainstreaming him into the regular classroom. Michael's grades began to vastly improve and he felt more like a "normal student." During elementary school he was given an aid who sat next to him to assist with his learning needs by giving him access to the auditory information. This aid would also take class notes for him and clarify verbal information as needed during classes.

Throughout high school Michael became a strong student, using his cochlear implant and cued speech transliterator in the classroom to communicate. He also began using tutors on a regular basis to assist with his writing, study skills and organizational skills. Throughout high school he had three different transliterators, and appreciated having a cued speech transliterator in class with him daily. Further high school accommodations for Michael included peer notes, note takers in class, an FM system speaker for each teacher and closed captioning on films or TV presentations. After being accepted to High Point University in North Carolina, he met with disability services over the summer to set up his college accommodations, which also included a cued speech transliterator. Since during high school he successfully used a transliterator and also relied on an in class note taker who sat next to him in each class, he decided to continue these accommodations in college. Michael requested and was approved for accommodations.

Michael's Approved College Accommodations

Classroom Accommodations:

- transliterator in class;
- peer notes;
- use of computer for essay writing and note taking;
- priority registration;
- reserved seating;
- foreign language substitution'
- closed captioning for films and YouTube

Housing accommodations included:

- emergency flashing light
- bed shaker alarm

Testing Accommodations included:

- extended test time
- testing in a distraction free environment
- use of computer for essay writing
- transliterator for testing directions

The college had access to sign American Sign Language (ASL) interpreters, but had never needed a cued speech transliterator in the past, so they researched the area in order to find a good fit for Michael. There are far fewer cued speech transliterators than ASL interpreters. Michael would need the transliterator for the freshman orientation seminars prior to classes starting, any campus presentations, as well as in the classroom daily. This takes a lot of pre-planning and coordination with the disability department and the transliterator, which is why Michael and his parents reached out to the campus disability coordinator in May.

A week before each semester began, the disability coordinator sent an email to each professor informing them that a transliterator would be assisting Michael in their classes. The transliterator was seated up front, off to the side in each of his classes. Michael also had a note taker sitting beside him whom he could ask for clarification when needed. Michael also took his own notes from the professor's PowerPoint presentations or Blackboard notes. His first-year college courses were mainly lecture based, so he needed more than one input of communication in order to receive all the information from the lectures. Each of the resources for Michael's hearing disabilities were put in place, and he looked forward to the fall semester at HPU!

The disability coordinator met with Michael as soon as he moved onto campus. She arranged for his transliterator to attend the freshman orientation and seminars. Michael's roommate was very open to taking him to the cafeteria and assisting with communication when he needed extra help. Michael chose to attend many of the orientation activities with his new peers, instead of with his cued speech transliterator in tow.

Fall semester was off to a great start, and he was very passionate about technology and eager to explore his major as a computer programmer. All too soon, however, new issues arose. During the first dorm fire drill Michael was sound asleep, and his roommate was out. Michael takes out his cochlear implant while sleeping, so he did not hear the loud fire alarm. Fortunately, the bright light blinking on and off in his dorm room irritated him enough to awaken him. As Michael walked into the hallway he realized it must be some type of emergency, so he followed a few straggling students outside. After the fire drill he contacted disability services to alert them to the potential emergency situation. He needed a back-up plan to alert him to fire drills and other emergencies. The resident assistant was asked to double check his room to make sure he was out of the building. The disability coordinator also met with the security staff to find an alert solution for Michael. They were able to find a mattress alarm that could be connected to the in-room emergency light alarm which would awaken him. This solution worked much better than just the light alert placed within the dorm room.

Academically, Michael learned that college was much faster paced than in high school and he began struggling in his calculus and English courses. The pace of the math calculus lectures, compounded with his hearing loss made it difficult to understand the math concepts as they were introduced. He was given tutors, and met with his professors for extra help, but still struggled with retaining the math concepts and formulas due to the fast pace. He met often with his advisor and together they began to explore possible new career options that would not require such high-level math skills.

Michael also struggled in his English writing course, and shared that writing papers had always been difficult for him due to his language/vocabulary disability. He met with his disability specialist and together they explored some options. He was given a writing tutor, and they worked together at least twice a week. He was also encouraged to meet weekly with his English professor to get direction with his content and clarification with directions. Putting both of these resources in place helped Michael to succeed in his English courses and built his confidence in writing, which he carried over to future writing assignments within his course work.

Attention deficit disorder was still a challenge in his academic progress, so Michael and his parents decided to enroll him in a fee-based academic coaching program at HPU where he was given guidance with time management, organization and new study strategies. He met with an academic coach weekly and was given tutoring in other courses as needed. He was also assigned a professional English tutor to give him extra guidance with writing his papers. Within this program his ADD problems were addressed, helping Michael to stay on track with assignments and test preparations.

Michael knew the importance of meeting independently with each of his professors at the beginning of the semester to discuss his accommodations and seating arrangements in each classroom. This helped the professors understand his needs and helped both parties feel comfortable communicating throughout the semester. If Michael was unsure of lecture information or oral directions given in class he would make sure to stay after class and get clarification from professors, especially with long-term assignments. He would often email professors while working on assignments to ask for clarification or assistance. Creating a relationship with each of his professors was a skill Michael perfected each semester.

Michael loved learning and was excellent with computers and art. He began college in the computer programing major, then after one year switched to a degree in Game and Interactive Media Design, where he combined his art and computer skills within a major that he was able to excel in. Michael became passionate about the gaming degree and enjoyed creating game scenarios with his course teammates.

Socially, Michael was very secure. He made friends easily and enjoyed being around his peers. His new major in interactive media and game design required a lot of group interaction, and Michael let his peers know to look directly at him when speaking so he could read lips and easily participate in the activity. He also met outside of class with teammates for group projects. Michael usually did not require his interpreter to attend these group sessions with him, instead he worked closely with his peers and they assisted with any communication needs. Michael's outgoing personality created an excellent relationship with students, professors and tutors.

Michael loved learning and was excellent with computers, and art. He began college in the computer programing major then after one year switched to a degree in game and interactive media design, where he combined his art and computer skills within a major that he was able to excel in. Michael became passionate about the gaming degree and enjoyed creating game scenarios with his course teammates. Michael worked hard, used all the resources available to him and successfully graduated college in four years with a very strong GPA.

Accommodations Deaf and Hearing Loss Students Can Request

Classroom Accommodations:

- translator/transliterator in class and other settings;
- peer notes or in-class note taker;
- preferential seating;
- use of computer for essay writing and note taking;
- closed captioning as needed;
- priority registration;
- speech-to-text technology: Cart (Computer Assisted Real Time Captioning) or G-Chat C-Print, and Typewell services;
- foreign language substitution (unless the student wants to pursue a foreign language);
- FM audio system; and
- reduced course load.

Housing Accommodations:

- priority housing;
- emergency flashing light;
- bed alarm/shaker; and
- closed captioning in residence hall and dorm room TVs.

Testing Accommodations:

- 50% extended test time;
- testing in a separate environment;
- use of computer for essay writing; and
- translator for testing directions.

Following are important tips for deaf and hearing loss students.

- Some students will prefer to test in the classroom so they can ask the professor for clarification during the test, or they can make arrangements to take the test in a separate setting with their professor. The professor can arrange the separate setting.
- Extended test time is provided when a student has difficulty processing the written language on the test, thereby requiring additional time to read and comprehend the questions (Brenner, 2007, p. 130).
- Priority registration helps the student to space out classes to assist with their fatigue levels, and with accommodating the translator/transliterator. Deaf and hard of hearing students can tire easily due to the constant focusing on translators and classroom communication along with studying.
- Make sure students and parents meet with housing and security to arrange emergency notification resources and procedures.
- Some hearing loss students have found "SMART PEN" technology helpful in recording lectures, taking notes and transferring these notes to their computers.
- Peer Mentoring—Some colleges provide peer mentors to assist students with the transition to college life. If a peer mentor is not offered the student can request one through the housing or counseling department.
- Tutoring—Most colleges will offer free tutoring services in most core subject courses and other advanced courses. Locate the academic services department on campus and inquire to policies for accessing tutoring. If there are none available the student can request tutoring as an accommodation; although they are not obligated to provide tutoring.
- "Residential facilities are responsible for purchasing and installing fire and smoke alarms in the residence halls. Additionally a door bell may be installed that connects to a lamp in order to signal that someone is at the

door. A peephole in the door is necessary for safety as the hard of hearing student may not be able to identify a visitor by asking for verbal identification" (Brenner, 2007, p.131).

• Alarm clocks—Deaf and hearing loss students have a history of not waking up on time because they do not hear alarms and sleep very soundly. To assist them with waking up in time for college classes, parents can invest in an alarm clock bed shaker (possibly two!). Mom and Dad will no longer be available to shake the student awake, so they need to rely on these devices in order to get to class on time.

• Accommodations may vary from class to class, depending on how the course material is presented and the individual student's needs.

Documentation for College Disability and Accessibility

• Medical records—Medical documentation should be up to date, and no less than two years old.
• Evaluation—On letterhead from medical doctor and ENT specialist/ audiologist.
• History should include onset and etiology.
• Current audiogram by a licensed audiologist.
• Current IEP with classroom and testing accommodations/teacher observations are also valuable.

IEP and 504 plans are not significant documentation by themselves.

Students who want to request SAT/ACT testing accommodations will need to locate the disability forms on each website. The forms need to be completed and signed and sent in with the appropriate documentation. Apply at least eight weeks ahead of the desired test date in order to give the board time to approve the accommodations requested. A letter will be mailed to your home, along with an email stating your approved accommodations and your unique access code. This code will need to be on the SAT/ACT from when requesting a test date. High school counselors should assist the families in completing and filing the appropriate paperwork. Some possible testing accommodations are

• 50% extended test time;
• testing in a separate distraction-free environment; and
• Translator/transliterator for testing directions.

For SAT testing accommodations the student and parent work with the school to submit their request online (College Board 2015). For complete SAT testing accommodations, go to http://professionals.collegeboard.com/testing/ssd/guidelines/sat or *http://www.collegeboard.com/prod_downloads/ssd/eligibility_form_instructions.pdf.*

For ACT testing accommodations, go to http://www.actstudent.org/regist/disab/chart.html or *http://media.actstudent.org/documents/ext-time.pdf* (application forms). Students and parents can work with the school counselor to complete all forms. Registration can be completed online at www.actstudent.org and the request can be mailed by the regular deadline for the test date.

The type of hearing loss the student is experiencing will determine the type of accommodations, resources and technology he or she will need. Vocational rehab services will assist the student in discovering the right hearing device to accommodate their needs. All colleges have access to ASL sign language interpreters and cued speech transliterators to be in the class with students, helping them access the lecture information and class discussions. Other students with only a mild hearing loss will benefit from using technology and software programs that provide either remote or in-class captioning services. Having access to lecture material and peer notes are essential to each student, regardless of the severity of their hearing loss. This population of students should have peer notes as well as a translator/transliterator in each class. They are usually focused on the professor and translator, working hard to keep up with the lecture information and they cannot always focus on note taking. Having access to peer notes online is a valuable tool to this type of student. Most colleges also have access to note taking software or a remote captioning service if the student does not choose to have a translator in class.

Another important accommodation to consider for hearing impaired and deaf students is housing. Being able to hear the fire alarms or emergency alarms in the dorm is a priority. The campus housing and security staff will assist in setting up the needed equipment. Michael needed housing to place a flashing light in his dorm room to alert him to emergencies such as fire alarms, which he could not hear. At night he slept without wearing his hearing aid for the cochlear implant, leaving him completely deaf. So it was imperative that Michael have another type of alarm to alert him to danger. Michael's roommates were made aware of the need for the flashing light inside their dorm room and practiced what to do in case of fire or other types of emergencies. Michael also used a vibrator alarm to wake him each morning, as he could not hear a radio or regular alarm. These tools helped him to be as independent as his peers. Alarm systems can also be programed into a student's phone to alert them of emergencies or awaken them.

The disability department needs time to set up housing and translator services for these students. Parents should contact the DSS or accessibility office in May before freshman year to discuss the needed accommodations. If you are certain of your choice of college before this, then let the DSS department know as soon as possible to give them time to ensure all your accommodation needs are in place—especially finding the interpreter or transliterator. Meeting once again with the DSS office a few weeks before classes begin is also important to review and finalize accommodations.

Vocational rehabilitation usually works simultaneously with the college to support deaf and hearing loss students by "creating goals and objectives to prepare for and engage in gainful employment for the individual student. Vocational Rehab services provide counseling and guidance along with testing and resources such as hearing aids, assistive listening devices, and other technology to help educate the signing deaf student" (Watson et al., 2007). VR begins to work with these students at age 17½, while still attending high school, to begin preparing post-secondary education plans by exploring and providing assistive listening devices along with technology resources. The vocational rehab counselor will also complete a comprehensive assessment which includes a variety of assessment tools, such as: Otologic evaluation, medical evaluation, communication assessment, comprehensive audiological evaluation, ophthalmological or optic exam, psychological assessment, rehabilitation technology assessment, and other specialty evaluations if a secondary evaluation is indicated (Watson et al., 2007). This information will help the VR counselor to assist the student with a solid individual plan of employment (IPE) by providing needed services along with clarifying educational goals. Once an IPE plan is in place the student can choose the right college fit and start connecting with the assistive departments on campus to incorporate the academic and housing accommodations into the plan in order to meet all needs.

As stated earlier, vocational rehab will work together with the individual college, ensuring that resources and accommodations are in place for the student. VR also helps to reimburse some of the costs the college undergoes for the interpreter or transliterator needed by deaf students. The students receiving any VR support must maintain a grade point average of 2.0 and above in order to continue receiving services from VR or they will no longer cover educational costs. The VR contact person from the student's hometown will need to be in contact with the college a couple months before school starts in order to get all the paperwork and procedures in place. Once the high school student turns 17½ years of age, the parent should contact vocational rehab to set up an assessment meeting and begin the process of sending in documentation to qualify for VR support services. The qualifying students can receive VR services while pursuing their undergraduate degree. Vocational rehab does not assist students with a masters or doctoral degree.

High school students who are under an IEP or 504 plan are required by the IDEA laws to have a transition plan in place. "Many state VR agencies have set up formal programs through cooperative agreements which allow for VR counselors, school counselors and teachers to work together to establish transition programs for eligible students. Typically these programs include career exploration, interest and aptitude testing, and information or referrals, in addition to work experience either on the job training, volunteer work, or actual employment. As a result the consumers have an IPE completed prior to graduation and plans are set for post-graduation goals" (Conway et al., [year], p. 107).

Choosing to tap into vocational rehabilitation services can greatly benefit the student on their academic and career journey. VR counselors also provide self-esteem counseling, advocacy training and address adjustment issues with the student while attending college or job training, along with communication and job site assessments as they later pursue their career.

The written by Jessica, a deaf high school student:

So you think being deaf is a curse?
You say "I'm sorry" when I constantly have to ask you to repeat yourself.
Apology accepted.
But if you are apologizing for me being "disabled"
You obviously don't know what you're talking about.

Yes, I struggle every day,
To understand simple conversations,
Being left out of family talks
Because it is too hard to follow ten people's mouths
And I don't want to bother them by asking what they said.
So I sit at the corner of the Thanksgiving table
Staring at my food hoping someone will talk to me.
But they rarely do.
It sucks.

Yes, I struggle at school,
To understand teachers,
To understand what videos are saying when there is no closed captioning.
I struggle to read the teacher's lips as they walk around the room.
Do I ask for help? Not usually.
Why? Because so many people have refused to help that I no longer have the courage to ask for it.

It's hard.
After countless times of teachers refusing
To repeat what they said even when they know
I'm deaf, I have given up.
I'm tired of giving myself headaches
When I concentrate so hard to understand the two sentence
Instructions the teachers give when it would help so much
If you would just stay in front of the classroom and face the damn class!

You don't understand,
My entire ability to communicate revolves around
Whether or not you face me when you talk.
So when you purposely turn away and speak,
Or say "nothing" when I ask what you said,
You have no idea how much that hurts.

So, Yes, I struggle,
I struggle every day, every hour, every minute.
Nothing is easy for me.
But would I change it?
Never.

I am part of a community of deaf people.
Some of the best people I have ever met are deaf.
We don't take anything for granted,
We don't complain because we know others
Have it so much worse than we do.

We know what it is like to be doubted,
To be missing a sense,
That's what brings us together.
I am part of a community of deaf people.

At night, when I take my implants off,
The silence is beautiful.
No TV, no birds singing, appliances humming,
Sheets rustling, or snoring.
Just silence.
I can turn off the world whenever I want.

So yeah, maybe I am disabled,
But I am a better person from it.
A blessing, not a curse,
And I am forever grateful for it.

Deaf students want to be treated the same as their peers. Their passions for learning, playing sports, playing musical instruments, singing, falling in love, etc., are as real as any other student; they just want others to treat them with respect and understanding. They need teachers and professors to help them by providing equal access to the course materials so they can reach their academic potential.

Parents of deaf students should help their child learn to advocate for themselves, so they will be able to communicate their needs once they are away from home and living on a college campus. These students will need to communicate with disability staff, professors, tutors, housing staff, cafeteria staff, health services and others on a daily basis. The more confident the student is when approaching these individuals and asking for assistance or accommodation needs, the more successful they will be.

A good resource for families is PEPNet, which was created to assist students and their families with transitioning to post-secondary education, providing resources for obtaining accessibility.

> In 1996 the US Department of Education, Office of Special Education and Rehabilitation Services funded four regional postsecondary education centers across the United States to serve as a collaborative organization to provide technical assistance to post-secondary institutions that enroll individuals who are deaf or hard of hearing. This technical assistance comes in the form of workshops, written materials, conferences, informational guides, and consultations to help such institutions initiate of enhance the accessibility of their programs to students who are deaf or hard of hearing. PEPNet works closely with two- and four-year colleges, vocational training and rehabilitation programs, adult education programs, private and community service agencies, secondary education programs, individuals who are deaf and hard of hearing, consumer and professional organizations, state and national organizations, and clearinghouses. Providing resources and training related to successful transition from secondary to post-secondary education and training is an important goal of this project. Readers are encouraged to contact the nearest PEPNet regional center for assistance. Additional information about PEPNet and the four regional centers can be found at http://www.pepnet.org/.

Other helpful resources to access include:
- Vocational rehab;
- Beginnings—family advocacy (birth–21 years of age); and
- DSDHH—Division under the NC Department of Health and Human Resources for Deaf and Hard of Hearing (information on equipment distribution/advocacy/ information/ counseling).

10

Achieving Success for Students on the Autism Spectrum
Student Testimony—Andrew

Since the 1990s people with Autism/Asperger's represent a growing population, and increasing numbers of these students are choosing to attend college—more than ever before, and colleges have been working to create accessibility to meet their needs. "Despite adequate cognitive ability for academic success in college many individuals on the autism spectrum find postsecondary education an insurmountable hill to climb. Often gaining admission without ever identifying themselves as individuals with Autism/Asperger's those students go unnoticed by their professors until their sensory, social, learning styles and organizational challenges combined with fatigue, cause them to fail" (Autism and Asperger's Association, 2013). Students attending college with Autism Spectrum Disorder (ASD) can face many unique learning challenges.

The ASD is presented differently in each individual student, with variations in social skills, academic ability, communication challenges, anxiety, organization, time management and executive functioning skills, fine or gross motor skills, and self-advocacy, to name a few. According to a study completed by McKeon, Alpern and Zager (2013), ASD students need extra support systems in place because they face more academic challenges, such as: information processing difficulties, poor ability to understand and apply concepts, distractibility and short attention span, weak organizational skills, difficulty understanding subtle cues or body language, poor time management, self-regulation problems, and hypersensitivity to particular sounds, smells and lighting.

Early and continued communication with disability services, housing and Student Life will be critical to the success of ASD students. It may also be helpful to find a college within two to four hours of home so the parents and student can stay better connected and easily travel back and forth for visits, personal assistance and emergencies. These students will benefit from a college with tutors, academic coaches, smaller class sizes and assistive technology. Take time to explore the culture and attitude of the college campus in order to avoid negative or extreme social situations later in the semester. Make sure to look for clubs and activities the student can join that complement their talents and interests.

Often students will be able to connect with peers and create friendships within these clubs. Finding the right college fit, considering the size of campus and student teacher ratio, as well as academic resources will be crucial to the success of these students. Parents need to find a specialized program that will give guidance and support to these students, especially during their freshman transition year, and some ASD students will need academic support services throughout their college education. Transitioning to college will be overwhelming in itself for students on the autism spectrum, and adjusting to the academic demands will tax all their skills, which may already be weak. Parents can check out the U.S. CAP, College Autism Program, for more information on colleges and resources to assist their child with the college process (http://www.usautism.org/uscap/).

Finding the Right College Fit

A small to medium sized campus with smaller class sizes will help these students with their distractibility issues. They will also need access to academic tutoring, a tutor who will work on improving executive functioning skills and a writing center tutor who will help these students build on their written communication skills which they need to be successful in their courses. The disability staff or a parent or other advocate will need to assist the student with contacting appropriate staff and putting each of these resources in place. When researching potential colleges make sure the college offers a *couple levels of tutoring* support and academic coaching, especially with executive functioning skills. These students usually do not seek out tutors without the assistance of a coach, counselor or their academic advisor. When visiting colleges make sure to explore the Academic Services Center and meet the director to discuss individual tutoring needs.

Assistance with improving executive functioning skills will benefit the majority of AS college students. They have frequently been observed with the following behaviors: "distractibility, poor time management skills, disorganization, and lack of impulse control" (McKeon, Alpern & Zager, 2013).

Some colleges will have minimal support for these students within their tutoring program and academic services; others will offer a more substantial support program. Colleges with *fee-based support programs* offer a large array of support with academic coaches to help with time management/organization, assistance with executive functioning skills, professional tutors and assistance with setting goals and new deadlines for project and research papers.

Enrolling the student in these types of programs from the very beginning will help to set up a firm academic foundation and extended support for their executive functioning skills. Some students will need a program like this the entire four years; others will only need it for three or four semesters. "To function successfully in the academic setting one must be able to attend, initiate and plan ahead. To do so requires organization of resources and time and the ability to generalize a set of skills to a variety of situations ... limited executive functioning also contributes to disorganized communication" (McKeon, Alpern, & Zager, 2013). Once they learn where the resources are and the benefits of accessing them the students often use them consistently to improve their academic progress.

Learning to Navigate the Campus Early

Students with Autism/Asperger's usually do not ask for directions, guidance or help easily. It will be important for the student's family members to help them learn to navigate the campus before they begin the first week of classes. The family needs to help them physically transition to the new campus environment. Moving into the college dorm can feel exciting yet overwhelming to the AS student because they often have difficulty adjusting to changes in schedules and routines. If he or she has roommates the family should introduce themselves to the other students and parents and share contact information in case a situation arises where they need some guidance. The parents or a friend should also take time to walk through the student's class schedule with them to make sure they can navigate the campus and find each classroom building before classes begin, thus lessening the first week anxiety.

Maneuvering around campus can become a daunting task to the AS student so the family should also help the student become familiar with the cafeterias, health center, library and academic services, disability support services, as well as the advisor's office. Take the time to walk with them to each building and locate offices and staff members they will need to access.

Some AS students may also need their family members to help them make initial contact with disability services, counseling or with their advisor to help ease the stress of that first meeting. Walking the student through their daily routine more than once will be extremely helpful. It is also beneficial to introduce them to a main contact person on campus, such as someone in disability services or student life, their resident assistant (RA), or a peer mentor so they have a familiar face they trust to touch base with and contact for guidance when situations arise.

Requesting Accommodations

Accommodations should be in place before classes begin, but can be put in place anytime throughout the semester. Parents can send the student's documentation to disability services and the AS student should also send in a personal statement to discuss which accommodations worked best in the past and which personal or social issues they may need guidance with. The student and parent should also meet with the DSS staff to discuss the approved accommodations, possible tutoring and other needs the student may have. If accommodations have not been set in place ahead of time the student can arrange a meeting with disability services and begin the accommodation process at any time.

Autism spectrum students often have trouble transitioning to lectures and discussions in college classrooms. The constant note taking, class discussions and small group interactions can create too much external stimulus on their senses, creating another level of anxiety. The accommodation of peer notes will help the AS student have the appropriate information they need in order to study for tests and exams. It is difficult for most of these students to pay attention to a lecture and take good notes, especially when external stimuli are added in. The student can access peer notes online at their leisure, and proceed to make notecards or other study materials.

Possible Classroom Accommodations:

- peer notes (students often struggle with following the lecture and taking strong notes);
- use of speech-to-text software;
- special housing needs (students often need a private dorm room);
- lighter or reduced course load (students may need to take summer courses or stay an extra year of they choose a lighter course load each semester);

- wearing sunglasses, hats or baseball caps in the classroom in the classroom (for light sensitivity);
- use of earphones in the classroom (to assist with higher frequency noises—distractibility);
- foreign language waiver or substitution;
- no cold-calling in class;
- record lectures;
- permission to bring drinks or snack to class; and
- permission to bring sensory object to class (e.g., squeeze ball).

Possible Presentation Accommodations:

- allow video presentation;
- allow presentation to professor only; and
- alternate assignment (if professor agrees to this, as they do not have to alter the curriculum).

Possible Testing Accommodations:

- extended test time;
- testing in a separate distraction reduced environment;
- use of computer for essay tests/exams;
- no scantron forms; and
- breaks during exams.

Possible Housing Accommodations:

- single dorm room.

Parents are welcome to call or meet with DSS to help with this process. Accommodations are provided after the student turns in their documentation and requests them.

Some Autism/Asperger's students will require a foreign language substitution or waiver due to their disability in language processing. "Support for language disabilities may be required for some students based on difficulties answering and asking questions and comprehending abstract linguistic information" (McKeon, Alpern, Zager, 2013).

Approved accommodations are legally protected under the ADA laws, and the college and professors are required to follow through with them. The student is never required to share their diagnosis with anyone, but they can chose to share their diagnosis or other personal information to professors in order to have them better understand their learning needs and the impact of their AS in the classroom setting.

Disability Support Services

Each college campus has a Disability Support Services office to provide students with support for accommodations, information on ADA laws and support and advocacy for their disability. Once the disability staff sets up the approved accommodations for the student, they are also available to assist with arranging tutoring and providing guidance with finding and using other campus resources and/or technology to assist with executive functioning skills. Parents can ask the disability office on campus to reach out to this student and set up a few meetings early in the semester to help them adjust to this new transition and create a comfortable relationship for support and advocacy in the future. The student can also request to meet with their disability specialist bi-weekly during the first semester to intercede with any accommodation and adjustment issues. These students often need an academic coach to assist them with time management and organizational skills. It would also be helpful to set up a weekly tutor who can assist the student with organization and time management so that they do not fall behind in readings, writing papers, completing research, writing lab reports and other assignments, especially since procrastination can be an impediment. Tutors can also assist with creating a weekly study schedule and to do lists to help the student stay organized.

Tutoring Resources

A majority of these students will need access to academic tutoring, and a tutor for executive functioning skills. Executive functioning help includes assistance with time management, organizing assignments, writing, and breaking large assignments into smaller segments. A parent or other advocate will need to assist the student with putting each of these resources in place. The student can also meet with disability services and academic services on campus and request help setting up the needed tutors.

Writing skills can become another hurdle for students with autism. Look for a college with strong *writing tutors and a writing center*. These students often need a writing coach to help them with the writing process, especially with required research papers. "While many students with high functioning Autism or Asperger's are proficient writers, others struggle with the writing tasks. Weaknesses in this area relate to executive functioning deficits and integration and synthesis difficulties: that is students struggle with organizing their thoughts into a cohesive paper and understanding how the details or evidence accumulate to prove a thesis" (Wolf, Brown, & Bork, 2009, p. 88). These students will require a writing tutor each semester to assist with papers, so having this in place the first semester will assist the student as they transition through each year and increased level of course material. The tutor can also help with clarifying the assignments or topic for the student. If the college does not have a strong tutoring program parents to can reach out to the community and find an educator that would be willing to become a private tutor for the student. Having the writing tutor in place and a personal connection and meeting times set up before each semester begins will greatly benefit the student.

Organizational skills are often difficult for AS students. Student services has tutors available who can work with the AS student on keeping up with weekly assignments as well as helping them break down larger assignments, such as research papers or projects and presentations. Some colleges will also offer a fee-based support program for any interested students. This would be extremely helpful for the AS student. These types of programs have an academic coach that meets once or twice with students and also monitors all tutoring and communication with professors. The AS student has difficulty keeping themselves organized and managing their time, so investing in a program like this will help keep them on a successful college path. If such a program is not available or the student cannot afford a fee-based program they may be able to work closely with a student tutor each week to help with keeping track of assignments, due dates and progression of research papers, labs, and projects. It is best to help the AS student set up a weekly routine of meetings, study time in the library or lab time. This keeps the student on a regimented schedule that is easy for them to follow. They may also need to set alarms on their phones with reminders of where and when they need to be somewhere, such as classes, tutoring, group projects, lab, or to study in a specified place on campus. disability services may also be willing to meet with the student throughout the semester to help address and solve these issues.

Self-Advocacy

Another important skill for the student will be self-advocacy. Parents and counselors can work together to help the student understand their Autism disability, with both its strengths and weaknesses. "Learning to self-advocate is a crucial skill for being a successful adult. Students with AS must be taught to self-advocate to be independent. Learning self-advocacy skills should begin in middle school, with students taking on increased responsibility each year" (Wolf, Brown, & Bork, 2009, p 29). It will be extremely helpful if the student meets individually with each professor at the beginning of the semester, hands them the accommodation letter and shares a little more about their disability. This will help the professor to better understand and assist the student throughout the semester. If the student is not comfortable, or socially ready to meet and discuss these issues with the professor either the disability staff or a parent can accompany the student to these initial meetings.

The student should also communicate their disability with the dorm resident assistant and build a trusting relationship. Housing staff should be aware of the student's Autism/Asperger's diagnosis in case of emergencies. I had an experience with an autistic student a few years ago who was scared of the fire alarm; it was loud and overwhelmed his sensitive hearing, so he stayed in his dorm room, balled up in a corner covering his ears. Fortunately the RA was aware of his Autism diagnosis and checked in on him. He was able to persuade the student to leave the building with him. From then on the RAs always checked in on this student during fire drills, tornado warnings and other emergency situations to help him exit the building and keep safe. Professors can also assist these students in the classroom with fire alarms and emergency situations.

Self-Care Skills

Some students with ASD will need assistance with personal care needs while attending college. This is not an accommodation that colleges support, but parents can look into special programs that do offer these services to students. An example would be Marshall University in West Virginia, which established the Autism Training Center in 2002, and it is still going strong today. The program supports 45 individuals with Autism/Asperger's, taking on 10–12 new students each year. The program creates a successful college experience for these students by providing academic, social and independent living skills support, and a student mentor who has successfully completed the program. This is a fee-based program, and qualified applicants need to apply by February 1. Any students interested in the summer transition program should complete that application by April 1.

Other colleges may have similar programs, but most are also fee-based due to the extent of services they supply for these students. Here is a list of other colleges with strong support programs for the ASD student with support that will vary from academics, social, peer mentoring, self-advocacy skills, and materials to assist with executive functioning. Unfortunately most of these programs are fee-based and are not cheap. Here is a list of "Ten Impressive Special College Programs for Students with Autism" from BestCollegesOnline.com:

1. Drexel University Autism Support Program
2. Rutgers Developmental Disabilities Center
3. Mercyhurst College AIM Program
4. Midwestern State University
5. St. Joseph's University Kinney Center for Autism Education and Support
6. Boston University Supported Education Services (free support program for admitted students)
7. University of Alabama College Transition and Support Program
8. Autism Collaborative Center at Eastern Michigan University
9. University of Connecticut SEAD Program
10. Marshall University Autism Training Center

Counseling Resources

Counseling is another valuable resource for students with Autism. Along with having sensory overload issues they often lack social skills, misinterpret body language/social cues and can have personal space issues (Wolf, Brown, & Bork, 2009). Meeting with a counselor weekly can help them discuss and work to improve these types of issues, plus any roommate concerns, dating issues, and general transitioning issues. The counselor will give them guidance and tips on working through their personal issues. Anxiety is another issue that counselors can help them address. The counselor can help the student build self-confidence so they can better function in the classroom and socially. Making contact with the counseling department before the semester begins will create a sense of comfort, a "safe place" and a positive connection with a counselor. Parents can bring their child in to meet or interview a counselor over the summer or during freshman move-in weekend. This creates a support system for the student and lessens the anxiety of making the initial contact alone.

Counselors can also assist AS students with communication skills both in the classroom and out. Professors have reported "they have observed frequent language and communication problems revolved around classroom discourse: difficulty with asking questions, answering questions, and going off topic in discussions" (McKeon, Alpern, & Zager, 2013). Counselors can help these students work on recognizing these habits and implement strategies to improve them. They can also assist with peer interactions and determining how and when to share with peers about their diagnosis.

Peer Mentoring

Many colleges are offering peer mentoring to their incoming freshmen, and this can be a real asset to students with ASD. The peer mentor can give these students guidance with possible clubs and activities that will meet their interest. They can join the student for lunch in a busy cafeteria. They can assist the student with using Blackboard or Moodle for their course assignments and readings. The ASD student may have trouble following directions for turning work in online, such as uploading an assignment to Blackboard or Moodle on a specific date and time. The campus peer mentors are trained to assist with the college transition and can refer students to appropriate resources on campus as needed.

Andrew

Andrew was very bright and enjoyed reading science fiction, computers, video games and learning. He was diagnosed with high functioning Asperger's in the seventh grade. His poor social skills interfered with relating to peers and family members. He also had some ADD, OCD and sensitivity to noises, which caused him to struggle with paying attention during class. He was usually an A student and often stressed over assignments as he worked diligently to attain all As. During high school he became more anxious and nervous, and his anxiety grew as the homework increased. His parents and doctor researched natural medications to help with his ADD and anxiety. They found a regimen of multivitamins and herbs that helped him focus and function throughout the day. His mother worked to teach him organizational and time management skills so he could keep up with assignments as he took rigorous high school courses. His mother also created a system for taking his medications regularly and independently as they prepared him for living away from home during college.

Andrew was very bright with strong math and science skills. He was interested in pursuing an engineering degree, and this required that he look into larger state colleges. He had a very close relationship with his family and knew he wanted to be within two to three hours driving distance from home.

He chose a state college about an hour and a half from home, close enough to visit on the weekends if needed. Andrew looked forward to the college experience, and his parents helped him to prepare for the change.

Transitioning to a large four-year college proved more stressful than Andrew anticipated. The campus itself was big and overwhelming at times. Class sizes were large and professors didn't have a lot of time to spend individually with him because they had many other students to meet with. Andrew made a few friends and relied on them to assist with coursework when he was confused or needed some extra assistance. Creating friendships was difficult at such a large campus, but he lived in an engineering community on campus, so he had peers he could reach out to when needed. Andrew also did not apply for any accommodations his freshman year, and became overwhelmed with the stresses of academic demands. He knew that he needed to make some changes soon, before he crashed emotionally.

Andrew and his parents discussed his moving closer to home and attending High Point University, a small private college in his hometown. Andrew was excited about making this change, yet still wanted to live on campus to maintain his independence from parents. He chose to live in a single dorm room, so he did not have other students touching or rearranging his things. His OCD made it difficult to live with a group of peers. He easily transitioned to his new campus and his new personal space. The new campus also had a cafeteria close to his dorm room that prepared fresh omelets for students, plus another healthy restaurant on campus, which greatly appealed to Andrew, as he enjoyed eating healthy. He was very comfortable with the campus size, maneuverability and meal options.

Andrew chose to apply for and use accommodations this time around, because he learned that he needed them in order to be a successful college student. He and his parents met with disability services and brought in his documentation. Andrew completed the ADA forms and requested accommodations.

Andrew's Approved College Accomodations

Classroom Accommodations:

- peer notes.

Testing Accommodations:

- extended test time; and
- testing in a distraction reduced environment (Andrew was very sensitive to noise).

Andrew picked up his disability letters from the disability department during the first week of classes each semester. He met individually with each professor and made special testing arrangements for extended time in a quiet environment nearby. He wanted to take his tests near his professors instead of at the disability center, because he felt more comfortable being closer to his professors in case he needed to ask questions during the test or exam.

Over the years Andrew's mother had taught him fairly strong organizational and time management skills, so he was proficient at keeping up with assignments and due dates. He took class notes, but would often become distracted with the classroom noises and lights due to his overly active sensory perceptions. This would often cause him to stop focusing on the lecture and focus instead on external noises, thus losing important information. His notes would ultimately have gaps of information missing. Once he was given peer notes he was taught to go back and fill in his notes with missing information from both the peer notes and his textbook. This strategy helped him best prepare for tests.

In class Andrew usually stayed quiet and reserved until he had a comment or opinion to add to the class discussion. He tended to be very outspoken with his opinions and did not realize that he could be offending his peers, sometimes to the point of becoming confrontational. "Some students with autism can often be extremely honest and verbally direct often not accepting other's point of view, which might inadvertently hurt others" (Wolf, Brown, & Bork, 2009). Andrew's professor knew he was working with disability services, so she met with the DSS coordinator to discuss her concerns regarding Andrew's outbursts. With Andrew's permission, the disability director shared his diagnosis and together they came up with a plan where the professor would signal to Andrew that his comments were too strong. A couple days later the three of them met to discuss the behavioral plan for his in-class outbursts. They agreed that when this happened Andrew could meet with her after class or during her office hours to further discuss his point of view without disrupting or offending his classmates. This solution worked well for Andrew. He understood his boundaries and still felt his professor was open to discussing his thoughts and opinions. Once in a while there were some uncontrolled outbursts, but they were much fewer than in the past. Andrew shared that he did not know that he was "blurting out" in classes until it was brought to his attention by his caring professor.

Andrew wants to encourage other students with Autism by stating, "Don't be offended if your professors come up to you to discuss a personal issue, just work with them to improve. The professor is going out of their way to help you because they want you to do well, not to embarrass you."

Andrew always felt more connected with his professors after they spoke about such issues. He felt more comfortable meeting with them after class or during their office hours, finding them very supportive and accommodating with his academic progress.

Andrew learned the importance of self-advocacy early on and chose to meet with each of his professors and share his Asperger's diagnosis, because he felt "professors can't help you with what you need unless they know your disability." He found that the majority of his professors were educated on Asperger's/Autism, but a few were not so he took time to explain the diagnosis and how it impacted him. This opened the door to better communication for both of them. Andrew found that each year he became better at communicating his academic needs.

Andrew had a very strong working relationship with the head of his department, who was his main professor, which helped him succeed as a student. Unfortunately this professor left to take a new position at a college across the country, and the new professor was not as easy to work with. Andrew approached him a few times, but never felt as comfortable with him. Andrew notes, "I did my best to work through this, but we never had as good of a relationship." The new professor was not as approachable, but Andrew knew that he had to meet with him for clarification and help with his courses. Andrew had to learn to communicate with him as best he could because this professor was important in completing his degree.

The curriculum for the interactive gaming major required students to work together as part of a creative team; Andrew had to learn to communicate with this team and contribute his ideas and creative work. This was not easy at first because sometimes the team leader would not consider his strengths, and would give him busywork or leave him out, which often made Andrew feel very uncomfortable. Andrew had to learn to speak up and share his interests and ideas. He also learned to volunteer for aspects of the project that he was good at. Some students would recognize symptoms of Asperger's and ask Andrew if he had this. He would always answer all of their questions honestly, but he never volunteered this information, because he did not feel comfortable talking about it with his peers unless they asked him first. Once his peers understood his diagnosis they were much better working with him both inside and outside of the class on group projects. Using self-advocacy was a little harder for Andrew when he was with his peers, but he eventually shared his diagnosis and was able to create positive relationships with classmates and friends.

Most students would text each other regarding meeting times and dates. At first Andrew did not want to text or receive texts, but the disability director taught him to text and his parents worked with him on improving these skills by texting him often so he would get used to this new type of communication. Texting back to peers and classmates assured that he would not miss meetings and details regarding projects they were working on. Andrew was now comfortable communicating with his classmates and began to join them for study sessions, as they helped each other prepare for tests and exams. Each semester his communication skills improved with staff, peers and professors.

Social skills were always a hurdle for Andrew. He spent his first couple years of college going home every weekend because he was more comfortable with his family. He did not like to attend sporting events because of the large crowds and the loud noises from the crowds, pep band and the buzzers. He did attend a couple of college plays. Once he settled into the gaming degree he met students with similar interests and joined the gaming clubs. He found his college peers were more accepting of his Asperger's and did not judge or label him. His first club was a Pokémon club and he quickly made good friends. He felt like he fit in and was finally free of labels. Andrew also has a comic book passion, which he was able to share with his friends. He found it much easier to build friendships in college due to their common major and interests, and for Andrew these were video games, movies, science fiction and superheroes.

Andrew also attended a couple of conferences during college for his interactive gaming degree. He quickly learned that he was very uncomfortable with larger conventions, because they had too many people and noises that overloaded his senses. He was able to successfully attend smaller conferences with his peers and professors. He learned to sort out what works for him and his disability, while still being successful in his career choice.

After switching to a smaller private college and changing his major to one that complemented his natural strengths and interests, Andrew had a very successful college experience. He joined the gaming and video clubs, making lasting friendships. He graduated within four years with a strong GPA, a major in interactive gaming and a minor in history. Andrew is aware of his social skills and works continuously to improve and communicate well with his peers within the workplace.

Andrew has advice for peers with Autism/Asperger's:

• When you need help, remember that you are not alone, because everyone is helping each other at college. Everyone needs different kinds of help.
• Part of life is doing stuff you are not comfortable with.
• Don't be afraid to speak up for yourself when working in teams with your classroom peers.

• If others ask about your diagnosis be honest and share about your Asperger's; once they learn about you the more accepting they will be.

• Find the right friends; they will never make you do anything you are uncomfortable with.

The Autism spectrum diagnosis should be shared with the student's advisor so they can guide the student towards a career that works with their strengths and to keeps them on track for graduation. The advisor can steer students towards professors who are more approachable and caring. They can also help the student to set up a schedule that that works with the times of the day when they are most productive as a student. The advisor can also communicate with the professors and other staff members, as needed. Andrew was majoring in the computer gaming design program but also had a passion for history. They explored adding a history minor to his degree program. He worked closely with his advisor to plan his courses each semester and was able to graduate within four years with a major and a minor, and a very strong GPA.

Colleges with Strong ASD Support Programs

Finding the right college fit for these students is imperative to their success. The severity or intensity of their AS diagnosis will require specific academic support needs. Having an academic coach to meet with weekly or being in a fee-based program could make all the difference in their success. Colleges with excellent support programs include

• Marshall University in Huntington, West Virginia;
• Landmark College in Putney, Vermont;
• Lynn University in Boca Raton, Florida;
• Beacon College in Leesburg, Florida;
• University of Alabama Autism Spectrum Disorders College;
• University of Arkansas Autism Support Program;
• University of Connecticut SEAD program;
• University of West Florida;
• Fairleigh Dickinson University COMPASS program;
• Rutgers University in New Jersey;
• Rochester Institute of Technology in New York;
• Defiance College—Ohio ASD Affinity Program;
• Wright State University in Ohio;
• St. Joseph's University in Pennsylvania;

- George Mason University in Virginia; and
- Bellevue College—Autism Spectrum Navigators College in Washington.

Each of these colleges has specific programs aimed at meeting the variety of needs for the Autism/Asperger's college student. Their support systems can include help with personal care skills, overseeing medication, teaching executive functioning skills, academic coaching, extra tutoring, and assistive technology support. These colleges have trained staff to better assist and understand the academic needs of the ASD student, and some professors are open to modified assessments, such as oral exams, essay exams or specialty projects. Take the time to visit these colleges and explore their programs at least two years before high school graduation to find the college that fits the student's academic and disability needs and to avoid unnecessary stress and anxiety for the student.

Each year more students with Autism and Asperger's are attending college with higher success rates. They may need to take an extra year to complete their degree program, but with the right accommodations, technology and a caring environment they can successfully complete their degree and move into independence and a successful career. Parents need to complete a thorough search to find the right college fit with the appropriate resources in place to assist their child with achieving their academic and personal goals, taking every opportunity to grow as a person.

Once the ASD student graduates college they may need to work with a life skills transition coach to assist them with transitioning into life after college and entering the job force. Assistance with finding more support services to help with career and life transitions can be found on the U.S. Autism and Asperger's Association website: http://www.usautism.org/uscap/college_connections.htm.

11

Psychological Disabilities
Student Testimony—Kate

Attending college as a freshman can be overwhelming for many students, but adding a psychological/mental health disorder can increase stress. For some disorders, the stress of beginning college can trigger episodes. Some students may attend college with a pre-existing psychological diagnosis, but others may experience depression, anxiety, bi-polar episodes or other psychological disorders for the first time as a college student. Psychiatric disorders may also be called "mental illness." "Mental illness refers to the collection of all diagnosable mental disorders causing severe disturbances in thinking, feeling, relating, and functioning behaviors. It can result in a substantially diminished capacity to cope with the demands of daily life" (Souma, Rickerman, Burgstahler, 2012) Under the ADA laws students with a psychological diagnosis can receive accommodations during college.

According to Souma, Rickerman and Burgstahler, a mental illness is a hidden disability; it is rarely apparent to others. However, students with mental illness may experience symptoms that interfere with their educational goals and that create a "psychiatric disability." These symptoms may include, yet are not limited to

- heightened anxieties, fears, suspicions, or blaming others;
- marked personality change over time;
- confused or disorganized thinking; strange or grandiose ideas;
- difficulty concentrating, making decisions, or remembering things;
- extreme highs or lows in mood;
- denial of obvious problems and a strong resistance to offers of help; and
- thinking or talking about suicide.

Students with a psychiatric disorder will need to disclose their disability and request accommodations with the disability support office on campus. Check the college website for appropriate documentation. Good self-advocacy skills will help the student share their diagnosis and request accommodations and counseling to support them while in college. The psychiatric disability can cause functional limitations, causing the student to need accommodations for their optimal academic performance. Some functional limitations, according to Sauma, Rickerman and Burgstahler, are difficulties with medication side effects, sustaining attention, maintaining stamina, handling time pressures and multiple tasks, interacting with others, and severe test anxiety.

Regrettably, a number of students with mental health disorders choose not to disclose their disability or seek services available to them. Some no longer want the label, don't want to be different than their peers or feel they can succeed without accommodations or counseling. Students with a mental health diagnosis "need to come to the acceptance that they really do need support services in place in order to succeed in college" (NAMI, 2015). Symptoms can worsen when transitioning to college, and students should have appropriate accommodations and counseling in place to assist them when episodes occur. It may take three to four weeks to get accommodations approved and in place, so start early and be prepared.

Possible Accommodations for Psychological Disabilities

Classroom Accommodations:

- peer notes (assists student when they cannot focus on lectures);
- record lectures (helps with filling in notes missed during class);
- class breaks; and
- preferential seating (preferably near the door for easier access when using breaks).

Testing Accommodations:

- 50% extended test time (helps ease anxiety);
- testing in a separate environment; and
- exams individually proctored, including in the hospital.

Housing Accommodations:

- single dorm room (less distractions and a quiet environment for appropriate sleep).

Accommodations will vary and are determined on an individual basis, depending on the individual diagnosis and how it impacts the student within the college environment.

If the student is under a high school IEP prepare a transition plan for college; this plan should include the following:

- Learning about college academic requirements and the services that might support academic and mental health growth.
- Developing the ability to describe one's illness and how it impacts their learning.
- Preparing a list of accommodations that may be helpful to them in college.
- Collecting and organizing appropriate documentation to share with the college disability office.

Before leaving high school the student should request a summary of performance, which describes their academic achievement and functional performance to date. It should also describe current and past services and supports, and include recommendations for future accommodations (NAMI, 2015). Documentation should state the specific psychiatric disorders as diagnosed. The diagnosis should be made by someone with appropriate professional credentials, be specific, and reference the *Diagnostic and Statistical Manual of Mental Disorders* (DSM-5 or whichever edition was current at the time of diagnosis) (College Board, 2015).

The Right College Fit

Take time to explore "right fit" colleges. Make sure to consider size, location, and services. Some students prefer to be closer to home for support, comfort and to enable them to continue meeting with their therapist. Larger colleges can sometimes be overwhelming, and may not offer the sense of community of smaller colleges. Larger colleges, however, may have a larger array of health services and housing options (NAMI, 2015). Services should include resources such as health clinics, counseling services, tutoring services, and a good disability support office to implement accommodations.

Kate

Kate had a very artistic personality; she plays piano, guitar, sings and draws. She was a natural with music from a very young age. When choosing a college she looked for a strong music department, and found the perfect fit at a small college a couple hours away from home. She looked forward to starting her freshman year, meeting new people and pursuing her passion for music.

At a young age Kate suffered numerous headaches, and was diagnosed with chronic migraines at age 11. She had always been a strong student, earning top grades and staying on the honor roll. Stress and mood swings continued to plague Kate, and by the age of 12 she was diagnosed with depression. Her grades began to slip as well as her motivation for academics. Her doctors placed her on medications for depression and her parents placed her in counseling. Kate faithfully attended counseling throughout high school and found it very beneficial. She learned coping skills, such as journaling and writing about her feelings. She stayed on her medications throughout high school, and as her body chemistry changed the doctors tried new medications, which worked for her. She eagerly looked forward to attending college and being on her own.

Kate made a conscious choice to forego college accommodations because she did not want her depression to be an excuse; she focused on moving forward with her life. She also chose not to use a college counselor; instead she would call her counselor from home when she began feeling stressed or depressed. She soon found that this did not work as well as a face-to-face session. She tried to hold it together as best she could, but soon found her plan was backfiring, and she was not becoming the independent college person she wanted to be.

Focusing on assignments became an overwhelming task. Kate did attend all classes but could not motivate herself to complete assignments or properly prepare for tests; she could not get past her mental block and increasing depression. The stress of transitioning to college and achieving passing grades triggered her depression and anxiety. She spent many sleepless nights battling with her thoughts instead of gaining the rest her body and brain needed to properly function. She would often skip meals or eat random, unhealthy foods. Her passions, even for music, waned. Succeeding academically was the farthest thing from her mind. She began thinking of dropping out of college, and envisioned herself living on her own pursuing music independently; she no longer cared about earning a degree.

The end of her first semester proved that changes needed to be made immediately. Her parents and counselor encouraged her to give college another try, with a few changes in place. Kate was not sure she wanted to continue with her education, but with her parents' encouragement she chose to return for another semester. During her second semester, she began meeting with an academic coach who encouraged her to work with a counselor. She chose to sign up for a counselor on campus and began to learn new coping skills. She gave permission for her counselor to speak with her mother and her academic coach, and they were able to alert the counselor to detrimental situations and potential "downward spirals." They all worked together in different capacities to support Kate.

Learning to live with roommates also created new anxiety. They did not all get along and Kate often felt frustrated and alone. She decided to meet with a college counselor to discuss her roommate issues, and found that she received support in many other areas as well. Kate shared that she did not always take her medication and felt that it did not make much of a difference. The counselor arranged an appointment with a psychiatrist, who looked into a medication change. The new medication made a big difference and Kate was able to better focus on academics and reignite her passions.

Even though Kate had some new resources in place she still struggled with anxiety attacks, which often led to depression. Sleepless nights still plagued her, leaving her head foggy during classes and she had no energy for coursework. Her college counselor worked on teaching her new coping skills involving her music and art. She also learned to reach out to good friends and her mother who would help to redirect her negative energy. They kept in touch with phone calls and visits when Kate was in a depressed mood.

Her academic coach set her up with tutors and also communicated with her professors to help get her back on track academically. Kate chose to share her medical diagnosis with her professors and they were more than willing to work with her. Kate still struggled with procrastination, especially when preparing for tests and exams, but she made high enough grades to attend the following semester.

Over the summer Kate chose to take an online class. For the first time Kate found herself enjoying a college course and excelling with tests and papers. The old Kate, who used to excel at academics, began shining through and confidence in her academics grew. The online class gave her flexibility; she was able to work on the assignments when she wanted to, and she used her strong writing skills to meet the weekly paper deadlines without any issues. The course was very challenging for her, but she kept focused and found that she could once again be a successful student.

She then took time to reassess her goals and made a commitment to stay motivated with her college academics. This included a big change in her major. Kate returned for her sophomore year with a new academic plan in place. She decided to change her major to communications/journalism and minor in music. With this new plan in place she was determined to improve her GPA and complete her degree. She felt renewed and her motivation and focus increased, although she did struggle with anxiety issues during mid-terms and finals when the stress of completing assignments and preparing for exams was most challenging.

Kate was usually very good about taking her medications regularly, although she would sometimes forget to order refills at appropriate times, and often had to wait a week or more for her needed medications to arrive. When this happened Kate would begin to lose her motivation, become more disorganized with course assignments and start to feel depressed. Her sleeping and eating patterns were also negatively altered, and she was often exhausted throughout the day, unable to focus or sleep. This would often happen around mid-terms and finals, which were the most demanding times of the semester, leaving Kate in a state of despair. The pattern was the same each time this occurred, so Kate learned that she needed to keep up with her medication refills ahead of time, or let her mother know that she was getting low so she could re-order for Kate. Learning to stay on her medication regimen became critical to Kate's academic success and to keeping this negative cycle from re-occurring. She realized that the medications kept her mind alert, her anxiety levels low, and her motivation high.

Kate began meeting regularly with her counselor and felt good about having someone on campus she could talk with, especially when anxiety levels rose. She still had panic attacks that would overwhelm her; the difference was that she now had a relationship with a counselor and would reach out to her for help. The counselor helped her learn which coping strategies worked best for her and often gave her validation for using healthy coping skills. The counseling session helped Kate share her feelings and thoughts without feeling judged.

She attended classes, took notes, and stayed fairly organized with assignments. She used a planner and a daily to do list. When Kate found herself struggling with some depression, she would use her new coping skills, and with the help of her counselor she found herself working through the depression instead of allowing it to control her. Once her emotional state became stable she was able to put more effort into her academics and her grades improved, which also bolstered her self-confidence. Kate began taking an interest in her coursework, meeting consistently with her academic coach and tutors in order to stay on top of assignments. She was rewarded with a much-improved GPA and a solid foundation for her journalism major.

She also had friends within her classes with whom she met for study groups before tests and exams (especially helpful were the ones who are task-oriented). Her network of close friends became a solid support system for her. She felt comfortable reaching out to them when she felt overwhelmed, or panic attacks coming on. Anxiety can still hit her quickly, and at inopportune times; the difference is that she now uses positive choices and relationships, instead of pushing friends and family away and sitting in her room alone for days. When this does happen, Kate will begin to paint or draw, or write a new song with her guitar. Kate has also tried jogging to help bolster a negative mood. Learning to occupy herself has saved her a lot of regret and self-disappointment.

Kate shares some personal tips.

- Use a planner and work at staying organized so you can visually see what needs to be done.
- Study with friends so you can stay on task; let your friends influence new study habits.
- Use the library; this puts your mind in a different setting where you know your job is to complete the task.
- Find your personal healthy coping strategies and *use them*!
- Journaling is a positive way to let out your feelings and monitor your moods, helping you to recognize when you need help or support.
- Work to earn good grades. This creates a sense of accomplishment and keeps you motivated.

College Counseling Support Services

The last ten years have shown a 50 percent increase in teens with anxiety disorders. Counselors are available at most colleges to assist students with these and many other types of issues. More students are using counseling services now than ever before. Transitioning to college can create new fears and anxiety, and knowing where your resources and support systems are can make a big difference. Students have many different types of coping skills, and some of these may be very unhealthy. Meeting with a counselor can help students develop good coping skills to reduce harm and help build stronger communication skills. College counselors are prepared to help students deal with a wide variety of personal issues. Counseling is available to all students on most college campuses, but *the student must seek out this service.*

Questions and Answers from a College Counselor

- How do I go about setting up a counseling appointment?

This will be different at each college, but start with going online to the college website. Information on the counseling center will be available. Some websites will include pictures and a short bio on their specialties. An email and a phone contact number will be available.

- Can I just walk in to the counseling center, or do I have to have an appointment?

Some colleges will be casual and have walk-ins available. Your larger colleges will have a receptionist and they will help you set up an appointment, or let you know if someone is available to see you immediately. Smaller colleges may have a counselor available to meet with you, or you can email the counselor to set up an appointment. The counselors check their email throughout the day and will let you know if they have an opening right away, or can help you schedule one for a later time.

- What if I am not comfortable with the counselor?

Students can "try a counselor out" by interviewing them. If you like the counselor and they are available you can set up weekly or bi-weekly meetings. Students can also switch to a counselor they are more comfortable with.

- Can I meet with the counseling department when I am making a college visit?

Yes, just contact the counseling center through their website and let them know the date and times you are available. They will set you up with a counselor who will give you basic information on their services and answer your questions. Students can also meet with a counselor over the summer, when they have more time, in order to explain their needs and interview a couple of counselors.

- What if I have an emergency or crisis during the night or on the weekends?
  - ○ Most colleges will have an on-call counselor or an *emergency contact number* to assist students. A counselor will speak with the student on the phone and determine whether the student needs emergency care.
  - ○ The campus *security* is always available to assist with emergencies.
  - ○ Students can also call the *resident assistant (RA)* on duty, and they will contact a counselor for crisis support.
  - ○ Other colleges will have a *24-hour open clinic.* The website should have contact information for the clinic.

- What types of issues do counselors help with? Does it need to be a serious clinical concern?
  - ○ Nothing is too small; counselors help students tackle many types of issues, such as
    - ✦ homesickness;
    - ✦ roommate issues;

+ family issues/home life;
+ advice on approaching professors;
+ self-esteem;
+ isolation;
+ making friends;
+ time management;
+ adjusting to independence and freedom;
+ self-advocating skills; and
+ grief and loss

o Other more clinical issues can be

+ depression;
+ anxiety/panic attacks;
+ bi-polar disorder;
+ PTSD (post-traumatic stress disorder);
+ OCD (obsessive compulsive disorder);
+ eating disorders; and
+ alcohol and drug abuse.

- Will my counseling session be kept confidential?

Yes, the student is covered under the HIPPA mental health laws and all sessions will be kept confidential, unless the student signs consent for release of specific information.

The counselor can break confidence if the student threatens to harm themselves or others.

Following are more helpful tips for students with psychological disabilities.

- Students with Asperger's will benefit from meeting with a counselor to talk through behaviors. The counselor will provide a different perspective than the parents or family members. Counselors are often less judgmental and assist with issues such as communication, personal habits, OCD, etc.

- If a student is thinking about counseling, they should do it sooner rather than later, before a real crisis occurs. Once a relationship is built the student knows where they are and will come see them as needed.

Academic Withdrawal for Medical Reasons

It may become necessary for a student to withdraw for a semester or longer due to their psychiatric disability. If this occurs the college counselor can help the student complete the forms for the withdrawal process. The student may need to return home to enroll in a support program, or take time off to become emotionally healthy enough to return to college. "Or you may want to ask to 'retroactively withdraw' from classes if your grades suffered in the weeks leading up to your medical leave. Under the ADA, retroactive withdrawal because of depression or other mental illness is considered a reasonable accommodation" (NAMI, 2015). See more at http://www.nami.org/Find-Support/I-am/Kids,-Teens-Young-Adults/Managing-a-Mental-Health-Condition-in-College#sthash.QyDnawv6.dpuf.

Managing a psychological disorder while in college will require coping skills, study strategies and accommodations in place to help promote academic success. Students with this diagnosis, or who receive this diagnosis while attending college are entitled to reasonable accommodations. Make sure to connect with the disability services office for more information for documentation and the process to request documentation. Setting up the needed accommodations before the first semester of college is highly recommended. The college counseling office will also assist students with individual counseling sessions and other support resources. Researching resources and accommodations as part of the college search, and utilizing them consistently will help create a successful college transition.

12

Blind and Visually Impaired
Student Testimony—John

The majority of college students who are blind or visually impaired have acquired skills and use assistive technology to help them succeed both academically and with life. Visual disabilities will vary greatly and students need to be aware of which support resources and assistive technology software and devices are available to them. "Low vision is a condition caused by eye disease, in which visual acuity is 20/70 or poorer in the better-seeing eye and cannot be corrected or improved with regular eyeglasses" (Vision Aware, 2015). Visual impairments range from low vision to being blind. Some visual disabilities are: macular degeneration, retinitis pigmentosa, glaucoma, and diabetic retinopathy. Low vision can also be caused by traumatic brain injury, injury to the eye, or multiple sclerosis. Allegheny College's disability website states, "A person is considered legally blind if his or her corrected vision is no better than 20/200." Students who are legally blind often use a cane or guide dog to assist with maneuvering campus. Low vision or visually impaired students may be able to maneuver campus better, but will require assistive technology to complete their academic courses. "A person who is visually impaired has difficulty performing ordinary tasks even with glasses or contacts, which substantially limits their daily living activities" (IDB Online, 2015). Along with putting the right auxiliary aids and services in place, the student needs to consider the physical setting and ease of maneuvering the campus. Identify your needs and know what accommodations and assistance you may need when choosing the right college fit.

Visual Variations

There are many variations on a person's visual ability. Some may be diagnosed with low vision and require assistive technology for reading, but have better peripheral vision. Others may see only directly in front of them, similar to tunnel vision, but have no peripheral vision. Students may want to share their exact diagnosis with their advisors and professors so that they better understand their abilities in order to aid the student with their academic needs. Knowledge is power, so the more they know and understand regarding the specific visual diagnosis the better they will be at helping make the college experience successful.

> Eighty to ninety percent of legally blind people have some measurable vision or light perception. A student who is legally blind may retain a great amount of vision. Many legally blind students are able to read with special glasses, and a few can even drive. It is also important to note that some legally blind students have 20/20 vision. Although these students have perfect central vision, they have narrow field or side vision and see things as though they were looking through a tube or straw. They often use guide dogs or canes when they travel. Some blind students with only central vision loss do not require a guide dog or cane. They are able to see large objects but have great difficulty reading. "Visually impaired" is the better term used to refer to people with various gradations of vision [Allegheny College, 2015].

Campus Maneuverability

Make sure to visit the college campus you are considering to explore the physical layout and check for any mobility challenges. All colleges will have pedestrian sidewalks; students with visual disabilities will also need alerts for crosswalks and intersections, so check to see whether they have an alert network throughout campus. The student should contact services for the blind to schedule mobility specialists to walk the campus, buildings and dorm with them before classes begin. They will teach the student and guide dog specific routes for mobility and best access to walkways and street crossings. The mobility specialist will also want the disability director to walk the campus with them the first time to ensure accessibility and address any specific problems.

Requesting Accommodations

The college website will have information regarding the specific documentation required in order to receive approved accommodations. The majority of colleges will require a letter or evaluation form from a vision professional with their credentials. The professional is usually an ophthalmologist or optometrist. A clear statement of the visual disability with an explanation of the current functional limitations and possible accommodations is required. Recent exam information is also helpful. If the student is blind a letter explaining the onset of blindness, functional limitations and possible accommodations is needed. If the college website does not have any specific guidelines, call or email the Disability Director and ask about their required documentation.

The following is a list of possible accommodations students with visual disabilities can request.

Classroom Accommodations:

- enlarged font (or Braille)—for handouts, tests, exams, etc.;
- use of computer with reading and writing software or Braille;
- textbooks in alternative format (Braille, if required);
- service animal in the classroom/lab;
- scribe in class;
- peer notes; and
- Assignments, syllabus and handouts given to student through email (student will access using assistive technology, such as Jaws or Kurzweil 1000).

Testing Accommodations:

- 50% or 100% extended test time (often blind students need 100% extended time when using Braille or other reading/writing formats);
- reader for tests;
- writer for tests;
- tests in Braille; and
- use of computer

Housing Accommodations:

- single dorm room;
- dorm room on first floor of building; and
- service/guide dogs permitted in dorm rooms.

The Right College Fit

Along with putting the right auxiliary aids and services in place, the student needs to consider the physical setting and maneuverability of the campus. Identifying their needs and knowing what accommodations and assistance they may need when choosing the right college fit is helpful. Maneuvering the physical setting of the campus is very important, along with the right major, location, size of the campus and available technology and tutoring resources. Students should make sure to visit the campus they are interested in attending and meet with the disability director to discuss accommodations, documentation and assistive technology. They should also plan to visit the student housing director to discuss personal housing needs. Once they make a final college decision, they can contact Services for the Blind and meet with a mobility specialist to help guide them around campus and review their housing situation.

Services for the blind will work in conjunction with disability services to make sure that all academic and housing needs are met. Tuition will be paid by services for the blind, as long as they keep a 2.0 GPA or higher. They will also supply the student with computer software, printer and updates. Disability services will provide them with academic and housing accommodations and will advocate for them if any problems arise. JAWS or Kurzweil 1000 software programs will give them access to all printed materials and provide them with comprehensive internet capabilities. The college disability services director will work with services for the blind to make sure all of their academic needs are met.

John

"I am John, with a visual disability. I have it, but it does not have me." John is currently married and a father of two children. He successfully completed both a graduate and an undergraduate degree at UNC Greensboro in North Carolina. John was diagnosed with retinitis pigmentosa by age nine. He was told that he would be totally blind by age 20, but he is currently not totally blind. He was able to drive a car until he was 27 years old. After high school he worked for a furniture company until his increasingly poor vision interfered with his work. John contacted services for the blind and they helped him acquire another job making brooms, but he was not satisfied with this type of work.

At first he just sat around feeling sorry for himself. He was angry and did not want to accept that he would soon become blind. He wanted his vision back, but this was not in the cards for him. "I gradually adjusted to being blind, but the adjustment part was the hardest part." He searched for his place in the world with his new low-vision life. John wanted to take control of his future and decided that he wanted to attend college and earn a degree to better support himself. Services for the Blind, in conjunction with vocational rehab, paid his college tuition and set him up with a laptop, printer, JAWS screen reading software, and a guide dog. He also went on Social Security disability for some income while he was attending college.

John chose to attend a community college close to home to help with the transition to college. He was overwhelmed with learning the college terrain and feared that he would walk into people and walls. This new college experience was frightening to John but the guide dog, Benny, was his mainstay. Services for the blind provided an orientation and mobility specialist who came out to campus to teach John and his guide dog how to best maneuver the campus. The guide dog was taught to find buildings on campus and easily guided John around. Most people are uncomfortable walking up to a blind or visually impaired person and just starting a conversation, but people loved to ask about Benny, so this broke the ice and John soon made new friends on campus. John could no longer drive, so his wife drove him to and from college each day. John quickly learned to advocate for himself and maneuver the campus.

The community college provided the following accommodations: extended test time, 100 percent, testing in a separate environment, reader for tests, talking calculator, a scribe in class, along with a math assistant in class and a personal tutor. John was able to complete his college assignments with the JAWS software program on his computer. His biggest challenge was the math courses. The professors would forget that he could not see the math problems they were writing on the board, and he would have to meet separately with them and with the help of the disability director train them with reciting each problem aloud so he could actively participate in working out the problems like the other students. John did not expect others to treat him differently, but he wanted to be included and contribute in each of his classes. Fortunately John enjoys people and soon built friendships with his college peers and professors. He quickly made friends and joined study groups. The disability director helped him resolve any problems that came up.

The decision to transfer to a four-year state college (with 18,000 students) to pursue a psychology and religion degree was once again overwhelming for John. He would be living on campus and needed housing accommodations. His family was very supportive of his career goals. He left his wife and young son at home, 80 miles away, while he pursued his education, and came home every other weekend. The disability director met with him to set up classroom, testing and housing accommodations.

John's Approved College Accommodations

Classroom Accommodations:

- scribe in class;
- peer notes;

- preferential seating;
- textbooks in alternate format (he would contact the professors ahead of time to get textbook information);
- use of laptop in class (with JAWS software); and
- priority registration.

Testing Accommodations:

- 100% extended test time (if he chose to take the test with the professor they would set up a different testing time and place);
- testing in a separate environment;
- reader for tests if it could not be scanned; and
- no scantrons.

Housing Accommodations:

- single dorm room (after first year he had a single with a private bathroom); and
- guide dog on campus.

The disability director met with John to discuss his academic progress, set up tutoring and help with any transition issues. The mobility specialist came to campus each semester to help John walk through his schedule to navigate each building and classroom. They would go through his schedule over and over until the dog and John were comfortable maneuvering the campus. The dog quickly learned where specific buildings were. John was able to tell the dog, "Take me to the café," and the dog would take him there directly. His new guide dog, Sarge, was able to easily lead him around campus and open doors, which calmed John's fears about maneuvering this large campus each day. John met more people because they came up to meet his dog. When inclement weather hit, John was still able to maneuver campus because the campus worked to keep paths clear. The cafeteria staff would often offer to send meals over to John's dorm room to assist him on inclement weather days. John was assigned the same dorm room for undergraduate and graduate school, which gave him a comfortable starting point each day to maneuver around campus.

The most challenging courses for John at the four-year college were math, foreign language and biology. He continued to use the JAWS software to assist with reading and writing skills, but in math courses he needed more assistance. The college gave him an independent tutor who went to class with him, took notes, and assisted with homework, preparing for and taking tests. He also used a small white board with special 20/20 black felt tip pens designed for low vision students. The tutor knew how to assist John with using formulas along with the JAWS software to complete math computations. He also joined study groups and met with his professors for extra help and to prepare for exams. With these resources in place he was able to successfully complete his math and statistics courses.

Biology provided a few challenges also. John was assigned a lab partner who was very willing to describe slides under the microscope and relay important visual information to him. They prepared their lab assignments together, and he often studied with his partner for tests, along with his tutor. John's biology professor gave him a separate oral test in labs. John would describe the parts of the microscope, or describe the parts of the organism they had been dissecting instead of labeling them. He still used the JAWS software for his written tests, but the lab sections often needed oral testing, which the professor happily accommodated.

John attempted his Spanish class using the JAWS software with his textbook and a tutor. The JAWS software has a foreign language component but he struggled with using the commands for JAWS in Spanish, since he was still learning the basics of the language. After attempting the Spanish course and struggling to pass his tests, he withdrew from this course at mid-term and requested a course substitution through disability services. He was granted a substitution with a cultural course instead of learning a foreign language. The cultural class was much easier for John to learn and succeed in.

John learned to adapt his learning needs to each specific course he took. For example, while taking a public speaking class he learned to memorize his speech because he could not read note cards. He was not proficient with Braille yet, so he relied on his memory. This helped him develop skills for other courses where he was required to give oral presentations. John also struggled with creating PowerPoint presentations, so he often worked with a group, contributing his information and ideas, while allowing his peers to create the actual presentation.

John had a very positive college experience. He successfully completed his undergrad degree in religion with a minor in psychology. While attending college he joined an honors fraternity and created strong friendships. He participated in social activities on and off campus with the help of his peers and his guide dog. He completed a master's degree in college counseling and student development in higher education, and an educational specialist degree. He credits his wife, children and mother for their unfailing support. John's ability to build strong relationships with his professors and peers kept him on a successful career path.

John has advice for visually disabled peers:

- Be comfortable with your disability, because if you are not no one else will be.
- Put yourself out there to peers, they will learn to see beyond your disability.
- Don't be afraid to ask for help from professors, peers, family and disability services.
- Communicate with professors early and often. I made a point of building relationships with professors.
- ASK for what you need. Others cannot read your mind, the worst they can say is "no."
- Use a guide dog on campus. They are extremely helpful and great companions. My guide dog helped me to overcome many fears.
- The first day of each class I would stand in front of the class and ask for a volunteer note taker. This worked very well for me. Take the initiative.
- Communicating with professors and peers was crucial to my college success.
- Contact your professors over the summer and in early December to get the textbook information for the following semester, so you will have your textbooks in alternate format ready when classes begin.

Assistive Technology

Technology devices and apps are a valuable resource to students with visual disabilities; these apps and devices help them gain independence. Technology is ever-evolving and creating new and accessible devices such as smart phones, iPads, tablets and e-readers such as Kindle and Nook, that provide access to reading and writing for the visually impaired. Technology has brought us a long way since the invention of braille to assist the blind and low vision population. Some examples of this technology include the following.

- JAWS—A screen reading software program for the blind and visually impaired that can also output text to a braille reader. The program uses "hot keys" and other standard commands instead of a mouse. It comes with many functions and is compatible with Microsoft Office, Excel, MAGic screen magnification and others. JAWS16 has MATHML support for science and math courses. Most colleges have this available to students, and it may be loaded on some library computers. Services for the blind will load and update it to your laptop.

• Braille—Braille is a raised dot code which forms letters and numbers, used by blind and visually impaired people. Each Braille cell consists of specific dots, which form words or numbers. They are used in language, math, music and foreign language.

• Kurzweil 1000—Text to speech software for the blind and visually impaired. The software reads printed and electronic text with natural sounding voices. It also sends files to braille. Reads text, magazines, books, E-books, and sends to other portable devices. It offers calendars, study supports for note taking, editing and outlining texts. https://www.kurzweiledu.com/products/kurzweil-1000-v12-windows-features.html.

The following technology information is from the "eyeSmart" web page (2015).

Speech-to-Text and Text-to-Speech:

• Dragon Dictation (free, iTunes App Store) / Dragon Remote Microphone (free, Google Play Store)—Enables users to dictate a text message, email, Facebook status updates or Tweet on any iOS or Android device.

• ZoomReader ($19.99, iTunes App Store)—Use the iPhone or iPad's built-in camera to take a picture of any text and then read it back to users.

• Voice Brief ($2.99, iTunes App Store)—Collects information that users want to read (calendar, weather, stocks, RSS news, social media, emails) and reads it aloud on iOS devices.

Reading:

• Spotlight Text ($30.00, iTunes App Store)—Ebook reader for the iPad designed for people with low vision. Text adapts to specific visual needs, and can easily be displayed on any television with an HDMI input.

Object Identification:

• LookTel ($9.99, iTunes App Store)—Currency identifier that uses the camera of your iOS device to read aloud the denomination of paper money. The developer is also working on other applications that will expand the technology to reading labels and more.

• TapTapSee (free, iTunes App Store, Google Play Store)—Enables users to photograph objects and have them identified aloud.

Navigation:

• Blindsquare ($29.99, iTunes App Store)—Describes the environment, announces points of interest and street intersections as you travel.

• Google Maps (free, iTunes App Store, Google Play Store)—Voice-guided GPS navigation and directions for driving, biking and walking.

Self-Monitoring:

• SightBook (free, iTunes App Store)—Allows patients to regularly monitor their visual acuity at home, and send their vision scores to their doctor.

Dr. Fontenot advises patients with low vision to ask their eye doctor for help and referral to a low vision clinic. Almost all clinics will be able to help with customizing digital devices and apps. Many low vision centers offer computer workshops or have occupational therapists that can provide training and support on how to use these tools effectively and tailor them to particular visual needs.

Resources

American Foundation For the Blind—Career Connect—www.careerconnect.com
eyeSmart—American Academy of Ophthalmology—http://www.geteyesmart.org/eyesmart/living/apps-offer-bright-spots-for-low-vision.cfm
JAWS—screen reading software for the blind and visually impaired—http://www.freedomscientific.com/Products/Blindness/JAWS
Services for the Blind (state by state contact information)—https://nfb.org/state-and-local-organizations
Technology Information—www.AFB.org

13

Veterans with Disabilities Transitioning to College

Interviews—Bruce, Beth and Bob

The past five years has shown a steady increase in the number of veterans attending college, and the United States currently has a record number of vets returning from war and attending two and four year colleges across the country. Each branch of the military provides their military members' access to their education center with classes in transition assistance, as they look forward to exploring new career choices.

Transitioning to college will require finding the right college fit for these veterans and their career goals; whether it is an online program they started while on active duty, or finding a college near their home, or starting life over in a completely new city. These men and women will have different educational levels and skills depending on their military training and experiences. Assessing these previous skills and education will help them to find the right college degree program, certificate program or career fit. The military education program can assist veterans with exploring their options. They will have access to the education center resources while on active duty and after they leave the military.

Some of the veterans returning to college will have disabilities related to their military service, and may experience more challenges with their college transition. These disabilities can range from traumatic brain injuries (TBI), post-traumatic stress disorder (PTSD), hearing loss, visual impairments, physical injuries, chemical exposure, and others. "Many of these veterans have the potential for earning postsecondary degrees and filling positions in challenging fields such as those in science, technology and engineering" (DO IT Returning from Service, 2015). These veterans with disabilities will require academic accommodations such as extended test time, testing in a separate environment, peer notes, assistive technology, etc. This is where the college disability/accessibility services office steps in to assist the disabled veteran with setting up appropriate accommodations to meet their educational needs. Each college has a disabilities website with specific guidelines for requesting accommodations and information on which type of documentation is required per the specific disability.

College Response to Veterans

Colleges have been gearing up to meet the needs of this new student population to help create a positive transition to academic life and new career goals. Veterans are unique in that they are usually older than the average college-aged student, and they have different world experiences. Some are married and have young families; others are looking for some direction with their life; while others may be the first in their families to attend college. Many veterans have military experience with computers, engineering and technology; guidance from their military education center and career services can aid in connecting them to a possible future. Career support for these veterans needs to be in place on college campuses to help them adapt to this new learning environment.

Bruce Pomeroy, who is UNC Greensboro's disability director and board member for their veteran's center, shared resources they have put into place to assist veterans as they transition to college life. Bruce suggests that veterans first look for a "veteran friendly campus," because these colleges will have more support resources in place than most campuses. Bruce's philosophy is to "help individuals gain as much independence as possible." He understands the value of an education to the veteran student and their family. Many veterans are still in their twenties and many have young families to provide for as they attend college and work to achieve their new career goals. They have served a few years or an entire career in the military and are now looking at opportunities to create a new career with continuing their education and often using their specific set of skills and talents. Some veteran students may struggle with asking for help, so they may need to be encouraged to seek out people and resources to help them move forward with their career goals.

The first step for these veterans is to investigate the campus academic services and interview disability services to decide whether this will be a good fit for them. Ask questions on how they implement accommodations like extended testing in a separate environment, or peer notes, and inquire as to the types of adaptive technology available to students. Veterans need to register with disability/accessibility services to request accommodations on their college campus after they have been admitted. They will need to provide appropriate documentation for their specific disability. Documentation requirements will be listed on the disability website.

The disability staff will meet with the veteran and review their documentation and accommodation requests. Appropriate accommodations will be approved for the classroom and testing environments, as well as any residential accommodations, if needed. An accommodation letter will be written for each professor at the beginning of every semester, and can either be delivered by the student, or sent to the professor by the disability director; this includes online classes. This letter will only state the student's accommodations, not the disability. It is recommended that the student meet individually with the professor during office hours to review the approved accommodations and testing environments. If the student wants to share with the professor that they are a veteran at this point, the student can make that choice. Students can share as little or as much as they want. The professor will implement the approved accommodations as requested by the student and assist with making sure students have all the classroom materials they need in appropriate formats.

Assistive Technology

Assistive technology can benefit the veteran student in creating independence as they gain enhanced access to course lectures, reading textbooks, writing papers, note taking, etc. The disability staff will provide adaptive technology training and show them how to apply the technology to the academic setting. Technology and software can include Kurzweil reading and vision software, Read and Write Gold, SMART Pens, Jaws, Dragon Speak, plus many Apple education apps such as Noteability, Zoom App, dictation apps, and course organization apps to name a few. Some of this technology will easily transition into appropriate technology for life success skills in the work force. For example, SMART Pens are used by many individuals in the business world for immediate review of meetings and access to their notes.

Approved accommodations are specific to each individual student, based on their disability.

Classroom Accommodations:

- peer notes;
- use of a SMART Pen for note taking and recording lectures;
- handouts in enlarged font;

- priority registration;
- not having to read aloud in class;
- reduced course load/ credits each semester; and
- use of assistive technology.

Testing accommodations:

- 50% extended test time;
- testing in a separate reduced distraction environment;
- use of laptop for essay writing;
- short breaks; and
- access to assistive technology.

Disability services can also help students learn how to be proactive with future assignments and learning campus resources to tap into, such as the writing center, speech center, math center, counseling center, veteran's center, and career and internship services. They will also guide them to academic resources with trained staff, tutors in each subject area, assistance with time management and organizational skills. Resources will be put into place to ensure that these students have equal access to all course materials, as well as learning study strategies that work with their individual learning styles. Once a student taps into these resources they will learn to apply study skills to assist with academic success and greater independence.

Hidden Disabilities

Along with the obvious physical disabilities, some of these veterans are returning to civilian life with "hidden disabilities" such as PTSD, depression, and anxiety. A majority of these veterans do not disclose their disability or request accommodations because they do not want added attention or identification. The sooner they disclose and request accommodations, and have them in place for classroom and testing situations, the more successful they will be as a college student. Campus resources outside of disability/accessibility services are also available such as the Veterans Center, Counseling Center and tutoring assistance.

According to a 2008 study in the *Journal of Behavioral Medicine*, roughly 80 percent of people exposed to PTSD eventually recover. Humans have a long history of sustaining enormous psychic damage and continue to function (Junger, 2015). Some PTSD is short lived and veteranS can get on with their lives. Requesting college accommodations, such as extended test time, testing in a separate environment and a lesser course load can help minimize the stress these veterans face while transitioning to college and create a positive academic experience. Veterans who start off using these accommodations gain confidence and ease into the demands of college academics, building success gradually. These students can choose to use accommodations for all or some of their classes, depending on the course structure and stress the student feels. Along with using academic accommodations, connecting to other veterans who can relate to their military experiences can add another layer of positive support to their transition.

Post-9/11 GI Bill

Many of these veterans have deployed to the war torn countries of Iraq and Afghanistan. These dedicated men and women have completed their service, are extremely positive about the next chapter and are ready for the challenge of preparing for a new career. For veterans, returning to civilian life may include pursuing a college degree or job skill using tuition assistance. Since 2009, one million vets chose to use the post–9/11 GI Bill to assist with the cost of a college degree (Hechinger Report, Nov. 25, 2013). In many cases, the GI Bill provides a basic allowance for housing and a book stipend; this is in addition to their tuition assistance. It's not technically for the family but can offset the cost of attending full time. Tuition and fee payments are sent directly to the college; a monthly housing allowance plus a stipend for books and supplies is sent directly to the student (U.S. Dept. of Veteran Affairs, 2015). Not all colleges take the GI Bill tuition assistance, so carefully look into college choices. Veterans need to apply for the post–9/11 GI Bill before they apply to colleges. The following website is an excellent resource for veterans who want to understand the educational benefits of the GI Bill: *http:// www.benefits.va.gov/GIBILL/resources/benefits_resources/rates/ch33/ch33rates 080114.asp.*

We currently have a volunteer military, and many of these veterans enlisted as young adults. "These veterans are unlike the usual 18 year old freshman as they have seen and experienced circumstances that have made them ready for adversity and tolerant to compliance." Their experience has also put them ahead of the pack by giving them much desired time-management skills. All active duty veterans have the opportunity for 100 percent tuition assistance based on a certain dollar amount per fiscal year. According to Budin, Kupur (2002), "13% of marines have taken advantage of this benefit while still on active duty. The system is dependent on their occupation and accessibility to take online courses or participate after working hours" (p. 4).

According to the U.S. Veterans Affairs website, the Post-9/11 GI Bill will pay

- all resident tuition and fees for a public school; and
- the lower of the actual tuition and fee. Only veterans entitled to the maximum benefit rate, as determined by service requirements, or their designated transferees may receive this funding. or the national maximum per academic year for a private school (Education and Training, 2015).

Actual tuition & fees costs may exceed these amounts if attending a private school or a public school as a nonresident student; in this case the veteran is responsible to pay the difference with possible loans available to supplement the VA Post 911 GI Bill. All veterans should complete the FAFSA form to learn which grants and loans they may be eligible for to assist with college costs.

Degree-granting institutions of higher learning participating in the post–9/11 GI Bill Yellow Ribbon Program agree to make additional funds available for the education program without an additional charge to the GI Bill entitlement. These institutions voluntarily enter into a Yellow Ribbon Agreement with VA and choose the amount of tuition and fees that will be contributed. VA matches that amount and issues payments directly to the institution. Some of the institutions participating in the Yellow Ribbon program have a maximum number of veterans they will take each year in their participation agreement.

Challenges in College

The majority of men and women join the military right out of high school, leaving parents and home to become part of a new military family. The military has strict rules with many policies and procedures to be followed, and teaches them to work together as a team and other values. The military also provides housing, food and medical benefits. These young adults are secure in this environment, knowing that all of their basic needs are being met, and usually feel a strong bond with their fellow veterans; especially those who have served together overseas and in battle. Once they have fulfilled their military commitment, chosen to leave the military, or have been injured and can no longer serve their country, some of these young adults find themselves overwhelmed with starting their lives over as a civilian. They no longer have an income and need jobs, possibly an education, a place to live, and medical benefits. Many have a spouse or young families they need to support. "Making good career decisions and completing an education, technical or training courses while meeting their basic needs can be extremely stressful, even more so with a young family to care for. Many also struggle with the isolation and disconnect from their close military family; losing this connection often leaves some feeling lost and alone because no one else can relate to what they have personally gone through" (Ingersoll, J., interview, 2015).

Veterans who make the choice to attend college can face some new stresses. Many feel isolated from their college peers because they are not the "typical aged college student," and they have different life experiences. Veterans who are focused and motivated and have access to a veteran support group usually do well with their coursework. Some find that they have to hold down a full or part-time job in order to support themselves or their family while attending college. "Many veterans find that trying to raise a family while attending college adds to their financial burden. This can cause more stress on the veteran and may trigger some PTSD moments or depression" (Ingersoll, J., interview, 2015). Adjusting to civilian life can create a culture shock that many vets find difficult to deal with on their own.

Family and community resources have been put in place to create support and guidance for vets. "Learning to find a good balance between home life, college and work takes planning and support from both family and local community and college veterans groups" (Pomeroy, Bruce, interview, 2015). Many colleges have a veteran's center which provides resources, counseling, peer group interactions, and assistance with understanding GI benefits. The veteran's center helps to ease the transition to civilian and college life, and provides a connection with other military members who have had similar experiences, thus easing that sense of loneliness.

"Learning new things and developing career goals can help veterans look to the future with hope and excitement" (DO IT Returning from Service, 2015). Veteran students need resources and support systems in place to help them become successful college students. According to the University of Washington DO IT veteran research, some issues veterans students face are: denying the impact their disability has on their learning, reluctance to self-identify as having a disability, fear of failure, challenges adjusting to civilian life, frustrations trying to navigate the veteran bureaucracies, and experiencing interruptions in sleep and depression as a consequence of military experiences. Both college and community resources are available to these veteran students. Spouses and family members can encourage their veteran to seek out this support and assist them with this transition process.

These young men and women are not only experiencing changes in their career and lifestyle, but some may be experiencing depression, adjustment issues after sustaining physical injuries or PTSD related to their military deployments. "Currently, many veterans have served over 19 months in Afghanistan, which increases one's chances of living through a traumatic experience; therefore increasing one's susceptibility to experiencing PTSD and depression" (Sargent, 2008). Others are dealing with physical injuries which limit their life activities, such as blindness, amputations, hearing loss, Traumatic Brain Injuries (TBI), and others. College disability/accessibility services have been preparing to meet the needs of these students by creating veteran friendly campuses, training faculty and staff, along with creating academic resources and assistive technology to help them succeed with college goals.

Veterans already come to college with many good skill sets. They know how to follow orders, meet deadlines, are more self-assured, are responsible group members, have leadership qualities, know how to problem solve, are very focused and dedicated, and bring their worldly experiences into classroom discussions. Their military experience has taught them the value of a strong work ethic and discipline, and they can be an asset to a classroom environment because they have world experience which they can relate to course information and lectures.

Counseling is available to veterans on a college campus. The counseling resources are free and will help them adjust to civilian and college academic life, along with adjusting to the loss of their military family. Military personnel experience extreme brotherhood both stateside and abroad, but once they leave this military environment and move back home they can feel extremely alienated, leaving them open to depression. "Many returning veterans are currently coping and living with PTSD. PTSD is a disorder that not only affects the veteran, but also his/her family, friends and co-workers" (Sargent, 2008). College counselors are trained to assist veterans with their transitions and will teach them coping strategies to help them to successfully move forward with their career and life goals.

The veteran's center on the college campus plays many support roles and supplies resources to help these students understand their military benefits and college life. These centers have numerous resources in place, along with the connection of other veterans who can relate to what they have gone through, which often eases the loneliness and despair these veterans feel upon leaving the military lifestyle and first attending college. "Student veterans face challenges that include social adjustments, financial burdens, new career goals, navigating veteran bureaucracies, accessing disability accommodations, depressions, and reluctance to disclose disabilities" (DO IT Returning From Service, 2015). The campus veteran centers have staff and programs available to assist the veteran student with each of these transitions; as well as "helping student veterans understand differences between the military, higher education and the corporate world" (DO IT Returning from Service, 2015).

Dealing with stress of daily life as a college student, as well as readjusting to civilian life can become challenging for many veterans. Veterans returning from Afghanistan and Iraq have experienced traumatic life and death situations on a daily basis, which contributes to stress. Returning veterans who leave traumatic stressful wartime conditions to enter academia are often faced with added stress from rigors of quizzes, papers and exams. "The stress from academia may be elevated when veterans are already coping and living with PTSD and other combat and war related diagnosis" (Sargent, 2008, pp. 8–10). Veteran students who take advantage of support resources will often have a positive and more successful college experience

Military Transition Education Program

Beth Barton, Ph.D., who is the deputy director of Marine and family programs division, shared valuable information on programs, policies and procedures they have in place to assist Marines with their transition to civilian life. Beth stated that the Marines are the first of the military service branches to put this new educational transition program in place, with other branches following suit in November 2012, per the Veterans Opportunity to Work (VOW) Act of 2012. The Marine Corps has created a "Life Cycle Approach" to educating their service members by preparing mandatory "Personal Readiness Seminars from as early as 90 days after a Marine has arrived to their first permanent duty station. The employment skills training program allows for on-the-job training while on active duty within six months of separation" (Barton, interview, 2015). This mandate for the Marine Corps began in 2013 with their new capstone program (MARADMIN 514–13) that outlines a transition plan, creates a personal readiness plan (MARADMIN 581–14) and workshops on how to prepare for educational goals while still on active duty. The new transition program begins helping the Marines create a plan 12–18 months prior to separation from active duty, and guides service members through resources available to them. Each service member must create an individual transition plan (ITP) and share this with their commanding officer at required steps in the program and again prior to their final departure date. "The capstone is a knee-to-knee counseling that occurs with a Marine's commanding officer while on active duty within three months of separation. So we are preparing Marines for transition as soon as they enter the Corps, and then they attend a Transition Readiness Seminar between 12–14 months prior, but no less than, six months prior to their EAS date (exit date)" (Barton, interview, 2015). Dr. Barton states that these programs and services are in place to help prevent unemployment, homelessness and other negative things. These programs and services are in place for not only Marines, but for all service members in all branches of the military and although the life cycle approach is unique to the Marine Corps, it will likely be implemented in all military branches soon.

These military education and transitions programs have created a roadmap to assist with various career choices after separating from the military. This capstone project offers valuable information to service members, veterans and their families on how to access benefits, resources and services. These programs offer college education assessment and assist with the application process, entrepreneurship training, employment workshops, financial planning, pre-preparation counseling and assessment, to name a few. They provide workshops and counselors to assist the service member with all steps involved in applying to college, building a resume, matching job skills with relevant available jobs, becoming an entrepreneur, and other related pre-separation topics.

The transition readiness seminars offer four pathways towards transition planning. These pathways are

- Employment Pathway;
- College/University Education Pathway;
- Entrepreneurship Pathway; and
- Career Technical Education Pathway.

Each pathway is "designed to give service members ownership of their transition from the military by providing resources, opportunities to make informed decisions when transitioning to the civilian sector."

Veterans who choose the higher education track will attend a two-day mandated program that provides information, resources and counselors to assist them with their educational track. Steps are put in place for each service member to complete as they prepare their individual transition plan, with checkpoints and numerous resources in place.

The higher education track provides the service members with information regarding

- post-9/11 GI Bill benefits information;
- how to find the right college fit;
- Yellow Ribbon programs;
- applying for and utilizing the post–9/11 GI Bill;
- FAFSA, financial aid and scholarship information;
- counselors to assist with the college application process;
- transferring military credits;
- credit for military training and experience; and
- personal financial management.

College Admissions Exams

Veterans should prepare to take the college admissions exams, either the SAT or ACT, which are required for college acceptance. The SAT and ACT websites have online practice tests to help review and prepare each sub-set being tested and military libraries often have free test preparation materials and websites for service members to use. Preparation practice books are also available through Amazon and local bookstores. The WONDERLIC website also has pre-employment testing, with results showing ability, competency, job readiness skills and industry-leading placement tests.

Yellow Ribbon Program

Veterans can explore online to find veteran friendly campuses who are participating in the Yellow Ribbon Program. Each year the website is updated; for example, veterans can go to "Yellow ribbon program-participating institutions for the 2015–2016 school year. This site will give you access to each state with a list of participating colleges and the amount of money each is willing to add to the veteran's tuition benefits." Veterans affairs training information for 2015 states, "Only Veterans entitled to the maximum benefit rate, as determined by service requirements, or their designated transferees may receive this funding." Please review all areas of qualification on the Veterans Education and Training, Yellow Ribbon website for participating in this program as a veteran or family member receiving veteran benefits. "Schools can limit the amount of tuition they waive, the number of students they choose to waive tuition for, and the specific programs they choose to participate in the Yellow Ribbon Program" (Military.com, 2015). This program helps students attend career programs for undergraduate and graduate programs at both public and private colleges.

College Advising Program—Bob Dannenhold

Bob Dannenhold, who has worked with veterans for many years with his nonprofit college advising for returning vets program (www.appnav.org), states that his successful vets have taken advantage of the veteran's centers, disability/accessibility support programs, and have spent time volunteering in their local community. Bob recommends that veterans who have experienced PTSD (also known as PTS) and wish to attend college wait at least six months before attending classes both on campus and online; and they should explore veteran friendly campuses who offer many resources; these colleges can be found on the Yellow Ribbon website. The military personnel do not completely agree with the six-month wait. They prefer that vets have an education plan in place and six months before exiting the services and do not end up on unemployment. Bob's experience with veterans has shown that it takes at least six months to mentally transition to civilian life and deal with the adjustment issues many vets experience during this time period. He recommends that these vets immediately get involved with volunteer work within their community and the local veterans support group. When these vets are ready to attend college courses they should not start off with the same high school courses that were difficult for them. Bob recommends that vets access the free tutoring available on college campuses, and they should look into signing up for tutors in courses that are difficult for them. Bob has also found that vets who take time for physical activity, both on campus and at home, feel less stressed, including stresses from PTSD.

Most vets feel disconnected from their military family whom they worked with daily. One way Bob has found for his vets to deal with these feelings is to get them involved with volunteering, coaching, or working at a college sponsored help-line to help them adjust to belonging to a community again. Bob has had great success in pairing vets with young autistic children in a volunteer program.

Counseling is an important step in moving forward with life and career goals. The veteran centers on campus and within the community have trained staff to counsel the veteran student as they traverse the academic world. Each campus also has a counseling center that is accessible to veterans, and each of these resources are free. Counseling can help the veteran deal with personal issues, along with the isolation and disconnection from the military family. Counseling will help veteran students address both personal issues and academic issues as they arise, decreasing their stress levels and helping them move forward.

Veterans have a strong need to feel safe on a college campus, so Bob recommends that they do not take any night courses, learn the campus grounds and look for an open campus, not one that is closed in by many buildings. Crowded parking lots and dark hallways can trigger some PTSD feelings and should be avoided when possible.

When exploring military friendly campuses, vets can also look for CLEP programs (college level exam programs for knowledge and experience learned outside of college), that give college credit for military training and experience, especially in the areas of medical, engineering, leadership, culinary skills, etc. Because the exams are funded by the United States government through the Defense Activity for Non Traditional Education Support (DANTES), you could save hundreds, even thousands, of dollars toward your degree (CLEP for the Military, 2015). CLEP tests are also available on military installations where testing centers are located and can be taken free of charge prior to leaving the military. Also look for colleges that recognize online classes for credit, as well as experiential learning.

Bob works with veterans across the country using SKYPE, FaceTime and email. His free program for veterans gives assistance with finding the right college fit, career counseling, completing college applications and writing college essays, understanding the GI Bill and finding quality yellow ribbon colleges who assist with college costs, and have excellent support resources for veteran students. Bob Dannenhold is able to offer these free services through donations from people across the country who believes in supporting our military as they transition to civilian life and the work force.

Some colleges with excellent Yellow Ribbon programs offer great veteran support and accessibility. Some colleges will have a limited number of students they will accept in the Yellow Ribbon Program, and or a limited amount of money for these students. Please check the Yellow Ribbon website for specific details: http://www.benefits.va.gov/GIBILL/yellow_ribbon/yrp_list_2014.asp.

The Right College Fit

Transitioning to college for veterans will require finding the right college fit for their career goals; whether it is an online program they started while on active duty, or finding a college near their home or starting life over in a completely new city. These men and women will have different educational levels and skills depending on their military training and experiences. Assessing these previous skills and education will help them to find the right college program, certificate program or career fit. The military education program can assist the veterans with these assessments and exploring their options. They will have access to the Education Center resources while on active duty and after they leave the military.

The following list shares some of the Yellow Ribbon colleges across the country:

West	Midwest	East
Academy of Art, San Francisco	Penn State	American Institute of
Art Institute, San Francisco	Texas A&M	Technology
Devry (many campuses)	Webster University	George Washington University
Drexel University	Methodist University	Campbell University
University of Washington—		Cornell
Do It Program		Fordham
UCLA (many campuses)		Harvard
		SUNY colleges
		UNC Greensboro

Family Members Interested in Using GI Benefits

Family members of veterans are eligible to use the GI Benefits, as long as the military family member has signed off on the form 3351B, in triplicate, and they meet all specified qualifications and guidelines. This form must be completed and signed in triplicate in order for the family members to receive the college aid. The veteran can designate and divide benefits to their children or spouse. Both public and private colleges accept the GI Bill. Some colleges will give students in state tuition if their parent is actively in the military and currently living in the state.

The Military.com website has more information on education and training for veterans as they transition into new careers and civilian life. The military will provide a one week transition program through their education center for each personnel member who has chosen to end their military career.

Resources for Veterans

ACE Toolkit for Veteran Friendly Institutions—www.vetfriendlytoolkit.org, *http://www.financialaidtoolkit.ed.gov/tk/outreach/target/military.jsp*

Application Navigation—www.appnav.org. Bob Dannenhold does nonprofit college advising for returning vets and offers free assistance filling out applications, college essays and the college search process, with assistance understanding the GI Bill and Yellow Ribbon funding.

BOOK—Military Defense Almanac, 2012 U.S. Military Retire Handbook

CLEP (College Level Exam Prep for the military)—*https://clep.collegeboard.org/military*

Debt Management Center—*DMC.ops@va.gov*

ED Student Aid for Military Families—*http://studentaid.ed.gov/types/grants-scholarships/military*

FAFSA (Free Application for Federal Student Aid)—https://fafsa.ed.gov/. This form should be completed between January 1 and June 30. The sooner the form is competed and submitted the better chance one has of receiving available student aid.

Operation College Promise—http://www.operationpromiseforservicemembers.com/. This is a training program for people who want to work with veterans.

Student Veterans of America—*http://studentveterans.org/index.php/what-we-do/million-records-project*

The Telling Project—*http://thetellingproject.org*

U.S. Department of Defense (DoD) Tuition Assistance (TA) DECIDE—http://www.dodmou.com/TADECIDE/

U.S. Department of education (ED) Financial Aid Toolkit—*http://vetfriendlytoolkit.acenet.edu/pages/default.aspx, www.vetfriendlytoolkit.org.* This is a federal student aid website for veterans and active duty personnel, plus grant and scholarship info.

U.S. Department of Veterans Affairs (VA) GI Bill—http://www.benefits.va.gov/gibill/, http://www.benefits.va.gov/GIBILL/resources/benefits_resources/rates/ch33/ch33rates080114.asp, and http://www.GIBill.va.gov/documents/factsheet/choosing_a_school.pdf

VA GI Bill Comparison Tool—*http://department-of-veterans-affairs.github.io/gi-bill-comparison-tool/*

Veteran Scholarship Aid—http://www.va.gov/stateedva

www.military.com—Information on education and training for veterans.

14

Role of the Parent
Testimonies—Sherry, Steve, Jennifer and Susan

The goal of a parent is to empower your children to become independent productive adults. As parents we each have academic and career hopes and dreams for our children, unfortunately life circumstances can places obstacles in this academic path. It is extremely difficult as parents when we have to watch our children struggle. Their particular challenge may be a learning disability, ADHD, dyslexia, Autism, Asperger's, medical condition, a traumatic accident or psychological conditions. As parents we want to take away all the physical and emotional challenges our children have to face, but we cannot. Instead, as parents, we must "assemble the team" that will provide all the resources they need, then step back and stay in the parent role, giving them love, encouragement and guidance as best we can.

Sending a child off to college often leaves parents feeling the need to remote parent and keep as connected as possible. Once a student turns 18 years of age the FERPA privacy laws kick in and the parent does not have the same rights as in high school. Parents have been advocating for their child since birth, but now that responsibility lies on the student's shoulders. Sending a child away to college with a disability does require some limited parental interaction, especially when setting up disability accommodations. Often parents feel they need to advocate for their child on a continuous basis, but that is not usually necessary on the post-secondary level. Some students will need parents to intercede on their behalf in order to communicate with the disability staff for the purpose of sending in documentation to put accommodations in place, or to relay personal medical situations and information. The student will need to sign a FERPA waiver in order to give permission for the college staff and faculty to communicate with parents.

Prior to the first semester of college parents will need to send in documentation and communicate to the disability staff with their student Once the student is on campus they are responsible for initiating communication with disability staff and following procedures to implement their approved accommodations and dealing with accommodation concerns. Students should come with good self-advocacy skills and knowledge of their disability. The student and parent can call, email or meet with disability staff at any time in order to discuss concerns or changes in their disability accommodations. There are some situations where the parent does need to stay a little more involved than normal, but this is usually on a special case by case basis, or for critical medical and physical conditions.

Accepting your child where they are is the most important job of a parent. Finding out what obstacles are in your child's path to academic success, and helping to set up a roadmap to conquer these obstacles is also your job. It is important that you find out which resources are available in your community, school system or college to give your child the support and tools they need to find academic success. Talk with your child and work together to create a plan for their career goals. Listen to their hopes and dreams and guide them to the path that will make these dreams attainable. Start with finding the right college fit with resources such as tutors, technology, academic coaches and writing and math labs available to assist the student with their disability needs.

Requesting Accommodations

Under the ADA laws the student must chose to disclose their disability. The student and parent of incoming freshmen should contact the disability services department at the college their student will be attending. Make initial contact with the department during your college visit, then again in the spring or summer prior to freshmen year to learn about required documentation needed for approval of their particular disability. Also get clarification on which types of accommodations they will offer your child, and discuss types of technology they may have available and which technology and apps you may need to purchase for your child.

Once you have faxed, emailed or mailed in your documentation remember to follow up with the staff to make sure they have received all the required documentation. Information for sending in appropriate documentation should be on each college website under disability support services. If you do not hear back from the DSS office within four to five weeks contact them again to inquire as to the status of your child's accommodations. Paperwork sometimes gets lost and you will not know that until you follow up. Once the requested accommodations are approved and in place the disability services department will send a letter home to the student stating approved classroom and testing accommodations. Review this with your child before they attend classes so they understand what should be on the accommodation letters given to the professors. The student's disability *will not* be stated in the letter to the professor, only the approved accommodations. If the student chooses to share more information about their disability or academic history they can, but it is not required. It is also helpful for the student to visit the disability department and acquaint themselves with the staff so they will feel more comfortable following through with DS their first couple weeks on campus. This should get them off to a strong start and help to build a positive relationship with the department.

As a parent of a college student you will also have the opportunity to attend family weekend each fall and possibly again in the spring , where you can meet with your student's professors as well as attend sporting events, theatre and music events as well as special guest speakers, artists and others from within the university. It will be important for you to explore all that the university has to offer your child. If your child is struggling in a course or two, you can *schedule a meeting with the professors* prior to the weekend to discuss options and explore resources to help the student improve. This would also be a good time to encourage your child to share with the professor any academic struggles, disabilities, etc., the student may be dealing with and find out if your child is following through and using their approved accommodations.

You and your child can discuss the approved accommodations in depth at this time, or share background on your child that will help the professor understand their academic challenges. This helps the professor understand where the student is coming from and which obstacles they are working to overcome. I have been very impressed with how empathetic professors can be when they are given insight regarding the student's abilities, needs and goals. As a parent you can take this opportunity to help a shy student bridge the gap between student and professor. Many students are uncomfortable meeting individually with a professor; as the parent you can assist in setting up the meeting and engaging the student in a personal discussion with the professor regarding their specific learning needs. After an initial meeting the student is usually more comfortable with initiating follow up meetings.

Parents can also take the time to meet with disability services during family weekend, or any time they are visiting campus to discuss any concerns you might have regarding the implementation of accommodations, or your child's lack of using these accommodations. The staff will usually encourage the student to try using the accommodations and will usually tweak any problems they are having with implementing these accommodations.

FERPA Waiver

The FERPA waiver is a form that your child must sign in order for parents to communicate with the college, especially with receiving copies of grades or speaking with the staff or professors if there is a critical concern or emergency. The form needs to be signed each fall. It is important to share with your child the importance of signing the form to create open communication throughout each semester. This way there should be no disappointing surprises at the end of the semester, and a smoother transition when an emergency situation occurs.

Resources

Some students will have difficulty contacting or reaching out to appropriate resources on their campus. The parent might need to help their child make the initial contact with a department, and then encourage the student to follow up with the meeting. Once a student becomes comfortable with the staff in the resource department, such as student academic services, tutoring, counseling, advising, housing, Greek life, they will continue to use the resources.

Parent Testimonies

The following testimonies are from parents who wanted to share some advice on how to support your child while still encouraging their independence once they leave home and attend college.

Sherry

"There is a time when you have to hand-hold in college in order to get them off to a good start."

Searching for the best fit college became a daunting task for Sherry and her son Zack. They found very few colleges that had appropriate resources to accommodate his academic needs. During first grade Zack was diagnosed with dyslexia, and throughout his education he attended private schools with special staff and helpful technology. Sherry worked closely with community member to build a private school for students with disabilities for grades one through eight. Zack attended this school and successfully progressed through each grade.

Psychological testing was updated during Zack's senior year to prepare for requesting college accommodations. The accommodations he received in high school made all the difference, and Sherry knew would be completely necessary in college. Sherry asked Zack's high school counselor for assistance in finding colleges that would have good academic support programs as well as assistive technology and strong staff support. Finding a college that offered use of assistive technology, unlimited tutoring, academic coaching, assistance with time management and organizational skills would keep Zack from falling behind in academic reading and writing assignments and would be key to his success.

Sherry also reached out to vocational rehab for more support resources. After registering her son they met with a counselor who assessed his learning needs and set up a program for his college academic goals. Vocational rehab will start working with high school students at age 17 to assist with transitioning to college or work. Vocational rehab provided Zack with a computer and software programs for college, and they also assisted with some tuition fees. They reminded Zack that he would need to keep a 2.0 GPA, or above to continue to receive their support.

The high school counselor also completed career assessments with Zack to explore his interests and talents. The counselor explored appropriate colleges and came up with a solid list: Eastern Carolina University, Marshall University, Lynchburg College, High Point University. Sherry and Zack toured each college, and visited the disability and academic services center where they could ask specific questions on accommodations and academic support. Sherry set appointments to meet individually with staff to thoroughly research aspects of each program.

Each of these colleges offered excellent technology resources, such as Kurzweil reading software, use of SMART Pens, Dragon Speak, editing software programs and tutoring support. They also each had a separate academic support program available for an extra fee. The support programs offer an academic coach, private tutors, writing resources, communication with parents and professors regularly, along with time management and organizational support tools. Zack finally chose High Point University because it offered the learning excellence program and a summer transition program for freshmen.

Zack agreed to sign the FERPA waiver so his parents could receive his grades and communicate with staff if necessary.

During the summer July transition program Sherry was very hands-off, and Zack had a successful experience, earning a strong GPA and eight college credits and adjusted well to the college campus. Fall semester proved to be a different story. When Sherry attended family weekend in early October she found Zack struggling in each of his classes and having anxiety regarding his coursework. He was not using any approved accommodations or any other resources his mother had put in place. Zack received his approved accommodations letters, and gave them to his professors, but did not meet with the professor to implement classroom or testing accommodations. He was not using tutors or any other resources available in the learning excellence program. After a long conversation with Zack Sherry knew she had to step in and assist her son.

Sherry immediately contacted the disability director and the learning excellence director. During their meeting a new plan was put into place to help Zack improve grades by using resources such as tutors, completing the mandatory study hall hours, learning time management techniques and implement his accommodations. Sherry also met individually with each professor to discuss Zack's learning struggles and approved accommodations. She was pleased to find that the professors were open to email exchanges and conference calls with her and Zack as needed throughout the semester. Before the initial meeting the professors thought Zack was just being lazy and disengaged. Once they understood his history of academic struggles they made sure to implement all accommodations and communicate frequently with Zack, parents, academic coach and the disability director. Communication was crucial in helping Zack work more productively to improve his course grades. Zack followed through with using tutors, accommodations and asking professors for help and was able to end the semester with a 2.4 GPA; keeping him in good academic standings with both the college and vocational rehab.

Sherry was aware that Zack was very shy and would never meet individually with his professors, so she and Zack decided to create a letter that outlined his specific learning struggles; which Zack hand delivered to each professor. Sherry or the disability director helped Zack meet with each professor at the beginning of spring semester to discuss his learning needs and approved accommodations. These meeting set the groundwork for continued support and communication for Zack throughout the semester. During family weekend each semester Sherry made appointments to meet with professor and helped Zack share more if his personal academic struggle and encouraged him to ask questions; once again assisting him to verbally communicate his needs. Zack was not able to advocate for himself at this point, so Sherry helped him until he learned this skill. His sophomore year of college was much smoother and Zack improved at communicating, using resources and self-advocating.

Sherry chose to step in and help her child learn which resources and people to access in order to achieve academic success. Once he started sophomore year Zack was a much better self- advocate, and became stronger with each academic year. When Zack became a college senior Sherry once again stepped in to encouraged him to reach out to career services to help him prepare a resume' and conduct job searches. Once he knew who to contact he sent emails and made positive connections. He also asked for assistance with practice interviews which helped with anxiety over meeting new people.

Sherry's early intervention made all the difference for Zack. He needed a little hand holding to reach out to staff and professors, but once he learned how to communicate his needs he was able to advocate better for himself.

Steve

Sending your first child off to college can really tug at your heartstrings, but sending them off with a new cancer diagnosis can add a whole new level of anxiety and concern for a parent.

Steve was devastated the summer after high school graduation when doctors told him that his daughter would probably not attend college, and would probably not live to graduate college. Remarkably the even bigger shock came when his daughter Kristy told him that she definitely wanted to attend her freshman year of college, even while finishing up her cancer treatments. Steve's initial instinct was to keep her home with him and close to her doctors, but her independent spirit led her to pursue her college dream, leaving Steve struggling with wanting to be overprotective and giving her hope by respecting her wishes.

Steve learned to let go of his fears for his daughter and began to put resources in place to help her transition to college in the fall. Once he realized how determined Kristy was, Steve gave her 100 percent support and worked to put every resource in place for her success. They met with her doctors to create a plan for her continued treatments while attending her freshmen year of college. Steve worked with doctors and his insurance company to make the move from the Johns Hopkins cancer center in Maryland to the Duke cancer center in North Carolina, where she would continue to receive the same chemo regiment. She would now only be one hour away from her doctors and chemo treatments.

The HIPPA laws state that once a child turns 18 years of age they can make their own medical decisions. Even though she was on his insurance she had control of her medical treatment, and as her father Steve had to take a back seat. He wanted what was best for her, but was afraid to let her go away from home and the unknown future.

Steve called the college disability services office to inquire about setting up housing accommodations and academic accommodations. After learning the process he sent in her medical documentation and required forms to request accommodations. His daughter was too sick at the time to communicate everything herself, so Steve handled the process. One important factor was setting up the housing needs. She would not be able to eat in the cafeteria due to germs and bacteria exposure, so she needed specific housing accommodations. Fortunately the college was able to provide a suite with individual bedrooms, bathroom, living area and a kitchen. Steve also chose to hire a student to aid Kristy in grocery shopping, laundry and running errands until she completed her treatments and gained back her strength. This student kept in close contact with Steve, especially when emergencies arose.

Steve felt that letting her go off to college saved her life because it gave her a new focus and motivation and kept her from feeling depressed. She stayed busy with course work, projects and making new friends as she transitioned to college. She finally had some control over her life. He watched her grow strong while her attitude and self-esteem did a 100 percent turnaround as she found an inner strength and determination to move forward and create her future.

Steve was pleased to see that his daughter's spirits rose as she continued to focus on planning for her move to college. He was afraid to leave her on campus after moving her in, but knew he had to let go. A few weeks later he was back taking her to the hospital for treatments. He would often sleep on the small couch in their dorm when she was very sick and right after treatments. He kept a close vigil on her medical condition because she often ended up with infections after the chemo treatments. Her energy often dwindled and she needed vast amounts of sleep. When she had spurts of energy she would complete course work and readings. He was pleased with the support she received for friends and professors visiting her at the hospital and bringing her work back and forth.

Steve learned that the best support he could give his daughter was to have all resources in place and allow her to become independent. He had to initiate services and accommodations for his daughter that first semester of college, but after that he only stepped in when there was a medical crisis, and allowed Kristy to handle her academic accommodation and housing needs.

Steve has advice to share with parents of students with medical issues.

- Keep in close communication with your child each week.
- Exchange phone numbers of roommates their parents and friends in case of emergencies.
- Contact disability services when there are changes in the medical conditions so they can reach out to the student and professors to monitor course work and tests and keep communication open.
- Participate in hospital support groups because as a human being you can only handle so much, and others who have gone through similar experiences can give guidance and support.
- Get to know child's friends, be involved so there is open communication during critical times.
- Find an advocate on campus, especially within disability services to your child with professor communication and housing needs
- Always keep a bag packed in case of emergencies
- Your child may need an extra year of college due to taking a smaller course load each semester to manage their illness and college.

Jennifer

"We worked so hard to get our child to college, we can't just give up, we need to keep support services in place while still allowing him some independence."

Jennifer and her husband realized that finding the right college fit was essential to their child's success. He initially wanted to attend a large college with his friends from high school, but this turned out to be a mistake. The college did provide support services and accommodations, but their son was overwhelmed with the size of the campus and finding all the appropriate resources, so he never used them. "We gave him his own space and tried not to interfere his first semester, but this proved to be our first mistake. In hindsight he needed our support and communication now just as he did in high school. We did not communicate as often as we should, and our son did not let us know how frustrated he was and how difficult college had become because he did not want to let us down." After his freshman year Jennifer and her husband researched potential colleges to help their son Ryan find another college that fit his academic needs and allowed him a new start.

The privacy laws in the college environment does not allow parents to be hands on as in the past, so parents need to rely on communication from their child. This proved to be the first biggest obstacle for Jennifer. The first college did not communicate that there were academic problems until January when a letter arrived for their son stating that he was on academic probation. Often parents need to make the initial call and work to discover whether there are any academic or personal issues going on. Jennifer and her husband have learned to look for signs that there might be academic trouble, and head it off as quickly as possible.

"When our son transferred to a smaller college we took him to meet with all resource personnel and put everything in place before leaving the campus. The second time around we chose a fee-based academic program to give him the guidance and academic support tools he needed for success." The academic support program took time to teach their son new study strategies, scheduled his weekly tutoring sessions as needed, and provided weekly communication regarding his academic progress. "This gave us the support and tools we needed to intercede as issues arose."

Here are Jennifer's tips for parents of students with medical issues.

• Take time to visit all potential colleges and explore their resources and the staff that work there to make sure it is a good fit for your child. Virtual tours always look good, but can often be deceiving form the reality of the college environment.

• Keep constant and open communication with your child so you can pick up on cues that things may not be going well.

• Smaller colleges are better for many students with learning issues. They offer smaller class sizes, available resources and accessible professors.

• Be vigilant the first two to three months of college; this is when most problems arise.

• As students get older parents feel they will become more independent, but parents need to stay involved and not drop the ball too soon.

• FERPA—make sure your child signs the waiver so you can intervene if needed, and be informed of their grades.

Susan

Susan knew she needed to be actively involved when her son Chase, who had physical disabilities, transitioned from community college and living at home to living on campus at a four-year college. She knew that her son wanted his independence and needed to learn to live on his own, but first she had to learn to let go and trust the professionals around him. During elementary school she had to fight hard for his rights because the school system wanted to place him in special education classes, and she would not allow this. Her son Chase had a physical handicap, not a mental one. She had to hire a lawyer and worked hard to win her case. She was ready to fight for him again on the college level if the need arose.

Things went fairly smooth at the community college, except for access to a couple of buildings, and the time when the elevator broke in a building and his mother had to come get him and ask security to carry Chase and his wheelchair down a few flights of stairs. After twenty one years of taking care of her son she was hesitant to let him live on campus. Chase and his mother met with the disability director, who organized a meeting with housing to discuss his accommodations needs. Together they created a list of suite room accommodations, down to changing the height of the bed and closets for easier access and independence. The hosing and enhancement immediately put her at ease and went out of their way to accommodate Chase. Susan knew he was in good hands.

During the summer Susan and Chase walked through the dorm suite and discussed alterations to the shower, bedroom and kitchen, giving the staff plenty of time to install the special assistive equipment. "Throughout the process there were plenty of things we did not think about, but the housing staff worked closely with the campus enhancement staff and they oversaw all of Chase's needs." The handicapped dorm room was across the hall from the RA (resident assistant) in case of emergencies, which made Susan feel better.

Susan was amazed at how accommodating the college staff were and how smoothly Chase transition to living on campus. Susan stayed with him for the first week to ensure he could get himself out of bed, in and out of the shower and maneuver the suite and campus before she would leave him on his own. She would contact the enhancement staff when adjustments were needed that first week. She admired her son's strength and determination. He quickly gained his independence, with a little help from his roommate, and Susan was able to go home. "The campus was small enough that he could easily maneuver to classes, café, restaurants, and the library. HPU was a small safe environment, much like a small city within the college boundaries." A few of the buildings had very large heavy doors, but peers would often assist with getting him inside. Susan left him on campus feeling that he was in good hands. Chase was able to follow up with any further accommodation tweaking from then on. She had taught her son to self-advocate, and knew that he would reach out and ask for help as needed.

Susan shares the following advice with parents of students with physical handicaps.

- Teach your child to advocate for themselves during high school.
- Your child should participate in all high school IEP and transition meeting; it is their future.
- Vocational rehab is a wonderful resource which will help with all of the following:
  - mobility access on campus;
  - occupational therapy to assist with teaching physical independence;
  - finding a campus environment that is comfortable for your child and their needs;
  - driving lessons, which provided Chase with handicapped accessible vehicle to drive;
  - paying up to $6,000 per year in tuition costs; and
  - providing assistance with job placement after graduation.

The parents who shared their experiences agree that there are times when the parent needs to help their child advocate on the college level. Circumstances arise and young adults are not always equipped to know which people and resources to approach for help. During this learning process have your child walk with you through the steps of communicating and requesting assistance, and then step back and let them take the lead. Parents will be amazed at how strong their child can be when they better understand their needs and the resources available to them.

15

Self-Advocacy and Working with Your Advisor

Self-advocacy is a term that has been used for years in the disability world, but what does it really mean? The Oxford dictionary states that self-advocacy is "the action of representing oneself or one's views or interests." In the postsecondary setting, it requires that the student be knowledgeable about their disability, understand how it impacts their learning and to speak up for themselves as they request college accommodations and other supports to achieve their goals.

In the college setting the student, under the ADA laws, is responsible for disclosing, requesting and getting the support they need. Students can develop or improve upon their self-advocacy skills at any time. The following tips will help the student in this process.

Understand Your Disability

Ask your parents, counselor, doctor or psychologist to explain your diagnosis or psychological report in terms that you can understand. Be aware of both your academic strengths and weaknesses, and which accommodations you need in place to succeed. Often parents will try to protect their child by not sharing everything within the psychological report, but this does not help the child overall. The more they know about their abilities and disabilities, the better armed they are to represent themselves in any setting. On the road to becoming self-sufficient, students need to take responsibility for their disability and learning struggles as they move forward with their career and life goals.

Actively Take Part in Your IEP and Transition Meetings

Throughout middle school and high school students with learning disabilities should take an active role in their IEP meetings. The school staff and parents should take time to answer the student's questions and encourage them to contribute while planning their academic and future goals. Along with academic reading, writing and math goals, the student should prepare social and personal goals to assist with overcoming stereotypes and maturing as a person. The sooner the student has a voice the more confident they will be in expressing their learning and personal needs and overcoming the labels. "It is especially important for the student to participate in creating their career transition plan. The current accommodations, support systems and familiar faces will not exist once the student graduates. Teaching them to understand their diagnosis, strengths and weaknesses, along with career goals will help prepare the student for meeting with the college disability staff when they request accommodations. Self-knowledge is the first step in developing self-advocacy skills. Learning about oneself involves the identification of learning styles, strengths, weakness, interests, and preferences. For students with mild disabilities, developing an awareness of the accommodations they need will help them ask for necessary accommodations on a job and in postsecondary education; students can also help identify alternative ways they can learn" (West, et al., 1999).

High school students will also need practice talking with teachers and expressing their academic needs, asking for help and sharing their weaknesses, so they can do this when they need to meet individually with professors to discuss implementing accommodations. The student will also become more confident when they need to request or change accommodations, or address issues as they arise. Actively participating in the IEP decision making and goal planning will help prepare the student for their future.

Know Your Rights

Professionals and parents should also introduce the student to the IDEA laws for grades 1–12 accommodations and rights, then the ADA laws for college accommodations and rights. Chapter 3 explained in detail the difference between these laws and how they affect the college student with disabilities. Under the ADA laws colleges must provide reasonable accommodations to all self-disclosed students. A solid understanding of the ADA laws will help the student when they request accommodations and utilize academic resources. The student may also need to meet with disability staff when their accommodations are not being met, or have been denied accommodations, and need to follow grievance procedures. The student is responsible for getting the support they need and discussing issues on their behalf. Speaking up for oneself becomes an important skill as they maneuver through life, facing challenges and obstacles.

Working Closely with Your Advisor

An advisor's job is to help students navigate their courses successfully while advocating for the student as they complete their career goals. The advisor is knowledgeable and resourceful, so it is in the student's best interest to build a working relationship early in order to benefit from their guidance. Your advisor should understand your strengths and weaknesses in order to guide you through your courses, and create a semester-by-semester schedule to help you graduate on time. Make sure that they understand your interests, talents and learning differences.

Students with diagnosed learning disabilities, medical disabilities or psychological disabilities should disclose early in order for the advisor to best serve their needs. Advisors will meet with you before and throughout the semester to determine how many credits you are capable of taking in a semester and guide you with course selection. The advisor will help you plan a schedule that fits your academic needs and will help each student stay on their appropriate curriculum track for graduation. If you have a diagnosed reading disability your advisor will help you plan out a schedule where you do not have more than one heavy reading/writing course per semester. For example, you should not plan to take history and English literature in the same semester. If you have a math disability you may want to take that difficult math course during the summer, where it is the only course you focus on, using tutors and meeting with your professor often.

The average college student takes 15–16 credits each semester. Honors students can take 17–20 credits. Students who have learning struggles will often take only 12 credits each semester. Choosing to take fewer academic courses has been a very successful option for students who struggle with the academic material because they can focus on fewer courses and achieve better grades. If you need to take fewer courses each semester in order to be successful, then you need to understand that you will also need to enroll in summer courses and/or plan to stay in college an extra semester or two. Make sure to discuss this thoroughly with your advisor and your parents. Many LD students take longer than the traditional four years to graduate, so don't let this give you anxiety; do what is best for your learning needs. Taking fewer courses each semester and being persistent with using accommodations, tutoring and other academic resources will result in you reaching your goals.

Your academic advisor will also guide you into a career path that is right for you. Often students will start out in a specific major as a freshman, such as education, and learn that they are better suited towards business, nonprofit or communication. The joy of being freshmen is that you can explore a couple of courses within different majors to help discover where your interests and talents lie. The majority of college students change their major twice before they find the right academic fit. Your advisor can help you select courses to explore while staying on a graduation path.

It is also important to *discuss a minor with your advisor*. Keep your options open to a minor in a second field which interests you. Often the minor you choose will complement your major, but it can also be in a field that is simply of interest. For example, you can be a mediated communications major, with a minor in music because you want to tap into your singing talent. Or you can be a graphic design major with a minor in marketing because you hope to run your own business one day. Speak with your advisor to explore all possible options for a minor.

Your advisor can also help you to understand what each major will require of you. For example, if you choose interior design you need to understand that you will have to put in numerous hours outside of class to work on your projects and with the CAD software, and a good night's sleep will become a thing of the past. Or a computer game designing degree requires strong math and computer skills as well as the ability to work as a team member on specific projects, each person contributing their part to the actual game design. Sharing your talents, hopes and dreams with your advisor will help you to explore all your academic options, understanding what works best with your schedule as well as your academic goals and timeline for graduation.

If you are completely unsure about the right major or career choice you can visit the career center on your college campus. They have trained staff members and many resources such as career tests and inventories to help you explore your interests and talents and find a career fit. Once a student finds the right career they become stronger, more focused students.

For example, I worked with a student who completed most of the required core courses and was majoring in Spanish. The student wanted to choose a second major to complement the Spanish degree, so took a few courses to explore majors but became even more frustrated. Eventually the student was advised to set up a meeting with career services, where they gave this student a battery of interest inventories and created a profile of her interests and strengths. This helped this student focus on a career path in strategic communications, which the student now also plans to pursue in grad school.

Advice to Students from a College Advisor

Advisors work with college students guiding them towards their educational goals. The advisor likes students to feel comfortable meeting with their advisor for assistance; they are often the go-to person on campus and can teach you how to advocate for yourself. They work to get to know each student during their session, catching up with them in order to connect as a person so they can help them navigate the university. Advisors have observed that many students stress out over trying to attain A's in their courses, as they did in high school, so they work to help them understand the different pace of college and accept that earning a C or a B in a course may be their best, and they have to move on, "One low grade does not define you; let's work on moving forward."

Along with assisting students with choosing courses each semester, your advisor will help with the following:

• exploring right fit majors, and has exploratory discussions with them when theirs is not a good fit;
• helping students discuss "politically correct" ways to handle difficult situations with professors or staff members;
• getting feedback from professors and creates a plan to move forward;
• referring students to support services;
• referring students for internships;
• making sure disability students use their approved accommodations;
• guiding students through an attainable course load each semester;
• introducing students to the Dean of a department they want to explore;
• intervening with parents as needed;
• advocating for students;
• encouraging and supporting students; and
• helping students navigate through university life.

Advice for Parents

Today's college students have parents who are actively involved with their academic progress and have more influence on their child than in the past. Often these parents contact their child's advisor for guidance and information on helping their child move forward. Unfortunately, the advisor cannot speak about the student without the student's consent. Colleges suggests that the student complete the FERPA waiver as a freshman, giving advisors and others permission to speak with parents on their child's behalf through graduation. Advisors have found that parents often call asking for an academic assessment, or assistance with changing a major. The advisor can evaluate the student's current progress within their major and help plan out a successful path to completion, but she is ultimately working with and for *the student* to meet their personal career goals.

Panicked parents often call near the end of the semester to see what can be done to salvage a bad semester. The advisor can help them address the immediate problem and look at resources to move forward. Sometimes the student is not able to turn around a bad grade and will need to accept the D or F and retake the course the following semester. There are also times when the advisor, the student and the parent have to have a difficult discussion as to whether college is the best place for the student. Sometimes mental health concerns are keeping the student from achieving success, and they need to withdraw for a semester or year and get healthy in order to return.

Deciding on a Major

Students either begin college with a very specific major in mind, or they are undecided. Your advisor can help you decide whether the specific major is a good fit for you, and if you are undecided they will help you explore majors within your talents and interests. Your advisor will encourage students to meet with career services and sign up to take some interests inventories and possibly the Myers Briggs or Strengths Test to get a good picture of their talents and interests. With these tools in hand the advisors can better assist students from the beginning, without having to backtrack after trying different courses in majors that prove to be too difficult or realizing the career path may be completely different than the student had originally anticipated.

Advisors also should take time with the student to look over required core courses and the curriculum for their major so that the student is aware of the upcoming courses and the academic demands they require. Together they plan out the entire four years, with a schedule that is attainable for the student.

An Advisor's Advice for Struggling Students

There are many different reasons why a student may have a bad semester. They range from difficult courses, poor effort on the students part, not utilizing support resources early enough, and not using accommodations, to family emergencies, personal situations, etc. The good news is that students can start over the next semester with resources in place to improve their grades and GPA. The following steps will help you improve academic outcomes the following semester:

- If a student has deficient grades in core courses they can retake the course with tutoring supports in place. The new grade will replace the old grade and improve a low GPA.
- Meet with professors often throughout the semester to get academic support and advice on how to improve as a student.
- Discuss your current study strategies and explore your learning style and better strategies to help you retain and recall information.
- Seek out academic services and set up tutoring and possible help with time management and organizational skills. Your advisor can get you connected with staff and services.

Advisors will reach out to students who have earned low grades after mid-term grades come out. The student should meet with their advisor and professor to see whether you need to drop a course or add support services to improve your grades. Some colleges have an "early alert" program in place, which allows professors to let academic services know that a student is struggling about a month before mid-term grades are reported. This information goes out to the advisors so they can contact the student and offer support.

Prepare for Your Advising Meeting

Students should come to their advising meetings prepared to discuss issues and concerns. If they are planning to discuss the next semester's courses, they should prepare a list of possible courses, times and professors ahead of time. Together the student and advisor can review these choices to tweak their schedule in order to keep them on track for graduation, and pair them with professors that complement the student's learning needs. The advisor's job is to guide them with course selection and course load while tailoring course schedules to their disability or learning needs.

Advisors believe in the "help me help you" approach by encouraging students to disclose any diagnosed disability, illness or other issues that may need to be addressed in order to help their students succeed academically. By sharing this information you allow the advisor to better understand your challenges and get advice to learn how to best advocate for yourself.

Four-Year Plan

Most students and their parents want to be on the four-year plan for graduation. Your advisor can help plan course selections and encourage you to stay on track by taking at least 16 hours per semester. Students need to keep a 2.0 GPA to stay off academic probation. Some majors such as education, engineering, pre-med, etc., will require higher GPAs in order to graduate with a specific degree.

If a student realizes they are failing a course they can withdraw by the withdrawal due date (usually mid-semester) and this will not affect their GPA. The student may need to attend summer classes in order to retake the course(s) and stay on track for graduation. Colleges usually offer two summer sessions with both online and on campus courses offered to students. Be aware that online courses usually require a 2.5 GPA to register. If a student is in a major, such as pre-med, and is failing an essential course (such as anatomy) they may want to change their major to a more appropriate and attainable science. Meeting with your advisor can help students with these decisions. It is advisable to email your advisor to set up a meeting, or show up at their office and get on their appointment schedule.

Advice for Graduating Seniors

All seniors need to set up an early fall appointment with their advisor and complete the "request for graduation" form. This form is processed by the registrar's office to make sure they will have met the graduation requirements for their major. Often students find that they have four to eight more hours to complete after spring semester and begin to panic. Fortunately most colleges will allow their seniors to walk the stage at graduation with eight hours or less left to take. The student will have to attend summer courses or online courses or partake in an internship in order to complete the requirements for graduation. Once these hours are completed the diploma will be mailed to the student. Students who have more than eight academic hours to complete will have to attend for another semester.

The college advisor is the student's advocate and cheerleader. Their knowledge and expertise will guide students through their course selection to attain the desired college degree. They assist students with finding appropriate resources and exploring possible majors. The advisor is a valuable resource, so it is imperative to meet with them at least a few times each semester and build a trusting relationship in order to benefit from their assistance.

16

Colleges Across the Country with Excellent Support Services for Students with Disabilities

Finding the right college fit for students with disabilities should include research on appropriate resources along with looking into the right major, size and location of the college. Students with learning disabilities must meet the general admission requirements for the college. The number of students with disabilities attending college has risen tremendously in the last 15 years, so colleges have adapted by providing extra support resources to help them successfully complete their course work. Fortunately, today's colleges have put many support services in place to meet the academic needs of students with disabilities to ensure retention and graduation. These support services include disability/accessibility services, accommodations, technology resources, tutoring services, a writing center, math centers, counseling, and assistive technology. Many colleges also offer fee-based programs with tailored resources that go beyond the regular disability resources. Many of these fee-based programs offer academic coaching, assistance with learning better study strategies, individualized tutoring, academic support labs with assistive technology and communication with professors and parents throughout the semester. These programs have successfully guided students through difficult core courses so they can move forward and excel in their major.

While visiting prospective colleges, make sure that your campus tour includes meeting with the disability/accessibility services director to explore possible accommodations. Ask about reading and writing software, and assess their testing rooms for computer availability during testing. Look into overall disability support along with benefits from extra fee-based programs to make sure all of your academic needs will be met in this educational environment.

A good fit college must take into consideration your type of disability and your individual accessibility needs along with a strong tutoring program, an appropriate and attainable degree program, suitable housing options, clubs, collegiate sports and activities to fit the student's interests. With a little extra effort and planning, along with a few possible career choices and knowledge of the right type of social environment, students can find a college with all the academic resources and accommodations they need.

Many successful students with learning disabilities have found that choosing a college with smaller class sizes and accessible professors, along with good resources made all the difference. Students who prefer a large college will need to make sure they can function in a class with 100–200 other students. Many other students on larger campuses will all require the resource services, so make sure to sign up with tutors and other services such as the writing center, math lab and counseling by the second week of classes to assure a time and space. *The K&W Guide to Colleges for Students with Learning Disabilities or ADHD* and the *College SOURCEBOOK for Students with Learning and Developmental Differences* are excellent resources to use when researching potential college fits.

Student Instructors

Some colleges will offer student instructors (SI) in many of their core course classrooms to assist the professor with helping students learn the course material. These student instructors can be very beneficial to students with disabilities as they navigate their college courses. The SI has previously taken the course and has been trained as a tutor. They will sit in on each class, assist the professor during classes, take notes and post them on an accessible website for students who receive peer notes. The SI's are also available to tutor students individually or in small groups, and will coordinate test and exam reviews with students. Advisors will often know which professors have student assistants and they can help students plan their schedules with this support service in place.

Athlete Study Hall

Colleges offer a study hall program with tutoring support and time management workshops for all collegiate athletes. If the athlete's GPA falls below a 2.5 they will usually be required to complete mandatory study hall hours (at least 10 per week) until their GPA rises above a 2.5. Professional and student tutors are available to assist the athlete with writing skills, math support, and most core courses. This is especially valuable to freshmen athletes who are still transitioning to the rigors of college academics.

I have researched colleges across the United States which provides excellent support services for students with disabilities. Fortunately, there are many colleges with excellent resources available in the United States. Each college has a disability support office, but their services vary from minimal (simply ensuring compliance with the ADA laws) to intensive, fee-based support programs. The minimal programs have a disability department to ensure equal access through accommodations and some available tutoring. Others offer accommodations, more intense tutoring, writing labs, and assistive technology. Support programs range from fee-based programs to no cost support programs. A majority of colleges have developed academic support services within a fee-based program in order to meet the academic needs of students with learning disabilities, ADHD, and Autism/Asperger's. Regardless of the disability, the student needs to take the initiative to want to learn new strategies for studying and learning. Students who participate in these programs and become actively involved in using new study strategies, self-advocacy skills, and tutoring services are often successful students

Comprehensive Fee-Based Programs

A number of colleges across the United States are offering a comprehensive fee-based academic support program. The support resources and fees will vary. Fees can range from $2,000 per semester to $8,000 per semester. These programs embrace a positive learning environment with many support tools in place to teach and empower students during their academic journey. Many parents are willing to invest the extra money for a year or two of extra academic support services in order to see their child succeed with their college goals, than to have their child fail out of college and have nothing to show for their initial financial investment in their college education. The student must take responsibility to attend classes, tutoring sessions and meeting with their academic coach in order for these programs to work. The academic support services will also vary, but the majority of these programs will have the following:

- individual weekly academic coaching;
- professional and peer tutoring;
- assistance with strengthening study skills;
- assistance with strengthening time management and organizational skills;

- regular communication with professors and parents;
- assistive technology; and
- guidance with course scheduling.

Colleges in the East

1. **Beacon College**—(Leesburg, FL): Exclusively for students with disabilities, offering bachelor degree programs, with a four-year graduation rate of 76 percent. Beacon offers six majors and 12 minors, with travel abroad options. They also offer an excellent center for student success, with a variety of support services:
  - academic and personal support services;
  - individualized academic mentoring with a personal academic plan;
  - professors trained to work with students with learning disabilities, ADHD, Autism and Asperger's and a variety of teaching modalities;
  - classes teaching study strategies/technology/time management; improve executive functioning skills, etc.;
  - a summer transitions program;
  - personal self-care skills;
  - math lab;
  - writing center; and
  - peer tutoring.

2. **Curry College**—(Milton, Massachusetts): Has a well-established academic support program as well as PAL (Program for Advancement Learning). Academic support offers professional tutors and student instructors to assist LD students, available technology, and writing and math labs. PAL is a fee-based academic support resource. The college also offers:
  - diagnostic center;
  - professional and peer tutoring (individual and small group);
  - required one PAL-credited course each semester to assist with writing skills, speaking, listening, reading comprehension, time management, etc.; and
  - events for counselors and educational specialist working with students with learning disabilities.

3. **Dean College**—(Franklin, Massachusetts): Claims "unparalleled learning support for students with disabilities." They offer comprehensive support services:
  - individual peer and professional tutoring;
  - writing center;

- math center;
- advanced assistive technology tools;
- academic coaching (fee-based); and
- personal and career counseling.

Arch Learning Community, a fee-based program, offers:
- individual and group academic coaching;
- smaller-size college courses;
- specialized academic advising; and
- weekly seminar.

4. **East Carolina University**—(Greenville, NC): Offers STEPP (Supporting Transition in Education through Planning and Partnership) Program, *no additional fees*. This is a large state college located on the coast of North Carolina. They have an excellent disability support program free to all students, with tutoring and technology services. They also offer the STEPP program to a limited number of students each year.

STEPP is a comprehensive support program that serves students with a documented learning disability. It
- accepts ten new students per academic year;
- has an application deadline of May15;
- starts each fall;
- provides academic support;
- provides social and life skills support; and
- requires students take a minimal course lead of 12 hours.

5. **Fairleigh Dickinson University**—(Teaneck, NJ and Madison, NJ): Offers comprehensive professional support at *no cost* to student and study skills course and technology training.
- Regional Center for College Students with Learning Disabilities offers:
  - professional support at *no cost* to students with language based learning disabilities at Metropolitan and Florham campuses;
  - offer academic support and counseling weekly;
  - requires students take a three-credit technology course; and
  - allows priority registration and requires a study skills course.
- COMPASS Program—fee-based—offered to Autism/Asperger students. It
  - accepts six new students each year;
  - offers a summer transition program;
  - has a comprehensive academic and social support program;
  - requires students be able to live in a semi-independent living situation; and

    ◦ requires students to receive academic support, counseling and group therapy.

  6. **Gallaudet University**—(Washington, D.C.): A small private college. "Gallaudet provides exemplary services to deaf and hearing loss students." It

- offers translators, hearing devices/software, tutoring;
- has professors educated in teaching deaf students;
- assistive technology;
- offers tailored comprehensive support services
- leads in technology for academic progress;
- offers hearing and communication technology;
- offers accessible bilingual education to international students;
- allows attending students to participate in a consortium of 13 colleges in the Metropolitan D.C. area;
- offers a wide variety of majors and minors; and
- offers SL CONNECT, an online sign language education resource.

  7. **Hofstra University** (Long Island, NY): A large private college located 25 miles from New York City with small class sizes. Important features include

- a student-faculty ratio of 14:1;
- accessible professors renowned in their field;
- SSD (Services for Students with Disabilities) for all documented students which includes
  - ◦ peer tutors—small group;
  - ◦ math center; and
  - ◦ writing center
- PALS, a comprehensive fee-based program (long-term) students must apply and interview for, offering:
  - ◦ academic coaching;
  - ◦ individual tutoring;
  - ◦ writing center/math center;
  - ◦ learning specialists who work with student from freshman year until graduation; and
- Academic Coaching Program, fee-based, short-term assistance, which is
  - ◦ to all students;
  - ◦ offers individual tutoring;
  - ◦ teaches study strategies;
  - ◦ enrolls per semester as needed; and
  - ◦ has a math center/writing center.

  8. **Landmark College** (Putney, Vermont): Small, private two-year college for students with learning disabilities and ADHD/ADD. "Since 1985 Landmark has

been known for its innovative educational model to teach students with dyslexia," and they have branched off into reaching students with other learning disabilities, including ASD and ADD/ADHD, by giving them the power, skills and strategies they need to learn. Their programs prepare students to transition to four-year colleges. Professors are trained to successfully teach to a variety of disabilities, and this is where students "learn how to learn"! Highlights include:

- excellent LD/ADD/Autism resources;
- excellent technology resources available to all students;
- individual and group tutoring;
- instruction in study skills;
- academic coaches who teach study strategies, learning styles, etc.;
- professional tutors;
- professors educated to teach to disabilities in various modalities;
- professors very accessible to tutor students;
- professors use Kurzweil 3000, Dragon and other assistive technology with students;
- professors constantly taught cutting edge learning strategies;
- students learn self-advocacy skills;
- counseling services available to all students;
- universal design; and
- small class sizes.

Drake Center offers academic support services, including:

- professors and staff available for individual support with reading, writing, math and study strategies (30- or 60-minute sessions);
- instruction in self-direction and independence;
- improve and refine academic and study skills;
- professors and staff available for drop in visits and appointments; and
- coaches who assist with improving executive functioning skills.

9. **Lynn University**—(Boca Raton, FL): Small, private college with excellent resources for students with disabilities. Also known as one of the top international colleges, with students from 90 countries.

Lynn's Institute for Achievement and Learning (IAL) offers:

- programs for LD/ADD/Autism, etc.;
- academic coaching;
- cutting edge assistive technology;
- individual and group content tutoring;
- learning labs with technology resources;
- math and writing labs with assistive technology; and
- iPads with appropriate assistive technology for disabilities.

Campus-wide resources include:

- professors are educated in teaching to students with different learning modalities;
- small student-teacher ratio at 15:1;
- iPad campus initiative for students and professors;
- iPad apps for reading/writing/ recording/time management of assignments; and
- learning labs with technology.

10. **Louisburg College** (Louisburg, NC): A 2-year college offering an associate's degree in a variety of majors, with rolling admissions. Academic support services

- are offered free to all students;
- include a writing center;
- include a math lab;
- offers science study sessions;
- include a reading lab;
- offers peer tutoring; and
- offers math focus groups.

The Learning Partners Program (fee-based) is

- open to students with learning disabilities/ADHD;
- takes a comprehensive approach;
- requires students to meet with a learning specialist times a week;
- offers independent coaching and instruction with learning strategies;
- and makes learning labs available to students.

11. **Mitchell College** (New London, CT): Small private college. Highlights include:

- 6:1 student teacher ratio;
- accessible technology instruction; and
- accessible professors.

Bensten Learning Center (BLC): Comprehensive, fee-based academic support program, offering

- four levels of support, each level addressing different student needs;
- learning specialists;
- individualized support plans;
- instruction in learning strategies;
- content strategy workshops;
- technology resources available;
- interpersonal skills;
- and encouragement in self-advocacy.

Colleges in the Midwest

1. **Marshall University**—(Huntington, WV): A large public university with a very strong disability support program for students who require accommodations, an academic support program and a program to assist students on the Autism spectrum.
   - H.E.L.P. program—an extra support service for students with a specific learning disability or ADHD/ADD. This is a fee-based comprehensive program offering the following:
     - study skills development;
     - time management and organizational skills;
     - individual academic tutoring;
     - test prep coaching; and
     - solid relationships between professor and student.
   - College Program for Students with Autism Spectrum Disorder—a fee-based program, applications for which are due by February 1. It offers
     - Person-centered positive behavior support approach;
     - social and communication skills;
     - academic skills;
     - personal living skills;
     - time management and organizational skills; and
     - summer transition program.

2. **Muskingum College** (Muskingum, OH): Small, private college with excellent disability support for students who require accommodations. They also have a fee-based program for students with dyslexia and other learning disabilities. Highlights include:
   - PLUS Program, a comprehensive fee-based program;
   - Student enrollment for entire four years of college;
   - professional tutors;
   - academic coaching; and
   - study skills.

3. **Texas Tech**—(Lubbock, TX): Large campus, over 35,000 students! They have a strong, well established disability support program for all students who request accommodation, excellent tutoring services. They also offer a fee-based program, TECHniques, which features
   - academic coaches;
   - individual tutoring;
   - assistive technology; and
   - limited instruction in study skills.

4. **University of Denver**—(Denver, CO): Offers strong disability support

services, plus the LEP support services program, a comprehensive, fee-based academic support program. Disability services assist students with accommodations, technology, and tutoring. Students may receive

- academic coaching weekly (student chooses which support services they want help with);
- instruction on organization and time management;
- learning strategies;
- individual tutoring;
- assistance with using other university resources;
- and faculty trained to support students with different learning styles (universal design).

5. **University of the Ozarks** (Clarksville, AR): Offer a strong disability support program plus a comprehensive fee-based program which includes

- assistive technology and
- peer tutoring.

The Jones Learning Center is a comprehensive fee-based program offering

- individualized personal instruction;
- professional tutors;
- academic coaching;
- instruction in study skills and exploration of learning styles;
- instruction in time management and organizational skills;
- instruction in life skills;
- accessible technology;
- a 4:1 student to staff ratio;
- and no SAT or ACT scores required for acceptance.

6. **University of Arkansas**—(Fayetteville, AR): Offers comprehensive support services, including

- free tutoring;
- math and writing centers;
- study skills workshops ;
- testing and anxiety workshops;
- time management workshops; and
- a comprehensive fee-based support program for academic and social skills for students with Autism.

Colleges in the West

1. **Mary Mount California University**—(Palos Verde, CA): A small, private Catholic University with a liberal arts program. They offer small class

sizes and a good disabilities program with specialized programs outside of disability services to meet the academic needs of their students.

The Learning Center is free and open to all students and offers

- a certain number of tutoring sessions per week, with both peer tutors and faculty tutoring in business, English, 2eading, math and study skills (two times per week per subject).

The MAAP (Mariner Academic Assistance Program) is a fee-based program open to all students who want extra academic support. It offers

- peer tutoring;
- standing appointments with faculty;
- tutoring in business, English, reading, math and study skills;
- instruction in academic skills and promotes self-advocacy.

MAST (Mariner Academic Strategies and Techniques Program) is fee-based program originally designed for students with learning disabilities, but is now open to all students who need extra academic support services. It offers

- individualized tutoring with peers and professors;
- intensive individualized support with standing appointments;
- instruction in academic skills with an emphasis on sound study habits;
- technology instruction;
- focus on metacognitive learning styles; and
- instruction in self-advocacy skills.

2. **University of Arizona** (Tucson, AZ)—SALT Center (Strategic Alternative Learning Techniques), a fee-based comprehensive support program for students who learn differently and serves over 5550 students. This is a nationally-recognized model that has successfully assisted students with completing degree programs since the 1980s. The SALT program assists a range of students with learning disabilities and attention disorders. Students must apply by June 30. It offers

- individual tutoring by professional tutors (many are retired professors);
- requires students to meet with a coach and create individualized learning plans;
- exploration of learning styles and teaches study strategies for all types of learners;
- offers writing labs;
- offers writing, math and science seminars;
- offers psychological services;
- offers assistive technologies;
- offers leadership and social programs.

3. **University of Oregon**—(Eugene Oregon): Offers a strong disability support program (Accessible Education Program) which includes
- individual peer and professional tutoring;
- assistive technology;
- accommodations (universal design);
- tutoring (peer and professional); and
- support with academic planning.

4. **University of Southern California**—(Los Angeles, CA): Offers a strong disability support program with no extra fees. It provides
- individual support structure for students with diagnosed learning disabilities with an LD specialist or grad assistant;
- tutoring;
- assistive technology; and
- assists students with learning good study skills.

The following colleges offer excellent disability support services, tutoring, and accessible professors and have successfully helped students with disabilities succeed:

Albright College, Reading, PA
American University, Washington, D.C.
Baylor University, Waco, TX
Boston University, Boston
Brown University, Providence, RI
High Point University, High Point, NC
Lewis and Clark College, Portland, OR
Lone Star College, Montgomery–Conroe, TX
Loras College, Dubuque, IA
Mount St. Mary's, Allentown, PA
Mount St. Mary's, Los Angeles CA
Northeastern University, Boston
Oberlin College, Oberlin, OH
Pacific Lutheran University, Tacoma, WA
Pacific University, Forest Grove, OR
St. Thomas Aquinas College, Sparkill, NY
Texas Lutheran, Sequin, TX
University of Arkansas, Fayetteville
University of Indianapolis
University of Kansas
University of North Carolina, Chapel Hill,
University of Tennessee, Chattanooga

University of Vermont, Burlington
West Virginia Wesleyan, Buckhannon, WV

The following colleges offer special support services exclusively for students with Autism and Asperger's:

Autism Collaborative Center at Eastern Michigan University
Boston University Supported Education Services
Drexel University Autism Support Program
Marshall University Autism Training Center
Mercyhurst College AIM Program
Rutgers Developmental Disabilities Center
St. Joseph's University Kinney Center for Autism Education and Support (not as comprehensive as most)
University of Alabama College Transition and Support Program
University of Connecticut SEAD Program

Technology Resources for Students with Disabilities
Student Technology—Miranda

Technology has been used to bridge the learning gap for many years. Advancements in technology help deaf students "hear," enlarge fonts for visually impaired students, read texts aloud for the blind; speech to text technology even helps students write. Each of these valuable resources assists students on the road to academic success. We are fortunate to live in a world where technology advances daily, empowering everyday individuals with tools and resources at their fingertips, allowing communication and knowledge to soar to new heights. Apple for Education, in particular, has created numerous apps available to every student for use in the academic arena.

Technology is used to assist students with accessing classroom lectures, reading textbooks, writing papers, organizing information, creating study cards and solving mathematical equations, giving students with disabilities complete accessibility in any given learning situation by leveling the playing field. Colleges have been investing in assistive technology resources for their students and training their staff to teach students how to enhance their learning skills, using technology resources from reading and writing software to SMART Pens to organizational and study apps.

Miranda had been diagnosed with dyslexia, dysgraphia and short-term memory and ADD disabilities in grade school. During high school she learned to use an Apple reading and writing software program to help her with her reading writing and test taking. Miranda knew college would require large amounts of reading and writing, so she made an appointment to meet with disability services in July, prior to her freshman year, to discuss technology options. Along with Offering Kurzweil reading software, and Dragon Naturally speaking for assistance with writing they offered the Echo SMART Pen, which would record lectures as she took class notes and send these notes to her computer. Miranda chose to stick with her Apple reading software and quickly learned how to use the other technology resources. She was a quick learner and enjoyed the new technology so much that she was soon teaching other students how to use the Echo SMART Pen. Disability services also taught her how to use the speech-to-text software called Dragon Naturally Speaking. After the initial training in the software she was able to easily prepare her college papers. Miranda was grateful that she took the time to meet with disability services early enough to learn how to use the technology before she became overwhelmed with her coursework.

Test taking accommodations for Miranda allowed her to use both the reading and writing software for test taking and essay writing. disability services would load her tests onto their computer and she would have the tests read aloud using the Kurzweil text to speech program, and would write out her short answer and essay answer using the Dragon software.

The Echo Smart Pen would record class lectures and send these notes directly to her laptop. Miranda was asked to sign a waiver to act responsibly with the recorded class lectures. She understood the importance of using technology responsibly and followed through accordingly.

Miranda majored in communications, interactive media and design. Each year she became very proficient with many different types of technology; both within her degree of study as well as for academic resources. She became very comfortable teaching other students with disabilities how to access technology and was often asked to assist with mentoring incoming freshmen each year. She continues to use and teach others about technology resources in her current career.

APPLE Apps for Education

The Apple research teams have worked to create many educational apps to facilitate an accessible learning environment for all students. The Mac comes loaded with accessible educational apps, plus many creative apps for photos, music and movies, which can help assist college students with PowerPoints, Prezi's and other presentations. Their calendar app sends reminders and alerts for appointments and assignments, which is very useful for college students who struggle with organization and time management. This app is also very helpful for students with ADHD, Autism and Asperger's, as they often need reminders to get to class, meet with study groups or professors and start working on long-term research papers and projects well in advance of due dates.

The text-to-speech app helps students with dyslexia read texts by engaging hearing and seeing senses, and will also highlight and create notes while they are reading course textbooks. Many college textbooks are now available as ebooks and/or iBooks, and can be downloaded onto computers, or accessed from a remote site. Many of these texts are filled with interactive technology, which assists all types of learners.

Students with hearing loss or deafness can use FaceTime apps or closed captioning on their phones, computers and iPads for easy communication with friends, family and professors. Apple states: "Closed captions offer all kinds of visual learners the ability to see captions in video to help with comprehension. Captions appear onscreen in easy-to-read white type on a black background. OS X supports closed captioning—as well as open captions and subtitles—across a wealth of educational materials, from podcasts in iTunes U courses to embedded videos in iBooks textbooks" (Apple, 2015).

Visually impaired students can easily access the Zoom App, which enlarges fonts, photos, maps, and graphs for visual assistance. "Zoom is a built-in magnifier that enlarges anything on the screen up to 20 times. Students can use it full screen or picture-in-picture, which allows them to see the zoomed area in a separate window while keeping the rest of the screen at its native size. So students can better read an essay, view a diagram, or focus in on maps. Activate it in a variety of ways, from a keyboard command to a trackpad gesture. And Zoom works with Voice Over, so students can better see—and hear—what's happening on their screen" (Apple, 2015). Braille apps with voice over are also available, which are compatible with blue tooth and USB (Apple, 2015).

The diction app helps students easily create papers, or just respond to emails. "Dictation lets students talk where they would type. They can reply to an email, search the web, or write a report using just their voice. Students can activate Dictation when their cursor is in any text field, then speak what they want to write. Dictation converts words into text with minimal physical touch" (Apple, 2015).

Enhance your academics and learn to work smarter by researching which assistive technology devices or apps work best for your disability and learning needs. Meet with the college Disability Director or technology specialist to explore the many tech resources available.

Types of assistive technology available may include:

Reading Software:
- Kurzweil 3000: Text-to-speech software with highlighting and note taking capabilities. Assists with reading, comprehension and study skills. https://www.kurzweiledu.com/default.html

- **Natural Reader:** Text-to-speech software:- http://www.naturalreaders. com/index.htm
- **Kindle or NOOK Readers:** For accessing electronic texts. Kindle Readers: Textbooks can be purchased and downloaded through the Kindle. Read aloud programs and zoom (for larger print) are programmed into the Kindle. Textbooks can be cheaper and students do not have to carry around large textbooks. Very convenient and easy to transport.

Note-Taking and Writing Technology:
- **ECHO Smart Pen / Live Scribe Pen:** Records lectures, send notes to your computer ... easy to return to specific parts of the lecture. Need to purchase Pen and notebooks.
  http://www.enablemart.com/Livescribe-Pulse-Smartpen?gclid= CMqex43s-K4CFc-a7QodyzUt0Q
- **G-Chat:** For use with peer note taking in real time. Send and receive instant messages. The note taker either sis tint eh classroom or is remote and takes class notes that instantly transfer to the student's computer. They can read and listen to the lecture. This is often used for students with hearing loss and visual disabilities.
- **Dragon NaturallySpeaking:** Speech to text software for computers. http://shop.nuance.com/store/nuanceus/html/pbpage.dragon-landing-2012?resid=T2o9LAoBAlcAACE8QYAAAAA2&rests=1339522828366

Software for Visual Disabilities:
- **JAWS (Job Access with Speech):** Screen reading software for blind and visually impaired. Screen reader with speech and braille output. Works with braille keyboards. Compatible with MAGic Screen Magnification Software; Openbook Scanning and Reading Program. DAISY built-in program. Uses "hot keys" and other standard commands instead of a mouse. It comes with many functions and is compatible with Microsoft.
  http://www.freedomscientific.com/Products/Blindness/JAWS
- **Braille:** Braille translation software translates electronic documents into braille code. From these files, a refreshable **braille** display can present tactile **braille** or a Braille embosser can produce a hard-copy on special paper. Commonly used products include Duxbury Braille Translator, MegaDots, and Braille2000 (Do IT, Washington University, 2015).
  http://www.brailleblaster.org/
  http://www.duxburysystems.com/
  Braille embossers: http://www.indexbraille.com/en-us/support

• **Office, Excel, MAGic Screen Magnification** and others. JAWS16 has MATHML support for science and math courses.

• **Kurzweil 1000:** Text-to-speech software for the blind and visually impaired. The software reads printed and electronic text with natural sounding voices. It also converts files to braille. Reads text, magazines, books, eBooks, and sends to other portable devices. It offers calendars and study supports for note taking, editing and outlining texts.

   https://www.kurzweiledu.com/products/kurzweil-1000-v12-windows-features.html

• **Zoom Text:** Screen magnifying software with text reader for low vision students.

   http://www.zoomtext.software.informer.com/9.1/

Apple Apps to Assist Students with Organization:

• Noteability: This app allows you to write, draw and record notes. Very versatile, students can highlight, text edit and create drawings within their notes.

   https://itunes.apple.com/us/app/notability/id360593530?mt=8

• Study Blue: Students will learn to study smarter as they create study tools, such as flashcards, review guides, and practice quizzes. Study anytime, anywhere, as this app easily transfers from computer to phone to tablet.

   http:www.studyblue.com

• iStudiez Pro: This app helps students create an electronic calendar and timeline for tracking progress of assignments and setting up schedule reminders.

http://istudentpro.com/

• Keynote: Helps students create PowerPoints and Prezi presentations.

• iBooks: Electronic textbooks that have podcasts and video embedded into the text.

iPad Apps (Apple for Education):

• **APPS for Dragon Speech:** Speech-to-text software

• **Noteability:** Note taking app … sends notes to your computer

• **Audio Notes:** Read-aloud app … this app records lectures.

   http://itunes.apple.com/us/app/audionote-notepad-voice-recorder/id369820957?mt=8

• **Complete Class Organizer:** One app to organize all your courses/notes, manage homework and exam dates, etc.

Other Free Apps:
- Apps to assist with APA/MLA/Chicago research citation formats
- Calculator HD Pro
- Google Docs
- Inspirational Maps
- Khan Academy
- Podcast

Glossary

ADA laws (American with Disability Act)—a civil rights law written for adults prohibiting discrimination on the basis of disability in employment, public services and accommodations.

ADHD—Attention Deficit with Hyperactivity Disorder/ADD Attention Deficit Disorder.

auxiliary aids—may include services and devices such as qualified interpreters on-site or through video remote interpreting (VRI) services; note takers; real-time computer-aided transcription services; written materials; exchange of written notes; telephone handset amplifiers; assistive listening devices; real time captioning; (TTY) text telephoning; video phones; Braille materials; screen reader software; optical readers; large print materials; screen reader software; and magnification software.

CLEP—college level exam programs for knowledge and experience learned outside of college, that give college credit for military training and experience, especially in the areas of medical, engineering, leadership, culinary skills, etc. Funded by the United States government through the Defense Activity for Non Traditional Education Support (DANTES).

dyslexia—"a specific learning disability that is neurobiological in origin. It is characterized by difficulties with accurate and/or fluent word recognition and by poor spelling and decoding abilities. These difficulties typically result from a deficit in the phonological component of language that is often unexpected in relation to other cognitive abilities and the provision of effective classroom instruction. Secondary consequences may include problems in reading comprehension and reduced reading experience that can impede growth of vocabulary and background knowledge" (International Dyslexic Association).

dysgraphia—a condition that causes trouble with written expression, impairment with written expression.

dyscalculia—severe difficulty in making arithmetic calculations, as a result of a brain disorder.

FAFSA—Free Application for Federal Student Aid.

FERPA—Family Education Right and Privacy Act. A Federal law that protects the privacy of educational records for students 18 years and older. (FERPA) (20 U.S.C. § 1232g; 34 CFR Part 99).

504 Plan—an educational plan with specific modifications and accommodations that gives students with disabilities individualized help to perform at the same level as their peers, throughout grades K–12. The disability must interfere with the child's ability to learn in a general education classroom. This plan is reviewed and updated each year to promote the student's academic success. This is not a standard plan, as the IEP, and only has the parent, special education teacher and principal involved. This plan follows Section 504 from the Rehabilitation Act.

hidden disability—disabilities that are not visible, such as psychiatric disabilities, Traumatic brain injuries, post traumatic brain injury, ADHD, learning disabilities, some medical disabilities, etc.

IDEA Law (Individuals with Disabilities Education Act)—a federal law that protects the rights of children with disabilities. The law requires schools to serve the educational needs of eligible students with disabilities. The students need to be evaluated for services and qualify under one of 13 kinds of disabilities. Students are then served within the school system under an IEP or 504 plans.

IEP (individual education plan)—a legal document that addresses a child's specific educational goals with accommodations and modifications, under the IDEA (Individuals with Disabilities ACT). The child must have a specific learning disability that affects their educational performance and/or ability to learn. Public schools are required to create an IEP for every child receiving special education services from ages 3–22. The child is assessed with a psychological evaluation. Once there is a documented disability the team, consisting of a special education teacher, general education teacher, school psychologist, and district representative all meet to finalize an educational plan providing individual educational and related services, written by the special education teacher. The IEP is updated each year, with a psychological revaluation every three years. Services are provided at no cost to the parent.

ITP (individual transition plan)—U.S. military transition plan for returning to civilian life and planning for a new career.

JAWS—screen reader software for the blind and visually disabled. Uses text to speech and output text to Braille and narration. JAWS is compatible with MAGic screen magnification, Word, and Excel.

Post-9/11 GI Bill—provides education benefits for individuals who served on active duty after September 10, 2001. Eligible service members can receive tuition assistance for college degree programs, vocational and technical training, apprenticeship training, flight training, licensing and certification reimbursement, correspondence training.

Predominantly Inattentive ADD—similar to ADD, but these students do not have much hyperactive/impulsivity symptoms.

psychological assessment or evaluation—another name is psycho-educational evaluation. This evaluation is given by a licensed psychologist to evaluate a student's intellectual and academic functioning to determine a learning disability or attention deficit disorder. The testing consists of aptitude and achievement testing. Aptitude testing for college students is the WAIS, Wechsler Adult Intelligence Scale, which measures verbal comprehension, perceptual reasoning, working memory and processing speed. The achievement test is usually the Woodcock Johnson III, which tests reading, writing and math abilities. The results of these tests will show discrepancies between intelligence and achievement indicating a specific learning disability. The completed written evaluation explains the tests administered along with the testing results, followed by a discussion of any learning issues and a formal diagnosis, along with recommendations for academic accommodations and strategies to help the student.

PTSD (post traumatic stress disorder)—"a mental health disorder that is triggered by a traumatic event. The individual can suffer symptoms such as flashbacks, nightmares, severe anxiety, as well as uncontrollable thoughts about the event" (Mayo Clinic).

self-advocacy—the action of representing oneself or one's views or interests. Students with disabilities on the college level learn to advocate for their academic accommodation and other needs by interacting with the disability staff and professors and other staff as needed.

self-efficacy—one's belief in their ability to succeed by executing behaviors to reach their goals. "I can."

TBI (traumatic brain injury)—injuries to the brain can range from mild to severe. Causes of TBI can be from car accidents, explosions, falls, penetration of the skull, metabolic disorders, lack of oxygen, tumors, infections, stroke, concussion, etc. The injury to the brain can cause memory problems, attention deficit, and impairment of cognitive functions, mood swings and frustration.

transition plan—high school students who are under an IEP or 504 plan work with their professional team to prepare a transition plan for career or a college degree.

universal design—involves accessible design that addresses the needs of people with disabilities; designing for human diversity to create things that will be functional and user friendly for all people. Universal design is always evolving and improving as architects, engineers and environmental design professionals work together to create space, products information systems, etc., to make accessibility safer and convenient for everyone,

VA (Veteran's Association)—provides a variety of services and benefit to assist service members, veterans, their dependents and survivors.

Yellow Ribbon Program—U.S. military program where college institutions across the country choose to participate in supporting veterans or their family members who are using the Post–9/11 GI Bill for college expenses. The institutions volunteer to enter a Yellow Ribbon agreement with the VA and choose the amount of tuition and fees that will be contributed.

Bibliography

Published Sources

ACT, Inc. (2015). ACT test accommodations for examinees with disabilities [chart]. Retrieved from http://www.act.org/aap/pdf/ACT-TestAccommodationsChart.pdf.

Allegheny College Disability Services. (2015). Students who are blind or have a visual impairment. Retrieved from http://sites.allegheny.edu/disabilityservices/students-who-are-blind-or-have-a-visual-impairment/.

American Foundation for the Blind. (2015). What is low vision? *Vision Aware*. Retrieved from http://www.visionaware.org/info/your-eye-condition/eye-health/low-vision/low-vision-terms-and-descriptions/1235#AFunctionalDefintion_of_LowVision.

American Psychiatric Association. (1994). Diagnostic and statistical manual of mental disorders: DSM-IV. Washington, D.C.: American Psychiatric Association.

American Psychological Association. (2015). DART Toolkit II: Legal issues—ADA basics. Retrieved April 16, 2015, from http://www.apa.org/pi/disability/dart/legal/ada-basics.aspx.

Americans with Disabilities Act of 1990, Pub. L. No. 101–336, 104 Stat. 328 (1990).

Antshel, K.M., and Barkley, R. (2008). Psychosocial interventions in attention deficit hyperactivity disorder. *Child Adolescent Psychiatric Clinics of North America 17*(2): 421–437. doi: 10.1016/j.chc.2007.11.005.

Antshel, K.M., Hargrove, T.M., Simonescu, M., Kaul, P., and Hendricks, K. (2011). Advances in understanding and treating ADHD. *BMC Medicine*. Retrieved from http:www.biomedcentral.com.

Buddin, R., and Kupur, K. (2002). *Tuition assistance usage and first-term military retention*. Santa Monica: National Defense Research Institute. Retrieved from http://www.rand.org/content/dam/ rand/pubs/monograph_reports/2005/MR1295.pdf.

College Board. (2015). CLEP for military Retrieved from https://clep.collegeboard.org/military.

DO IT. (2015). Academic accommodations for students with learning disabilities. University of Washington. Retrieved from http://www.washington.edu/doit/academic-accommodations-students-learning-disabilities.

DuPaul, G.J., Weyandt, L.L., O'Dell, S.M., and Varejao M. (2009). College students with ADHD: Current status and future directions. *Journal of Attention Disorders 13* (3): 234–250. doi: 10.1177/1087054709340650.

Hadley, W.M. (2007). The necessity of academic accommodations for first year college students with learning disabilities. *Journal of College Admissions 195*: 9–13.

International Dyslexia Association. (2015). Definition of dyslexia. Retrieved from: http://eida.org/definition-of-dyslexia/?gclid=CLiuxLPht8YCFUY8gQod9BUF6w.

Iowa Department for the Blind. (2015). Legal definition of blindness. Retrieved from http://www.idbonline.org/legal-definition-blindness.

Junger, S. (June 2015). How PTSD became a problem far beyond the battlefield. *Vanity Fair*: 7–8.

Lightner, K.L., Kipps-Vaughan, D., Schulte, T., and Trice, A.D. (2011). Reasons university students with disabilities wait to seek disability services. *Journal of Postsecondary Education and Disability 25*(2): 145–159.

Retrieved from http://files.eric.ed.gov/full text/EJ994283.pdf.

McKeon, B., Alpern, C.S., and Zager, D. (2013). Promoting academic engagement for college students with autism spectrum disorder. *Journal of Postsecondary Education and Disability 26*(4): 353–366. Retrieved from http://files.eric.ed.gov/fulltext/EJ1026894.pdf.

Military.com Education. (2015). The Yellow Ribbon Program explained. Retrieved from http://www.military.com/education/gi-bill/the-yellow-ribbon-program-explained.html.

Mukamal, R. (2015). Tablet and smartphone apps offer bright spots for low vision. *Eyesmart.* Retrieved from http://www.geteyesmart.org/eyesmart/living/apps-offer-bright-spots-for-low-vision.cfm.

National Alliance of Mental Illness (NAMI). (2015). Managing a mental health condition in college. Retrieved from https://www2.nami.org/Template.cfm?Section=Check_Out_Resources&Template=/ContentManagement/HTMLDisplay.cfm&ContentID=146793&MicrositeID=0.

National Center for Educational Statistics. (2011). Students with disabilities at degree-granting postsecondary institutions. U.S. Department of Education, Institute of Educational Sciences. Retrieved April 20, 2015, from https://nces.ed.gov/pubsearch/pubsinfo.asp?pubid=2011018.

Pope, L. (2006). *Colleges that changed lives.* New York: Penguin.

The Princeton Review. (2015). Learning disabilities and the SAT/ACT. Retrieved from http://www.princetonreview.com/college-advice/learning-disabilities-sat-act.

Quinn, P.O. (April 1998). Top ten things I wish students with ADHD knew about their medications. *The Official Newsletter of the Association on Higher Education & Disability 22*(2).

Quinn, P.O. (2001). *ADD and the college student: A guide for high school and college students with attention deficit disorder.* Washington, D.C.: Magination Press.

Sarkis, S.M. (2008). *Making the grade with ADD: A student's guide to succeeding in college with Attention Deficit Disorder.* Oakland: New Harbinger Publications.

Sargent, W.M. Jr. (2009). Helping veterans transition into academic life through the creation of a university veteran support group: So we can better serve those who serve us. University of West Georgia (pp. 7, 8, 11). Retrieved from Eric database.

Sauma, A., Rickerman, N., and Burgstahler, S. (2012). Academic accommodations for students with psychiatric disabilities. University of Washington, Do-IT. Retrieved from http://www.washington.edu/doit/academic-accommodations-students-psychiatric-disabilities.

Tiedemann, C. W. (2012). *College success for students with physical disabilities.* Waco: Prufrock Press.

U.S. Department of Veteran Affairs. (2015) Post 9/11 G.I. Bill payment rates for 2014 academic year. Tuition and fee payments for higher learning. Retrieved from http://www.benefits.va.gov/GIBILL/resources/benefits_resources/rates/ch33/ch33rates080114.asp.

U.S. Autism and Asperger Association. (2013). About us college autism project (uscap). Retrieved from http://www.usautism.org/uscap/index.htm.

U.S. Department of Education. (2015). Transition of students with disabilities to postsecondary education: A guide for high school educators. Retrieved from http://www2.ed.gov/about/offices/list/ocr/transitionguide.html.

U.S. Department of Veterans Affairs. (2015). Education and Training. Retrieved from http://www.benefits.va.gov/gibill/school_resources.asp.

U.S. Department of Veterans Affairs. (2015). Yellow Ribbon Program. Retrieved from http://www.benefits.va.gov/gibill/school_resources.asp.

Watson, D., Schroedel, J., Kolnitz, M., DeCaro, J., and Kain, D. (2007). *Hard of hearing students in post secondary settings.* Knoxville: University of Tennessee Center on Deafness.

West, L., Colby, S., Boyer-Stephens, B., and Jones, B., et.al. (1999). Transition and self-advocacy. LD online. Retrieved from http://www.ldonline.org/article/7757.

Wolf, L.E., Brown, J.T., and Bork, G.R.K. (2009). *Students with Asperger syndrome: A guide for college personnel.* Shawnee Mission, KS: Autism Asperger Publishing (APC) Company.

WordPress. (2016). Quotedly [blog]. Retrieved from https://quotedly.wordpress.com/2012/

06/12/develop-success-from-failures-discouragement-and-failure-are-two-of-the-surest-stepping-stones-to-success-dale-carnegie-2/.

Resources

ACT test accommodations chart: www.act.org/aap/pdf/ACT-TestAccommodations Chart.pdf.

ADA LAWS—Americans with Disabilities Act: http://www.2.ed.gov/about/offices/list/ocr/transition.htm.

Association of Higher Education and Disabilities (AHEAD): https://www.ahead.org/.

College Board's "College Matchmaker": http://collegesearch.collegeboard.com/search/index.jsp.

DART Toolkit II: Legal Issues. Major requirements under the ADA: http://www.apa.org/pi/disability/dart/legal/ada-basics.aspx.

Differences between the IEP and 504 plans: https://www.understood.org/en/school-learning/special-services/504-plan/the-difference-between-ieps-and-504-plans.

Disability friendly colleges for students with physical disabilities: http://www.disabilityfriendlycolleges.com.

DO IT Program—University of Washington: http://www.washington.edu/doit.

Example of College Disability Documentation Guidelines, UNC Chapel Hill disability website (documentation guidelines): https://accessibility.unc.edu/eligibility/documenting-your-disability.

Financial aid info (also from DO IT program): http://www.washington.edu/doit/Brochures/PDF/financial-aid.pdf. See also Eeoc.gov.

Free Application for Federal Student Aid (FAFSA): www.fafsa.gov/

G.I. Bill Benefits: http://www.benefits.va.gov/GIBILL/resources/benefits_resources/rates/ch33/ch33rates080114.asp.

HEALTH Resource Center (online clearinghouse for post secondary education for individuals with disabilities): http://www.health.gwu.edu.

LD Online—learning disability informational website: http://www.ldonline.org.

National Center for Education Statistics: http://nces.ed.gov/programs/digest/d14/tables/dt14_304.80.asp.

National Center for Learning Disabilities (NCLD): http://www.ncld.org.

National Center on Secondary Education and Transition (coordinates national resources for secondary education and transition for youths with disabilities): www.ncset.org

Office of Civil Rights (OCR): http://www.2.ed.gov/about/offices/list/ocr/complaint process.html. See also Students with Disabilities Preparing for Postsecondary Education: Know Your Rights and Responsibilities, www.ed.gov/zbout/offices/list/ocr/transition.html.

Self-advocacy guides (Arizona Center for Disability Law) (provides self advocacy information on ADA laws, Technology, IEP meetings): http://www.acdl.com/self guides.html.

State Vocational Rehabilitation Agency (contact info for all state vocational rehabilitation agencies): http://askjan.org/cgi-win/TypeQuery.exe?902.

2Study Guides and Strategies: http://www.studygs.net/index.htm.

U.S. Autism/Asperger's Association: http://www.usautism.org/index.htm.

U.S. CAP program (College Autism Program): http://www.usautism.org/uscap/index.htm.

Assessments

http://vark-learn.com/the-vark-questionnaire/.

http://vark-learn.com/the-vark-questionnaire/?p=results.

http://www.edutopia.org/multiple-intelligences-assessment.

http://www.educationplanner.org/students/self-assessments/learning-styles-quiz.shtml.

http://www.howtolearn.com/learning-styles-quiz/.

http://www.learning-styles-online.com/inventory/.

http://www.personal.psu.edu/bxb11/LSI/LSI.htm.

Brain Dominance Assessments

http://personality-testing.info/tests/OHBDS/.

http://www.web-us.com/brain/braindominance.htm.

Index